한 달이면 귀가 트이고 입이 열린다

박찬영 지음

리베르

한달이면 귀가 트이고 입이 열린다

2007년 1월 20일 개정판 4쇄 발행

지은이 / 박찬영

펴낸이 / 박선우

발행처 / 리베르

주소 / 서울시 용산구 한강로 2가 2-11
대우아이빌 1102호

등록번호 / 제2003-43호

TEL / 790-0587

FAX / 790-0589

e-mail / skyblue7410 @ hanmail. net

값 / 13,500원

박찬영

한국외국어대학교 영어과 졸업. 중앙일보 기자와
美 시사주간지 'NEWSWEEK' Korean Edition의 Editor(부장)를 지냈다.
현재 프리에이전트로서 문학 비평 및 어학교재 연구.

저서

일상영어 7일이면 충분하다
체험영어회화 1000장면
토익독해 문제에 답이 있다
Let's go 기초영어(김충원 그림)
인생에는 아무런 의미도 없다(인생을 노래한 세계의 명시)
함께 서되 너무 가까이 서지는 말라(사랑을 노래한 세계의 명시)

Prologue

　전통 영문법, 번역식 해석, 무작정 듣기, 생활 영어 지상주의는 이미 실패가 검증된, 한쪽 기능에만 치우친 학습 방식이다. 아무 의심 없이 받아들였던 전통 영문법과 번역식 해석이 사실은 영어 능력 향상을 막아 왔다는 사실을 이제는 누구나 안다. 실제로 잘 쓰이지도 않는 영문법을 백과사전식으로 공부하는 것은 시간 낭비다. 반드시 알아야할 기본 문장 형태를 철저히 익히는 것이 더 시급하다. 또 영어를 읽을 때 우리말로 멋을 부려 번역하면 정작 영어는 우리와 멀어진다. 영어에 관한 것은 영문학자에게, 번역은 번역가에게 맡기자. 무작정 듣기는 마치 아기에게 링컨의 연설문을 들려주는 것과 같다. 아기도 무작정 듣지는 않는다. 상황에 맞는 말들을 엄마와의 관계를 통해 익힌다. 영어회화의 극히 일부분에 불과한 생활 영어가 마치 영어의 전부인양 매달리는 것도 시간 낭비다. 영어회화는 생활 영어보다 주로 폭넓은 읽기를 바탕으로 한 토론으로 이뤄진다. 생활영어는 생활하면서 익혀나가도 충분하다.

　영어 학습 비법이 죽어야 영어가 산다. 비법이 아닌 영어 그 자체를 익혀야 한다. 많이 읽고 듣고 말하고 쓰는 것, 이 4가지 영역을 총체적으로 반복하는 것만이 비법이라면 비법이다. 영어 학습의 주된 목표인 정확한 영어 읽기가 모든 영어 학습의 기초가 돼야 할 것이다. 영어 원문을 정확히 이해한 후 큰 소리로 동시에 따라 읽는 것은 읽기, 듣기, 말하기를 한꺼번에 익히는 가장 확실한 방법이다. 이 책으로 매일 두 시간씩 한 번만 큰 소리로 따라 읽어도 한달이면 30번을 읽고 듣고 말할 수 있어 사실상 90번을 반복하는 셈이 될 것이다. 한달 만에 입이 트이고 귀가 열리지 않으면 그것이 오히려 이상한 일이 아닌가. 이 책이 그 길잡이가 돼 줄 것이다.

지은이 씀

Contents

PART 1 읽기, 듣기, 말하기를 동시에 하라

1. 영어를 있는 그대로 받아들이자 ······ 10
2. 영어와 우리말의 어순은 거의 똑같다 ······ 12
3. 전통 영문법이 죽어야 영어가 산다 ······ 13
4. 아기에게 링컨의 연설문은 소음이다 ······ 14
5. 생활 영어는 7일이면 충분하다 ······ 15
6. 발음은 구강 구조에 유의하면 당장 좋아진다 ······ 17
7. 영작은 영어 읽기보다 더 쉽다 ······ 19
8. 영어 단어에는 기본적으로 하나의 뜻밖에 없다 ······ 21
9. 만능 영어 학습법인 암기에도 요령이 있다 ······ 22
10. 성인이 외국어 학습에 더 유리하다 ······ 24
11. 가슴 벅찬 명문 읽기, 가장 완벽한 영어 공부다 ······ 25
12. 토익 시험은 가장 쉬운 시험이다 ······ 26
13. 이 책의 활용법 - 미친듯이 큰 소리로 따라 읽어라 ······ 27

PART 2 영어를 있는 그대로 이해하는 新구문론

1. 명사+전명구/동사+(명사)+전명구 ······ 30
2. To do~+동사/동사+to do~ ······ 31
3. It is~ to do ··· / It is for~ to do··· / 동사+it+보어+to do ··· ······ 32
4. 명사+to do ······ 33
5. wh-+to do ······ 34
6. 행동동사+to do~/To do~, ······ 35
7. 형용사 + to do ······ 36

8. too ~ to … / enough to ································· 37
9. 무의지동사 + to do / so ~ as to / never to do / ········ 38
   only to do
10. 감정동사, 형용사 + to do / would, should + to do / ···· 39
    must be, cannot + to do
11. be to + 시간 / no(not) + be to / if + be to / ········· 40
    be never to
12. 독립부정사 ·· 41
13. -ing + 동사 / 동사 + -ing ···································· 42
14. 전치사 + -ing / 명사 + of -ing ······························· 43
15. 소유격, 목적격 + ing ·· 44
16. 동사 + 동명사 / 동사 + 부정사 ······························ 45
17. -ing, -ed + 명사 ·· 47
18. 명사 + -ing, -ed + 수식어구 ·································· 48
19. -ing ~, 주어 ·· 49
20. -ing / 명사 + -ing …, 주어 / with + 명사 + 분사 ······ 50
21. 독립분사구문 ·· 51
22. 동사 + that + 주어 + 동사 ···································· 52
23. It ~ that … / 동사 + it + 보어 + that ···················· 53
24. 동사 + (that) + 명사 + 동사 ·································· 54
25. 5w1h + 주어 + 동사 ··· 55
26. whether + 주어 + 동사 / 동사 + if + 주어 + 동사 ····· 57
27. It is + 강조되는 어구 + that(who) ·························· 58
28. 명사 + who, whose, whom, which, that ················· 59
29. 사람 + who + 동사 ··· 60
30. 사람 + whose 명사 + 동사 / 사람 + whom + 주어 ···· 61
31. 동물, 사물 + which (+주어) + 동사 ························ 62
32. 사람, 동물, 사물 + that (+주어) + 동사 ·················· 63
33. 명사 + (that) + 명사 + 동사 ·································· 64

34. what + 주어 + 동사 ·· 65
35. 명사 + when, where, why, how ···················· 66
36. whenever, wherever, however ························ 68
37. whoever, whichever, whatever ······················ 69
38. 동격 명사 + that ··· 70
39. as ~ as ··· / such ~ as + 명사 ····················· 71
40. so(such) ~ that 주어 ···/ so that 주어 may(can) ··· 72
41. either ~ or ···/ ,nor / no sooner~ than··· / ··· 74
    no more ~ than ···
42. 되다·이동·정지·감각·판명·인생 동사(2형식) + 보어 76
43. 되다동사 + 보어 ·· 77
44. 이동·정지동사 + 보어 ····································· 78
45. 감각동사 + 보어 ·· 79
46. 판명·인생동사 + 보어 ····································· 80
47. be + 과거분사 ·· 81
48. 타동사(3형식) + 목적어 ··································· 82
49. 주다동사(4형식) + 사람 + 사물 ··················· 83
50. 동사(5형식) + 명사 + 보어 ··························· 84
51. 생각 동사 + 명사 + 명사, 형용사, 준동사 ··· 86
52. 호칭·임명 동사 + 명사 + 명사 ····················· 87
53. 명령·허락·부탁 동사 + 명사 + to do ········· 88
54. 감각동사 + 명사 + 원형부정사(분사) ·········· 89
55. 사역동사 + 명사 + 원형부정사 ····················· 90
56. 기타 5형식 동사 ·· 91
57. 가정법 ·· 92

PART 3 세상에서 가장 아름다운 영어 명문 30

I 세상 사랑하기

1. On Being in Love / Jerome Klapka Jerome — 96
   우리가 사랑할 때는
2. On Three Kinds of Love / Erich Fromm — 100
   세가지 종류의 사랑
3. On Love / André Maurois — 104
   사랑에 대해
4. Love / Corinthians 13:1-13 Teachings of Paul the Apostle — 108
   사랑이란
5. Romeo and Juliet / by Shakespeare — 116
   로미오와 줄리엣
6. The Prophet – On Marriage / by Kahlil Gibran — 124
   예언자 – 결혼에 관해

II 세상 살기

7. The Diary of Anne Frank — 130
   안네 프랑크의 일기
8. Walden – To Be Alone / Henry David Thoreau — 138
   월든 – 혼자 있는 것
9. On Friendship / A. clutton-Brock — 142
   우정에 관해
10. How to Win Friends and Influence People / Dale Carnegie — 146
    친구를 얻고 사람을 움직이는 비결
11. The Little Prince / Antoine de Saint Exupéry — 150
    어린 왕자
12. The Conguest of Happiness / Bertrand Russell — 158
    행복의 정복

III 세상 가지기

13. Of Studies / Francis Bacon — 164
    학문에 대해
14. Dead Poets Society — 176
    죽은 시인의 사회

15. The Autobiography of Lee Iacocca / Lee Iacocca 188
아이아코카 자서전

16. On Achieving Success / Ernest Hemingway 200
성공하는 것에 대해

17. How to Enjoy Music / George R. Marek 204
음악을 즐기는 방법

18. Painting As A Pastime / Winston Churchill 212
취미로서의 그림 그리기

IV 세상 바꾸기

19. Why We Cannot Wait / Martin L. King 222
왜 우리는 기다릴 수 없나

20. Inaugural Address / John F. Kennedy 226
케네디 대통령 취임사

21. Gettysburg Address / Abraham Lincoln 230
게티즈버그 연설

22. Julius Caesar / Shakespeare 238
율리우스 시저

23. The Prince / Niccolo Machiavelli 242
군주론

24. Learning and Citizenship / Marvin lazerson, Judith B. 250
학교 교육은 왜 죽었는가

25. The Worthless Ivy League? / by Robert J. Samuelson 262
아이비리그는 소용이 없나?

V 세상 버리기

26. Freedom From The Known / J. Krishnamurti 272
아는 것으로부터의 자유

27. Jonathan Livingston Seagull / Richard Bach 284
조너선 리빙스턴 시걸

28. Illusions / Richard Bach 296
환영

P·A·R·T

 읽기, 듣기, 말하기를 동시에 하라

---

1. 영어를 있는 그대로 받아들이자
2. 영어와 우리말의 어순은 거의 똑같다
3. 전통 영문법이 죽어야 영어가 산다
4. 아기에게 링컨의 연설문은 소음이다
5. 생활 영어는 7일이면 충분하다
6. 발음은 구강 구조에 유의하면 당장 좋아진다
7. 영작은 영어 읽기보다 더 쉽다
8. 영어 단어에는 기본적으로 하나의 뜻밖에 없다
9. 만능 영어 학습법인 암기에도 요령이 있다
10. 성인이 외국어 학습에 더 유리하다
11. 가슴 벅찬 명문 읽기, 가장 완벽한 영어 공부다
12. 토익 시험은 가장 쉬운 시험이다
13. 이 책의 활용법 - 미친듯이 큰 소리로 따라 읽어라

1. 영어를 있는 그대로 받아들이자

　언어는 뇌 속에서 스스로 복제된다. 인간사회에서 스스로 복제하는 정보 '밈'(meme)은 머릿속에 들어가 자신이 기억되도록 뇌를 재배열한다. 밈은 생물학자 리처드 도킨스가 만들어낸 용어다. 모든 언어는 뇌세포가 자라 형성된 시냅스를 통해 뇌 안에서 전달된다. 그러나 대부분 전달 과정에서 원래의 의미가 상실되고 원 뜻을 잃은 채 무의미하게 방황한다. 불필요한 '언어 밈'은 뇌의 재구성 과정에서 뇌를 공격해 정신병까지 야기한다.

　불필요한 언어 정보의 대표적인 예로 영어를 받아들일 때 우리말 사고 구조에 맞춰 번역하는 것을 들 수 있다. 영어를 읽을 때 영어의 어순 그대로 받아들이지 않고 우리말에 맞춰 뒤죽박죽 받아들이는 것은 영어를 공부하는 것이 아니라 영어와 우리말을 비교 연구하는 것이나 다름없다. 주객이 전도돼서는 안 될 것이다. 밈 이론에 근거해 '밈 공해'를 제거하려면 있는 그대로 가감 없이 받아들여야 한다. 영어를 있는 그대로 받아들이면 영어 그 자체로 자연스럽게 뇌에 입력된다.

　있는 그대로 받아들이는 것은 단순화시키는 것을 의미한다. 일본의 경영학자 사토 유시나오는 단순화 능력이야말로 경영자의 첫째 가는 자질이라고 주장한다. 조직이나 의사 결정 과정을 단순화하고 직원의 자율적이고 창의적 능력에 맡기면 그만큼 효율도 오른다는 것이다. 마찬가지로 학습자의 첫째 가는 자질도 단순화 능력이다. 영어 학습자의 단순화 능력이란 바로 영어를 있는 그대로 받아들이는 능력이다. 있는 그대로 받아들이는 것 이상 단순한 것은 없다.

제2외국어로서 영어를 배우는 입장에 있는 우리는 영어와 우리말을 불가피하게 대응시켜야 한다. 언어간의 대응은 문화 교류를 위해서도 필요하다. 영어를 우리말 사고 구조에 대응시키는 것이 아니라 영어를 있는 그대로 우리말과 1대1로 대응시키는 것이 중요하다. 그래야 언어적 혼란이 제거된다. 하나의 영어 문장이라도 수많은 번역이 가능하기 때문이다.

영어를 읽거나 들을 때 우리말 구조에 대응시키기 위해 해석의 순서에 신경을 쓴다면 정보가 거미줄처럼 혼란스럽게 자가 복제돼 이해의 속도는 물론 질도 떨어진다. 우회되는 정보는 뇌를 혼란에 빠뜨리고 직관적인 성찰을 방해한다. 정보를 우회한 형태가 아니라 있는 그대로 받아들여야 하는 이유다. 영어를 있는 그대로 해석하면 애매하게 이해되던 것이 분명하게 이해된다.

영어가 복잡하게 생각되는 것은 불필요한 정보들이 뇌에 혼란을 주기 때문이다. 처음부터 불필요한 과정을 버리면 영어 그 자체가 있는 그대로 부각된다. 우리가 영어를 공부하는 목적이 바로 영어 그 자체를 받아들이는 것이라고 말할 수 있다. 있는 그대로 받아들인다는 것은 마치 도를 닦는 것과도 같다. 원효 스님은 해골 물을 마신 뒤 사물을 있는 그대로 받아들이게 됐다. 사람도 있는 그대로 선입견을 버리고 받아들이면 갈등은 있을 수 없다. 나와 그의 차이에 대해 왜 시비를 거는가. 나와 그의 차이가 서로를 존재하게 하는 이유일 것이다. 있는 그대로 받아들이는 것 이상 명백한 것은 없다. 영어 학습에도 명경지수와 같은 구도 정신이 필요하다. 구태여 절에 가지 않아도 영어 공부하면서 도를 닦을 수도 있다.

2. 영어와 우리말의 어순은 거의 똑같다

영어를 있는 그대로 받아들이는 것은 읽는 순서대로 받아들이는 것을 의미한다. 영어를 순서대로 해석해도 이해하는 데는 거의 지장이 없다. 우리말은 도치법이 잘 발달돼 있기 때문이다.

우리말은 정말 세상에서 가장 뛰어난 언어다. 그 근거는 과학적 창제 과정 보다 도치법에 있다. 그러나 영어는 어순에 얽매인다. 예를 들어 'K love you'는 어순을 바꾸면 'love You K'처럼 문장이 성립되지 않거나 'You love K'처럼 뜻이 바뀐다. 그러나 '나는 너를 사랑한다'는 어순을 바꿔 '사랑한다 나는 너를' 혹은 '너를 사랑한다 나는'이라고 말해도 의미가 바뀌지 않는다. 다만 우리말은 조사가 의미를 결정짓는 경우가 많다는 점에 유의해야 한다.

영어의 순서대로 해석하면서 도치법을 활용하면 영어를 있는 그대로 이해할 수 있기 때문에 영어와 우리말은 어순이 달라 한국인이 영어를 배우기가 어렵다는 주장은 변명에 불과하다. 오히려 영어와 한국어의 어순은 거의 비슷하다.

영어 읽기란 영어를 있는 그대로 받아들이는 것이다. 영문을 정확히 있는 그대로 파악하면 번역은 우리말 실력의 문제다. 있는 그대로 자연스러운 번역이 가능하면 영문의 순서대로 번역하는 것이 좋다. 구태여 힘들게 말을 돌려가며 번역하는 것이 반드시 잘 하는 번역은 아니다. 다만 전치사, 조동사, 접속사, 부정어 등은 말의 자연스런 연결을 위해 뒤에 해석해 주는 것이 좋다.

3. 전통 영문법이 죽어야 영어가 산다

일제의 잔재가 새 천년을 맞이한 지금도 영어 교육에서는 사라지지 않고 있다. 우리가 지금까지 배워온 영문법은 대부분이 일제 때의 영문법 그대로다. 마치 약속이나 한 듯이 반세기 이상을 의심 없이 사용해온 일제식 영문법의 틀이 우리의 발목을 잡고 있다. 우리는 지금까지 영어를 공부하지 않고 영어에 관한 것을 공부해 왔던 것이다.

이제는 영어 공부를 위한 영문법을 자체 개발할 필요가 있다. 우리말과 영어의 구조를 1대1로 대응시켜 영어의 기본 문형을 확실하게 익히도록 하는 것이 하나의 대안이다. 영문법 용어도 알기 쉽게 고치고 필요 없는 용어는 가능한 사용하지 말아야 한다.

영문을 순서대로 정확히 읽기 위해서는 기본 문형에 익숙해야 한다. 대충 이해하면 영어도 대충 지나가 버린다. 10년을 공부해도 영어에 자신감을 가질 수 없는 이유를 바로 여기서 찾을 수 있다. 영어 읽기는 이 책에서 소개한 57가지의 문장 패턴만 익히면 수많은 영문법 규칙을 공부한 사람보다 훨씬 더 자신감을 가질 수 있다. 기본에 충실해야 실전에 강해진다. 세부적인 문법 사항은 그때그때 영문을 접하면서 기본에 입각해 파악하면 된다. 기본만 갖춰져 있으면 응용은 자연스럽게 할 수 있다. 무릇 실전에 강하지 않은 지식은 장식품에 지나지 않는다.

'part II 新구문론'에 있는 예문의 해석 부분을 보면서 테이프를 동시에 듣고 따라서 말하는 연습을 하면 필수 문형들이 쉽게 몸에 익고 동시 통역의 감각도 익힐 수 있을 것이다.

4. 아기에게 링컨의 연설문은 소음이다

아기가 언어를 습득하는 과정에 따라 무작정 듣기를 권하는 학습법이 유행인 것 같다. 그러나 아기는 전혀 모르는 내용을 무작정 듣지 않고 상황에 맞는 말들을 엄마와의 관계를 통해 몸으로 익힌다. 아기에게 링컨의 연설문을 계속 들려준다면 그 아기는 정신 장애를 일으킬지도 모른다. 성인도 마찬가지다. 모르는 내용을 듣기만 하는 것은 일종의 고문이다. 그렇다고 쉽게 알아들을 수 있는 수준 낮은 내용을 계속 듣는 것도 곤란하다.

최근 영어 공부를 하지 말라고 하면서 사실은 재미도 없는 영어 공부를 엄청나게 시키는 학습법이 인기를 끌고 있다. 공부(study)하지 말고 배우라(learn)라는 주장에서 공부하는 것과 배우는 것의 차이점이 무엇인지 도무지 알 수가 없다. 외국어에 소질이 있고 어느 정도 궤도에 오른 특정인이 성공한 방법이라고 해서 누구나 성공할 수는 없다. '성공 시대'를 보고 따라한다고 해서 누구나 성공할 수 없는 것과 마찬가지다.

무릇 비법은 간단한 데 있다. 듣기 능력이 부족한 것은 듣는 양이 그만큼 적었기 때문이다. 영어 공부에 비법이 있다면 많이 읽고 듣고 말하는 방법밖에 없다. 다만 정확한 읽기가 밑바탕이 돼야 한다. 이것이 포인트다. 읽을 때 이해하는 수준 이상으로 들을 때도 이해할 수는 없기 때문이다.

무작정 듣기 이론도 영어의 리듬을 익히는 데는 상당한 효과를 발휘하지만 초보자가 적용하기에는 적합하지 않다. 어쨌든 듣기의 리듬 감각을 집중적으로 익히기 위해서 상황을 잘 아는 10분 정도 분량의 뉴스를 반복 청취한 후 꼼꼼히 받아쓰기를 하는 것도 하나의 방법이 될 수 있다. 약 2시간 정도 걸릴 것이다. 모르는 내용을 무작정 두어 시간 듣는 것보다는 훨씬 효과적이고 성취도도 높다.

5. 생활 영어 7일이면 충분하다

영어 회화란 토막 생활 영어 몇 마디 하는 것은 아니다. 생활 영어는 영어 회화의 극히 일부분에 지나지 않는다. 영어회화는 생활 영어보다 주로 폭넓은 읽기를 바탕으로 한 관심 분야의 토론으로 이뤄진다. 영어 회화 교재에 수록된 생활 영어 표현만 모으더라도 수 만 개는 될 것이다. 수십 년을 미국서 생활한 사람도 모르는 표현이 수두룩할 것이다. 우리가 그런 표현들을 다 모른다고 해서 부끄러워할 이유는 없다. 우리는 기본적인 생활 영어 표현만 제대로 구사할 수 있어도 충분하다.

상황에 따른 수 만 가지의 생활 영어 표현들을 모두 암기해도 실제로 외국에서 살거나 외국인과 생활하지 않는 한 사용할 일이 별로 없다. 외국 식당에서 음식 주문하는 영어를 잘 몰라도 메뉴를 적당히 가리키기만 하면 된다. 쇼핑을 할 때는 그냥 입어보고 신어보고 사면된다. 생활 영어는 생활하면서 익혀나가면 되는 표현들에 불과하다.

일반 영어 회화 책에서 인사에 관한 표현만 모으더라도 수십, 아니 수백 가지는 될 것이다. 화장실 묻는 간단한 표현만 하더라도 슬랭 등을 합치면 수십 가지나 된다. 우리가 하나의 내용을 표현하기 위해 그 많은 표현들을 모두 외울 필요는 없다. 어떤 생각을 100가지로 표현할 수 있다 하더라도 대표적인 표현 한 두 개는 우선적으로 익혀야 한다. 이것이 바로 생활 영어 학습의 비결이라면 비결이다. 생활 영어는 일종의 관용 표현이므로 하나의 단어처럼 외는 것도 잊어서는 안 된다.

실제 생활 영어라고 할 수 있는 것은 2,3백 개 정도밖에 없다. 좀 더 많은 표현을 익히고 싶으면 기본 표현들을 뼈대로 삼아 살을 붙여 나간다는 기분으로 정리를 하면 된다. 백과사전 식으로 모든 표현들을 익힌다는 생각은 버리고 기본적인 표현들 만이라도 확실히 내 것으로 하는 것이 중요하다. 1만가지 일상 영어 표현을 건성으로 공부한 사람보다는 200가지 표현을 입으로 확실히 외운 사람이 실전에서는 훨씬 더 영어를 잘 하는 것처럼 보이는 법이다. 별책 '일상 영어 7일이면 충분하다' 에서 실전에서 반드시 쓰이는 461가지의 문답을 정리해 놓았다. 일주일 동안 미친듯이 큰 소리로 테이프를 따라 읽으면 어떤 상황에서도 필요한 말이 즉시 튀어 나올 것이다. 큰 소리로 따라 읽기보다 더 빠른 영어 공부 방법은 이 세상에는 없다. 읽기, 듣기, 말하기를 동시에 완성시키기 때문이다.

한국외국어대학교의 이상준 교수도 '평범의 진리' 라는 수필집에서 영어 회화는 전체적인 영어 학습의 작은 일부에 지나지 않는다고 지적했다. 그의 주장 중 학습자가 되새길만한 부분을 인용해본다.

"생활 영어의 범주에 든 영어의 문장들은 극히 제한돼 있고 일반 영어 속의 관용적 표현들에 불과하다. 다른 관용적인 표현들과 함께 그런 표현들이 효과적으로 학습되는 것이 바람직하다. 생활 영어란 영역을 인정하더라도 그 표현들의 수는 겨우 2,3백 정도밖에 되지 않는다. 방대한 일반 영어의 규모에 비한다면 소위 생활영어는 빙산의 일각에 불과하다...

나는 중학교 때 영어 발음이 좋다고 평이 나 있는 선생을 접촉해 그의 발음을 흉내내고 미국 영화나 미군들과의 대면을 통해 열심히 발음을 다듬어 나갔다. 그렇게 하면서 동시에 일상 회화에 가장 많이 쓰이는 How do you do? Excuse me 등과 같은 생활 영어의 문장들을 약 2백여 개 공책에 기록하여 그 문장 하나 하나를 정확한 발음으로 큰소리로 외웠다. 그것을 약 한 달 동안 계속한 결과 나도 모르게 그 문장들이 나의 입에서 저절로 튀어나오게 되었다. 그래서 나는 도 내에서 영어 회화를 가장 잘 한다는 명성까지 얻게 되었다. 나는 그 때, 즉 중학교 3학년 때 영어를 정복했다고 감히 말할 수 있다."

6. 구강 구조만 유의하면 당장 발음이 좋아진다

사마란치 IOC 위원장이나 키신저 前 미국 국무장관은 영어 발음이 별로 좋지 않다. 리드미컬하게 말이 연결되지 않고 끊기는 느낌이 들어 답답한 느낌마저 들 정도다. 그러나 그들은 발음이 정확하지는 않지만 유려한 표현을 자유자재로 구사한다. 영어를 네이티브 스피커처럼 발음하지 못해도 의미를 이해하는 데 지장이 없다면 의사 소통에 문제가 없을 것이다. 그렇다고 해서 우리도 그들을 흉내내 발음보다 표현에만 신경 쓰는 것은 바람직하지 못하다. 영어를 못하는 사람이 발음마저 무시한다면 영어와 친해지기는 어려울 것이다.

최근 발음이 좋아야 귀도 뚫리고 입도 열린다는 발음 중심의 영어 학습법들이 소개되고 있다. 발음이 좋아야 영어의 리듬을 타며 자연스럽게 말을 할 수 있고 기억도 잘 된다는 데는 이론의 여지가 없다. 기억은 리듬에도 의존하기 때문이다. 그러나 문제는 그 학습법을 열심히 따라 해도 발음은 금방 좋아지지 않는다는 것이다. 발음 연습을 열심히 하면 발음이 좋아진다는 미신에서 이제는 벗어나야 한다. 발성법, 혀의 위치, 발음 구구단 등을 아무리 연습해도 과거의 버릇은 쉽게 사라지지 않는다. 발음은 개별적인 발음기호를 열심히 연습한다고 해서 좋아지는 영역은 결코 아니다. 아무리 개별적인 발음을 열심히 연습해도 긴 문장을 읽을 때는 과거의 습관이 다시 나오게 돼 있다. 결국 영어 발음은 구강 구조적으로 접근해야 한다는 결론을 내릴 수밖에 없다. 영어를 말할 때와 한국어를 말할 때의 호흡법과 구강 구조가 다르기 때문이다. 이것이 한국인의 발음이 좋아지지 않은 근본적인 이유다.

만약 구강 구조에 유의한다면 지금 당장 발음이 달라질 수 있다. 영어의 구강 구조에 적응되면 개별적인 발음이나 연음 등은 저절로 해결된다.

서양인들은 육식을 주로 해서 그런지 입 속이 우리보다 훨씬 크다. 따라서 영어를 발음할 때 입을 크게 벌려야 하는데 그러려면 입을 가로로 벌리고 턱을 목 쪽으로 당기듯이 뚝 떨어뜨려야 한다. 우리말을 할 때는 세로로 입을 벌리는 경우가 많지만 영어를 말할 때는 가로로 입을 벌리는 경우가 80% 이상이다. 다음 요령을 동시에 적용시키며 발음을 하면 매끄러운 영어 발음이 가능하다. 몸 전체, 특히 입 주변의 안면 근육과 어깨의 긴장을 푸는 것을 잊어서는 안 된다.

1. 어깨에 힘을 뺀다(몸 전체의 긴장이 풀린다).
2. 아랫배에서 가슴으로 소리를 끌어올린다 (배가 들어간다).
3. 안면근육의 긴장을 풀고 아래턱을 목 쪽으로 당기듯이 떨어뜨리면서 입은 옆으로 벌린다.

개별음을 발음할 때는 혀끝의 위치에 유의해야 한다. 평상시 한국인의 혀끝은 윗니와 위 잇몸에 닿아있으나 미국인의 혀끝은 아랫니와 아래 잇몸에 가볍게 붙어 있다. 개별음을 발음할 때의 혀의 위치는 다음과 같다.

1. 위 잇몸 /t d tʃ dʒ n l/
2. 입안 공간 /r s ʒ/
3. 윗니와 아랫니 사이 /θ ð/
4. 아랫니와 잇몸 사이: 그 외의 자음 및 모음 모두

혀의 위치에 유의하며 다음 단어들을 발음해 보자.

Jew[dʒuː]   zoo[zuː]
walk[wɔːk]   work[wəːrk]
late[leit]   rate[reit]
face[feis]   pace[peis]
vase[veis]   base[beis]
thank[θæŋk]   they[ðei]

7. 영작은 영어 읽기보다 쉽다

영작은 생각하기에 따라 읽기 보다 더 쉬운 영역인지 모른다. 영문을 읽어가다 모르는 부분이 나오면 해석이 불가능한 경우가 얼마든지 있다. 그러나 영작은 자신이 아는 표현만 쓰게 되므로 영작 자체가 안 되는 경우는 없다고 볼 수 있다.

기본적으로 아무리 긴 문장이라도 우리말의 주어와 동사를 먼저 영역한 후 나머지 부분은 뒤에서부터 앞으로 올라가며 영역하면 거의 틀림없다. 주어와 동사가 접속사로 계속 이어지는 경우에는 접속사를 기준으로 동일한 방법을 적용하면 된다. 대개 복잡하게 느껴지는 긴 문장은 접속사, 주어, 동사가 계속 이어지거나 수식어가 길 경우다. 따라서 아무리 긴 문장이라도 '주어 + 동사 / + 접속사 + 주어 + 동사 / + 접속사 + 주어 + 동사…'의 형태를 벗어나지는 못한다.

전체 문장의 주어와 동사를 먼저 찾아 영역한 다음 나머지는 뒤에서부터 영역하면 자연스러운 영작이 된다. 첫 단추(전체 문장의 주어와 동사)를 잘 끼우면 나머지 단추들은 저절로 자리를 찾아가게 돼 있다. 이런 식의 구조화 훈련을 계속하다 보면 아무리 복잡한 우리말 문장이라도 영어로 어순이 순식간에 재배열되는 것을 느낄 수 있다. 영어 코드와 한글 코드가 마음대로 전환될 때 비로소 영어와 친해졌다고 할 수 있을 것이다. 영어와 우리말의 코드를 쉽게 바꾸려면 '영어를 있는 그대로 받아들이는' 훈련을 꾸준히 하는 것이 첩경이다.

결국 영작은 주어와 동사 찾기가 거의 전부라고 말할 수 있다. 주어가 우리말에 표면적으로 나타나지 않는 경우에도 숨어 있는 주어를 찾아내야 한다. 우리말은 문맥에 따라 주어를 생략하는 경우가 많지만 영어는 대명사를 써서라도 주어를 나타내려는 경향이 강하다.

영작을 할 때는 대체로 다음과 같은 원칙이 적용된다.

1. 전체 문장의 주어와 동사를 먼저 찾는다.
2. 수식어는 수식 당하는 말 다음에 놓는다.
3. 접속사로 이어진 절 안에서도 주어와 동사를 먼저 찾는다.
4. 주어와 동사 외의 부분들은 뒤에서 앞으로 올라가며 영역한다.

이상을 도식화하면 다음과 같다.

> 우리말: (수식어+) 주어 + (수식어+) 목적어, 보어 + (수식어+) 동사
> 영어: 주어(+수식어) + 동사(+수식어) + 목적어, 보어(+수식어)

실제 영작문의 예를 들어본다.

1. 우리 모두는 대학에 가는 것이 경제적 성공에 필수적이라는 사실을 알고 있다.
   → 우리 모두는 알고 있다 / 대학에 가는 것이 / 필수적이라는 것을 / 경제적 성공을 위해
   → We all know that going to college is essential for economic success.
2. 원래 같은 능력을 가진 사람들은 명문대를 졸업함으로써 일을 더 잘 하고 더 많이 돈을 번다.
   → 사람들은 / 원래 같은 능력을 가진 / 일을 더 잘 하고 돈도 더 많이 번다 / 졸업함으로써 명문대를.
   → People with the same raw abilities do better and earn more by graduating from an elite school.

8. 영어 단어에는 기본적으로 하나의 뜻밖에 없다

영어에는 다의어가 많다. 심지어 사전에 수록되지 않은 뜻도 있다. 글쓴이가 비유적으로 만들어 쓰는 의미까지 포함한다면 영어 단어의 의미는 매우 많다. 영어와 우리말의 구조가 다른데다 영어 단어의 뜻도 워낙 다양하므로 영어가 어렵게 느껴질 수밖에 없다.

그러나 어떤 단어든 기본적인 의미는 하나 밖에 없다. 극단적으로 영어 단어에는 하나의 뜻밖에는 없다고 말할 수도 있다. 영어 단어의 의미는 기본적 의미에서 파생적 의미, 비유적 의미로 분화될 뿐이다. **파생적 의미는 품사의 변화, 다른 단어와의 결합, 즉 합성어에서 생긴다고 할 수 있다.** 이는 어법과 관련된 경우가 많다. 비유적인 의미가 사실 가짓수가 가장 많다고 볼 수 있다. 글을 쓰거나 말을 할 때 기본적 의미보다 비유적 의미를 제대로 구사하면 생기를 불어넣을 수 있다. 비유적 의미는 기본적 의미에서 쉽게 연상할 수 있다.

영문을 읽을 때 기본적 의미를 우리말과 1대1로 대응시키며 순서대로 읽으면 영어가 우리말처럼 다가온다. 영어 단어에 하나의 뜻만 적용할 수 있다면 영어가 매우 쉬워질 것이다. 비유적 의미는 문맥에 따라 자연스럽게 드러나는 경우가 많으므로 걱정할 필요가 없다. 비유적 의미를 애써 생각해내려고 하면 읽기의 정확도와 속도가 떨어진다. 영어 읽기는 번역이 아니라는 것을 잊어서는 안 된다.

9. 만능 영어 학습법인 암기에도 요령이 있다.

좋은 텍스트의 암기는 이미 검증된 whole language 학습법이다. 하나의 텍스트를 대상으로 읽기, 말하기, 듣기, 쓰기를 모두 완성할 수 있기 때문이다. 이 과정에서 정확한 발음은 영문 텍스트의 암기에 상당히 도움을 준다. 어떤 사람들은 외국인이 영어를 할 때는 발음은 그다지 중요하지 않다고 주장한다. 이런 사고는 경계해야 한다. 리듬과 강세를 지닌 영어는 단음 구조의 우리말보다 입으로 기억하기가 훨씬 쉽다. 정확한 발음과 리듬 감각이 바로 기억의 실마리를 제공하기 때문이다.

한 고시 3관왕은 학창 시절 수업 내용을 쉬는 시간을 이용해 불과 1,2분에 통째로 암기했다고 한다. 그 요령은 간단하다. 먼저 수업 내용을 정확히 이해한 다음 그 요점을 적은 노트를 마치 사진을 찍듯이 순간적으로 떠올리며 암기한 것이다. 처음에는 의미 단위 별로 내용을 떠올린 다음 전체를 하나로 연결해 순간적으로 떠올리는 방법을 쓴 것이다. Time誌를 즐겨 읽었다는 故 성철 조계정 종정도 이 방법을 사용한 것으로 알려지고 있다. 이 방법은 명상의 원리를 적용한 것으로 개인차는 있겠지만 집중력만 높이면 누구나 활용할 수 있다고 본다. '명상 기억법'의 장점은 복습시간을 엄청나게 줄여준다는 것이다. 이 방식대로 암기를 한다면 1,2시간의 학습량을 복습하는 데는 5분 정도면 충분하다.

트로이의 유적을 발견한 독일의 고고학자 슐리만은 15개 국어에 능통한 것으로 유명하다. 그의 학습법은 통째 암기하는 것으로 의외로 간단하다. 소리내어 읽기, 결코 번역하지 않기, 흥미 있는 대상을 영작한 후 교사의 지도에 따라 정정하기, 전날 지도 받은 것을 암기하기 등이다. 그는 스콧의 '아이반호' 등을 전부 암기하며 6개월만에 영어를 정복하기도 했다. 다른 사람은 10년 걸려도 못하는 것을 6개월만에 해낸 것이다.

Richard Bach의 '환영(Illusion)'이란 소설에는 다음과 같은 말이 있다. '배우는 것은 당신이 이미 알고 있는 것을 발견하는 것이다. 행하는 것은 당신이 그것을 알고 있다는 것을 보여주는 것이다. 가르치는 것은 다른 사람들에게 그들도 알고 있다는 것을 상기시키는 것이다'
　우리가 이 세상에서 모르는 것은 하나도 없다. 다만 잊고 있을 뿐이다. 기억법이란 이미 알고 있는 것을 이용해 새로운 것(잊고 있는 것)을 되살리는 방법이다. 즉 未知의 사실에 의미를 부여해 旣知化하는 것이다. 세상일이든 영어든 의미를 부여할 때 우리에게 다가오는 법이다.
　학습을 위한 효과적인 최면법 한가지를 소개한다. 여류 소설가 비키 바움이 길을 가다가 넘어져서 울고 있자 근처에 있던 할아버지가 달려와 이렇게 말하며 그녀를 달래주었다. "얘야, 네가 넘어진 것은 어깨를 편안하게 하는 방법을 몰랐기 때문이다. 네가 잠들 때 안고 자는 헝겊 인형처럼 어깨를 부드럽게 해보렴. 자, 이렇게." 서커스의 소품을 담당했던 할아버지는 광대처럼 넘어지며 재빨리 일어나는 재주를 보여주었다.
　어깨에 힘을 뺀 뒤 몸을 축 늘어뜨리고 "나는 쉬고 있다. 나는 쉬고 있다"라고 중얼거리면 에너지가 얼굴에서 신체의 중심부로 흘러내리는 것을 느낄 수 있을 것이다. 그러면 긴장에서 해방되고 점차 원하는 대로 행동할 수 있을 것이다.(데일 카네기의 '생각이 사람을 바꾼다'에서)
　무엇인가를 받아들이거나 행하기 위해서는 먼저 자신을 비워야 한다. 자신을 비우는 데는 명상이 하나의 방법이 될 수 있지만 일상 생활에서 늘 행하기는 힘들다. 그러나 어깨에 힘을 빼는 일은 평소에 쉽게 할 수 있다. 긴장을 하면 그만큼 어깨에 힘이 들어가게 된다. 글을 읽거나 말을 할 때도 집중력이 떨어진다. 어깨에 힘을 뺀 상태에서 글을 읽거나 말을 하면 몰라볼 정도로 편안하고 부드럽게 글이 읽히고 말이 나오는 것을 느낄 수 있을 것이다. 기억력도 놀라울 정도로 향상된다.

10. 성인이 외국어 학습에 더 유리하다

자기 나라의 언어로 수준 높은 대화를 나누고 웬만한 독서를 할 수 있을 정도가 되는 나이를 15세 정도로 본다면 어느 정도 언어를 능숙하게 구사할 수 있는 기간을 태어나서부터 대략 15년까지로 볼 수 있을 것이다. 물론 기본적인 의사 표현을 할 수 있는 나이는 5세 정도로 볼 수 있겠지만 수준 높은 독서 및 사고 기능을 갖추려면 15세는 돼야 한다고 가정해볼 수 있다. 또래의 미국인과 비슷한 독서와 사고 능력을 가진 우리나라의 성인은 영어 학습을 할 때 기존의 지식과 사고 능력을 활용해 영어를 우리말과 단순히 대비하며 익히기만 해도 된다. 따라서 우리가 영어를 어느 정도 원활하게 구사하는 기간은 15년이나 될 필요는 없다. 오히려 성인의 논리와 사고 수준을 고려할 때 언어적인 차이점만 보강하면 되므로 2,3년 내에도 일정 수준의 언어 습득이 가능하다고 본다. 이미 언어적 사고력은 형성됐으므로 그것만큼 접고 들어갈 수 있다. 어린 아기가 언어를 습득하는 것과 같은 불필요한 과정을 거칠 필요가 없는 것이다.

슐리만은 암기를 통해 6개월만에 영어를 정복했다고 한다. 따라서 우리도 이론적으로 1년 정도면 가능하다. 이를 위해 네이티브 스피커가 아닌 우리로서는 성인이 가진 높은 사고력을 활용해 완성도 높은 글들을 정확히 읽고, 듣고, 말하고, 쓰는 것을 동시에 반복하는 것이 가장 이상적인 영어 학습이다.

성인은 암기에 약하다는 주장도 설득력이 없다. 성인의 논리력은 오히려 암기 능력을 강화시켜준다. 슐리만이나 양주동 등은 오히려 성인이 돼서 탁월한 암기력을 발휘한 사람들이다. 그들은 기본적인 학습 내용을 논리에 입각해 철저히 암기함으로써 창의력을 최대로 발휘했다.

11. 가슴 벅찬 영어 명문 읽기, 가장 완벽한 영어 공부다

요즘 글을 다루는 사람들 사이에서 품격 높은 글에 대한 정열이 사라지고 있는 것 같다. 그들의 글 수준은 우리 나라 문화 수준의 척도일 수도 있다. 그러나 신문이든 교과서든 기교나 부린 雜文이나 梵文들이 지면을 메우고 있고 가슴에 간직하고픈 아름다운 글들은 찾아보기 힘들다. 정보 통신 기술은 오히려 저질 언어를 확산시킨다.

우리가 고등학교를 다니던 시절만 해도 국어, 영어 교과서에서 페이터의 산문, 우리를 슬프게 하는 것들, 청춘 예찬, 안네의 일기 등 너무나 아름다운, 그리고 인생을 성찰하게 해주는 명문들을 접하곤 했다. 이제 우리 교과서에는 살다보면 그냥 터득하게 되는 무의미한 실용문들이 그 자리를 대신하고 있다.

우리의 학창 시절에는 여학생(혹은 남학생)에 대한 경모와 설렘이 있었고 젊음의 고뇌에 대한 철학적 사변이 있었다. 명문들이 있었고 그 명문들을 이야기하는 사람들이 있었다. 그녀에게 한 통의 편지를 쓰기 위해 - 비록 가식일지언정 - 수십 권의 아름다운 책들을 읽었다. 그녀 혹은 그는 우리들의 진정한 문학 스승이었다. 우리의 삶을 아름답고 순수하게 한 원동력이었다. 이제 그 아름다운 글들을 되살리고 싶다. 그래서 이 세상을 아름답게 하고 싶다.

품격 높은 대화와 완벽한 글쓰기를 위한 진정한 텍스트, '세상에서 가장 아름다운 영어 명문 30'은 소중한 사람에게 들려주고 싶은 내 마음이다. 사랑과 영원의 길을 밝히는 삶의 지침이다. 가슴 벅찬 영어 읽기, 이 세상에서 가장 완벽한 영어 학습이다.

12. 토익 시험은 가장 쉬운 시험이다

영어 실력을 단기간에 향상시키는 것은 힘들지 몰라도 토익이나 토플 시험에서 단기간에 고득점하기는 쉽다. STRUCTURE 은 전통 영문법보다는 기본 문형을 철저히 익히면 간단히 해결된다. LISTENING 은 기본 질문 유형에 유의하면서 문제 중심으로 반복해서 듣기 연습을 하면 짧은 시간에 쉽게 고득점 할 수 있다. 문제는 독해다. 독해는 실력이 밑바탕이 되지 않으면 고득점이 쉽지 않다. 그러나 방법은 있다. 그 방법에 대한 설명은 독자들이 북맨에서 출간된 'TOEIC 독해 문제에 답이 있다' 란 책을 읽고 출판사로 보내온 수많은 e-mail 중 하나를 있는 그대로 소개하는 것으로 대신하고자 한다.

저는 한국자산관리공사에 재직중인 박형진이라고 합니다. 먼저 메일로라도 저자분과 반갑게 인사를 나누게 되니 매우 기쁩니다. 아울러 이 책을 쓰신 노고에 심심한 감사를 드립니다. 학창 시절 어학에는 어느 정도 자신감이 있었지만 바쁜 업무중에 수년간 영어를 뒷전으로 미루어 둘 수밖에 없었던 직장인으로서 막상 토익 시험을 준비하려고 해도 무엇을 어디서부터 시작해야 할지 난감할 수밖에 없었습니다. 토익 시험을 60번이나 치렀다는 김대균씨의 책으로 방향을 잡은 저는 파트별로 교재를 선택해 공략하기로 마음을 먹고 점수를 올리기가 가장 힘들다는 독해 부문의 교재를 고르던 중 저자분의 책을 접하게 되었습니다. 각 주제별로 구분이 잘 되어 있었고 왠지 서로 베낀 듯한 다른 교재들과는 달리 저자의 노력한 흔적이 보여 참 흐뭇했습니다.

대입 공부를 할 때도 노량진 어느 학원에서 직독직해로 공부를 한 적이 있는데 시간에 쫓기는 토익 시험에서 이 방법은 아주 효과적이라는 생각이 듭니다. 아울러 이 교재의 방법으로 전체 문장 내에서 질문의 핵심과 관련된 문장을 찾아내는 훈련을 반복하다보니 실제 시험에서 굳이 전체 문장을 해석하지 않아도 답을 골라낼 수 있게 됐습니다. 문장의 수준이 중급 이상이라서 실제 토익 시험의 문장이 상대적으로 쉽다는 인상을 받았습니다. 끝으로 저자의 무궁한 발전을 기원합니다.

13. 이 책의 활용법 – 미친듯이 큰 소리로 따라 읽어라

이 책은 다음과 같은 순서로 학습하거나 지도할 것을 권한다.
(1) PART1의 기본 구문 해설과 기본 예문을 한번 죽 읽은 후 테이프를 들으면서 읽은 다음 다시 들으면서 동시에 큰 소리로 빠르고 정확하게 따라 말한다.
(2) 기본 예문을 다시 한번 더 읽고 응용 예문을 읽는다. 역시 테이프를 들으면서 큰 소리로 따라 말한다. 응용 예문은 PART3에서 예문을 뽑은 것이 대부분이므로 PART3와 연계해서 공부할 수 있다.
(3) 응용 예문 해석을 보면서 영작 연습을 한다. 영문을 있는 그대로 해석해 놓았으므로 부담 없이 영작할 수 있을 것이다. 동시 통역의 감각을 익히기 위해 해석 부분을 보면서 테이프를 동시에 듣고 따라서 말하는 연습도 병행한다.
(4) PART3는 영문을 있는 그대로 정확히 읽은 후 역시 테이프를 들으면서 큰 소리로 따라 말한다.
(5) 테이프 전체를 매일 들으면서 큰 소리로 따라 말하기를 반복한다.
(6) 내용을 잊어버릴 때쯤 다시 읽기와 듣기, 따라 말하기를 반복한다.
(7) 평소에 듣기의 생활화를 위해 우리에게 친근한 내용을 많이 방송하는 아리랑 TV, 위성 방송 등을 자주 시청한다.
(8) 1개월만 지나도 어휘, 구문, 듣기, 말하기 능력이 몸에 축적된다.
(9) 이 책의 기본적인 학습 순서를 다음과 같이 도식화할 수 있다. 복습할 때는 들으면서 따라 말하기 위주로 해야 한다. 이때 본인의 잘못된 발음을 스스로 찾아 고칠 수 있도록 원어민의 소리가 학습자가 동시에 따라 말하는 소리보다 반드시 커야 한다.

> 읽기 → 읽기 + 듣기 → 읽기 + 듣기 → 말하기 → 듣기 → 듣기 + 말하기

아무 의심 없이 받아들였던 전통 영문법과 번역식 해석이 사실은 영어 능력 향상을 막아왔다는 사실을 이제는 누구나 안다. 실제로 잘 쓰이지도 않는 영문법을 백과사전식으로 공부하는 것은 시간 낭비다. 반드시 알아야할 기본 문장 형태를 철저히 익히는 것이 더 시급하다. 또 영어를 읽을 때 우리말로 멋을 부려 번역하면 정작 영어는 우리와 멀어진다.

P·A·R·T

 영어를 있는 그대로 이해하는 新구문론

1 명사 + 전명구 / 동사 + 전명구

(1) 전명구(전치사 + 명사) 앞에 명사가 오면 '**~하는**'으로 해석하고 동사가 오면 대체로 '**~에**(서), **로**'로 해석한다.
(2) 동사와 전명구 사이에는 동사의 목적어가 올 수 있다.
(3) 시간을 뜻하는 두 개 이상의 명사도 전치사가 생략된 전명구다.
(4) 전명구는 보조 요소이므로 생략해도 문장은 성립한다.

> 1. The book **on** the desk is mine.
> 2. He lives **in** the house **on** the hill.

1. 그 책은 / 책상 위에 있**는** / 나의 것이다.
2. 그는 살고 있다 / 그 집**에서** / 언덕 위에 있**는**.

1. He is a man **of** ability.
2. Beauty lies **in** the eye of the beholder.
3. What is essential is invisible **to** the eye.
4. I went **to** the park with him.
5. Flowers, **by** their brilliant color, attract insects.
6. I must say goodnight **for** the last time.
7. He takes a walk **every evening.**
8. If you want to give a man credit, put it **in** writing.
   If you want to give him hell, do it **on** the phone.

영작

1. 그는 능력 있**는** 사람이다.
2. 아름다움은 존재한다 / 구경꾼의 눈**에** (=제 눈에 안경)
3. 중요한 것은 눈**에** 보이지 않는다.
4. 나는 갔다 / 공원**으로** / 그와 함께.
5. 꽃들은, / 그것들의 현란한 색깔**로**, / 곤충을 끈다.
6. 나는 말해야겠어요 굿 나잇이라고 / 마지막**으로**.
7. 그는 산책한다 / **매일 저녁**.
8. 만약 당신이 주기를 원하면 / 한 사람에게 신뢰(칭찬)를, / 서면**으로** 하라.
   만약 당신이 주기를 원하면 / 그에게 지옥(꾸중)을, / 전화**로** 하라.

2 To do ~ + 동사 / 동사 + to do ~

'to do~'가 동사 앞에서 주어 역할을 하거나 동사 뒤에서 보어 · 목적어 역할을 할 때 '것' 으로 해석한다.

> 1. **To** teach is **to** learn.
> 2. He began **to** read the book.

1. 가르치는 **것이** 배우는 것이다.
2. 그는 그 책을 읽는 **것을** 시작했다.

1. **To** live with an ideal is a successful life.
2. **To** be in company, even with the best, is soon wearisome and dissipating. I love **to** be alone.
3. Friendship is a gift that we offer because we must; **to** give it as the reward of virtue would be **to** set a price upon it.
4. **To** spend too much time in studies is sloth; **to** use them too much for ornament is affectation; **to** make judgement wholly by their rules is the humor of a scholar.
5. Your only obligation in any lifetime is **to** be true to yourself.
6. "I want **to** learn **to** fly like that," Jonathan said.

영작

1. 산다는 **것은** / 이상을 가지고 / 성공적인 삶이다.
2. 사람들과 같이 있는 **것은** / 최고의 사람들과 같이 있는 경우에도 / 곧 지루하고 낭비적이다. // 나는 좋아한다 / 혼자 있는 **것을**.
3. 우정은 하나의 선물이다 / 우리가 내놓는 / 왜냐하면 우리가 그래야 하기 때문에; 그것을 주는 **것은** / 미덕의 보답으로 / 가격을 매기는 **것이** 될 것이다 / 우정에.
4. 소비하는 **것은** 너무 많은 시간을 / 학문들에 / 게으른 짓이다; / 사용하는 **것은** 그것들을 너무 많이 / 장식을 위해 / 허식이다; / 판단하는 것은 전적으로 / 그것들의 규칙들에 의해 / 학자의 기질이다.
5. 당신의 유일한 의무는 / 일생에서 / 진실해지는 **것이다** / 당신 자신에게.
6. "저는 원합니다 / 배우**기를** / 그렇게 나는 **것을**," / 조너선은 말했다.

3 It is ~ to do … / It is for~ to do … / 동사 + it + 보어 + to do …

(1) 주어로 쓰인 'to do …'가 길 경우 It를 주어 자리에 놓고 'to do …'는 문장 뒤로 보낸다.
(2) 'to do'의 의미상의 주어는 for~로 나타낸다.
(3) 목적어로 사용된 'to do …'가 길 경우에도 it를 목적어 자리에 놓고 'to do …'는 문장 뒤로 보낸다.

1. **To** finish the work in a day is impossible.
2. **It** is impossible **to** finish the work in a day.
3. **It** is impossible **for** me **to** finish the work in a day.
4. I think **it** wrong **to** tell a lie.

1. 그 일을 끝내는 **것은** / 하루에 / 불가능하다.
2. (그것은) 불가능하다 / 그 일을 끝내는 **것은** / 하루에.
3. (그것은) 불가능하다 / 내가 그 일을 끝내는 **것은** / 하루에.
4. 나는 생각한다 / (그것을) 나쁘다고 / 거짓말하는 **것은**.

1. **It** is too rash, too sudden **to** swear anything now.
2. **It**'s better **to** attend Yale or Stanford than Arizona State.
3. How sweet **it** was **to** worship!
4. I guess **it** is easy **for** those who have never felt the stinging darts of segregation **to** say "wait."
5. I find **it** wholesome **to** be alone the greater part of the time.

영작

1. (그것은) 너무 성급하고 너무 갑작스러워요 / 맹세하는 **것은** 무엇인가를 지금.
2. (그것이) 더 낫다 / 다니는 **것이** 예일大나 스탠퍼드大를 / 애리조나 주립大보다.
3. 얼마나 달콤했던가 / 숭배하는 **것은**!
4. 나는 생각한다 / (그것이) 쉽다고 / 느껴보지 못한 사람들**이** / 인종차별의 날카로운 화살들을 / "기다려라"라고 말하는 **것은**.
5. 나는 생각한다 / (그것이) 건전하다고 / 혼자 있는 **것이** / 대부분의 시간을.

4 명사 + to do

(1) 명사 뒤에 오는 to do는 '~할, ~하는' 으로 해석한다.
(2) 보통 명사가 to do의 목적어로 해석되지 않으면 to do다음에 적당한 전치사를 넣어야 한다.

> 1. I have some books **to** read.
> 2. I have no house **to** live in.

1. 나는 가지고 있다 / 읽**을** 약간의 책들을.
2. 나는 가지고 있지 않다 / 집을 / 들어가서 **살**.

1. Give me a chair **to** sit in.
2. I need a desk **to** write on.
3. He says (that) the deepest urge in human nature is "the desire **to** be important."
4. He's never risen to the top ranks, because he just doesn't have the ability **to** handle people.
5. The best way **to** develop ideas is through interacting with your fellow managers.
6. All there is **to admire** and how little time there is **to see** it in!

영작

1. 나에게 달라 / 한 개의 의자를 / 앉**을**.
2. 나는 필요하다 / 한 개의 책상이 / 글을 **쓸**.
3. 그는 말한다 / 가장 깊은 충동은 / 인간 본성에서 / '중요해지려**는** 욕구' 라고.
4. 그러나 그는 결코 오르지 못했다 / 최고 계급(경영직)에는 / 그는 단지 가지고 있지 않기 때문이다 / 능력을 / 사람을 다루**는**.
5. 가장 좋은 방법은 / 아이디어들을 개발**하는** / 상호작용을 통해서다 / 당신의 동료 경영자들과.
6. 모든 것이 있다 / 찬양**할** / 그런데 얼마나 적은 시간이 있는가 / 들여다 **볼**!

5 wh- + to do

what, when, where, which, who(m), how 뒤에 오는 to do는
'~할 지' 로 해석한다.

> 1. "Tell me **what to** do."
> 2. Would you like to know **how to** make a girl fall in love with you?

1. "말해주세요 나에게 / **무엇을** 해야**할 지**를."
2. 여러분은 알고 싶은가 / **어떻게** 만들 **지**를 / 한 소녀가 당신에게 사랑에 빠지도록?

1. Twain learns **how to** navigate the river at a young age.
2. A prince, being thus obliged to know well **how to** act as a beast, must imitate the fox and the lion.
3. It dazzles them, and they don't know **what to do** with it all.
4. I can't decide **whether to** postpone or cancel it.
5. The boy didn't know **which to** choose.
6. Nobody knew **which way to** go.

영작

1. 트웨인은 배운다 / **어떻게** 그 강을 항해**할 지**를 / 젊은 나이에.
2. 군주는, / 따라서 잘 알아야 하는 / **어떻게** 행동하는 **지**를 / 짐승으로서 / 모방해야 한다 / 여우와 사자를.
3. 그것은 눈부시게(어리둥절) 한다 그들을, / 그리고 그들은 모른다 / **무엇을** 해야**할 지**를 / 그것 모두를 가지고.
4. 나는 정할 수 없다 / 그것을 연기해야 **할지** 그만두어야 **할지**.
5. 그 소년은 몰랐다 / **어느** 것을 선택해야 할 **지를**.
6. 아무도 몰랐다 / **어느** 길로 가야할 **지를**.

6 행동동사 + to do ~ / To do ~,

to do 앞에 go, come 등 구체적 행동을 나타내는 동사가 오거나
to do 뒤에 코마(,)가 올 경우 '~하기 위해'로 해석한다.

> 1. He went abroad **to** study economics.
> 2. **To** study economics, He went to America.
> 3. We stopped **to** eat.

1. 그는 갔다 / 외국으로 / 경제학을 공부**하기 위해**.
2. 경제학을 공부**하기 위해** 그는 미국으로 갔다.
3. 우리는 멈췄다 / 먹**기 위해**.

1. Most of them follow the current fashions **to** catch the attention of men.
2. I will send a messenger to you **to** hear your word, and **to** fix the time and place for our marriage.
3. The little prince went away, **to** look again at the roses.
4. The kind of people I look for **to** fill top management spots are the eager beavers.
5. We have come **to** dedicate a portion of that field, as a final resting place for those who here gave their lives that that nation might live.
6. **To** make a plan, thorough reconnaissance of the country is needed.

영작

1. 그들의 대다수는 따른다 / 최신 패션들을 / 끌**기 위해** / 남성들의 관심을.
2. 내일, 나는 보낼 거예요 / 한 심부름꾼을 당신에게 / 듣**기 위해** / 당신의 말을 / 그리고 정하기 **위해** / 시간과 장소를 / 우리의 결혼을 위한.
3. 어린 왕자는 떠났다 / 보**기 위해** 다시 / 장미를.
4. 그리고 내가 찾는 종류의 사람은 / 최고 경영직에 채우**기 위해** / 열성적인 비버들(일꾼들)이다.
5. 우리는 왔습니다 / 바치**기 위해** / 그 싸움터의 한 부분을 / 마지막 안식처로 / 사람들을 위해 / 여기서 목숨을 바친 / 그 나라가 살 수 있도록.
6. 구상을 **하기 위해서는** / 시골의 철저한 정찰(현지답사)이 필요하다.

7 형용사 + to do

형용사 뒤에 오는 to do는 '~하기에, 하는 데'로 해석한다.

> 1. English is very easy **to** learn.
> 2. This water is not good **to** drink.
>
> 1. 영어는 매우 쉽다 / 배우**기에**.
> 2. 이 물은 적당하지 않다 / 마시**기에**.

1. Some flowers are pretty **to** look at, but have no fragrance.
2. What one learns beyond the basic skills is hard **to** measure.
3. It's really a wonder that I haven't dropped all my ideals, because they seem so absurd and impossible **to** carry out.
4. If he be not apt **to** beat over matters, and **to** call up one thing to prove and illustrate another, let him study the lawyers' cases.
5. Medicine, Law, business, engineering, these are noble pursuits and necessary **to** sustain life.
6. Best of all and easiest **to** acquire are sketching and painting.

영작

1. 어떤 꽃들은 아름답다 / 보기**에는** / 그러나 향기가 없다.
2. 사람들이 배우는 것은 / 기본 기술들을 넘어서 / 어렵다 측정**하기에**.
3. 정말 놀라운 일이다 / 내가 버리지 않았다는 것은 / 모든 나의 이상들을 / 그것들은 보이기 때문에 / 너무 터무니없고 불가능하게 / 실천**하기에는**.
4. 그가 적합하지 않다면 / 철처히 파헤치는 데 문제들을 / 그리고 한 가지 사실을 불러내**는 데** / 증명하고 예증하기 위해 다른 것을, / 그가 공부하게 하라 / 판례집을.
5. 의학, 법률, 사업, 기술 / 이런 것들은 숭고한 추구 대상들이고 / 필요하다 삶을 유지**하는 데**.
6. 모든 것 중에서 가장 좋고 가장 쉽다 습득**하기에** / 스케치하기와 그림 그리기는.

8 too ~ to … / enough to

(1) 'too~to…'는 to do 앞에 형용사가 오므로 '**너무 ~하다 …하기에는**'으로 해석할 수 있다. 따라서 '너무 ~해서 …할 수 없다'로 해석하는 것은 엄격히 말하면 오역이다.
(2) enough to는 직역하면 '~ 하기에 충분한'이므로 '**~할 정도로**' 로 해석한다.

> 1. He is **too** young **to** marry.
> 2. He is rich **enough to** buy the book.
>
> 1. 그는 **너무** 어리다 / 결혼**하기에는**.
> 2. 그는 부자다 / 그 책을 **살 정도로**.

1. Books are **too** nearly akin to the ordinary daily round of the brainworker **to** give that element of change essential to real relief.
2. Let us devote our life to worth-while actions, feelings and thoughts. For life is **too** short **to** be little.
3. The sky knows the reason and the patterns behind all clouds, and you will know, too when you lift yourself high **enough to** see beyond horizons.
4. A handkerchief of his wife's seen in Cassio's hand, was motive **enough** to the deluded Othello **to** pass sentence of death upon them both.

영작

1. 책은 **너무** 유사하다 / 정신 노동자들의 평범한 매일의 업무 순환(일상 업무)과 / 주기**에는** / 변화의 요인을 / 실제적인 휴식에 필수적**인**.
2. 우리의 생애를 바치자 / 가치 있는 행동, 감정, 사상에. // 왜냐하면 인생은 너무 짧기 때문이다 / 보잘 것 없이 보내**기에는**.
3. 그러나 하늘은 안다 / 그 이유와 그 형태들을 / 모든 구름들 뒤에 있는, / 그리고 당신은 알 것이다, 역시 / 당신이 높일 때 당신 자신을 / 높게 / 수평선 너머 **볼 정도로**.
4. 아내의 손수건은 / 카지오의 손에 보이는 / 동기가 되었다 / 속고 있는 오델로에게는 / 사형선고를 내릴 **정도의**.

9 무의지동사 + to do / so ~ as to / never to do / only to do

(1) 주어 마음대로 할 수 없는 grow, live, awake 등 무의지동사 뒤에 오는 to do는 '~한 결과 …했다'로 해석한다.
(2) so ~ as to do는 일반적으로 '매우 ~해서 …하다'로 해석되지만 as는 '만큼'을 뜻하므로 '너무 ~하다 …할만큼'으로 해석하는 것이 영어의 원래 의미에 더 가깝다.
(3) only to do는 '했으나 ~ 했을 뿐이다', never to do는 '했으나 ~하지 못했다'로 해석한다.

---

1. He **grew** up **to** be a doctor.
2. He worked **so** hard **as to** pass the exam.
   = He worked **so** hard **that** he passed the exam.
3. He did his best **only to** fail in the exam.
4. He went to America, **never to** return.

---

1. 그는 **자라서** 의사가 되었다.
2. 그는 **매우** 열심히 일했다 / 시험에 합격할 **만큼**.
   = 그는 **매우** 열심히 일**해서** 그는 그 시험에 합격했다.
3. 그는 최선을 다**했지만** 시험에 실패**했을 뿐**이다.
4. 그는 미국으로 **가서는** 돌아오**지 못했다**.

1. He **lived to** be eighty years old.
2. One fine morning he **awoke to** find himself famous.
3. He got up **so** early **as to** be in time for the plane.
   = He got up **so** early **that** he was in time for the plane.
4. Have you never rushed dripping from the bath, or dazed from the bed, **only to** be told that you are a wrong number?

영작

1. 그는 살**다보니** 80살이 되었다. = 그는 80살이 되었다.
2. 어느날 아침 / 그가 일어**나보니** 알게됐다 / 자신이 유명해진 것을.
3. 그는 **매우** 일찍 일어났다 / 비행기 시간에 늦지 않을 **만큼**.
   = 그는 **매우** 일찍 일어**나서** 비행기 시간에 댈 수 있었다.
4. 당신은 경험이 없습니까 / 물을 뚝뚝 흘리면서 쫓아 나오거나 / 목욕탕에서 / 부신 눈을 하고 쫓아 나왔**지만** / 침대에서 / **단지** 듣게 되는 / '전화 잘못 걸었습니다'라는 말을.

10 감정 동사, 형용사 + to do / would, should + to do must, be, cannot, 감탄문 + to do

(1) smile, weep, rejoice, regret 등 감정 동사나 glad, happy, sorry, surprised 등 감정 형용사 뒤에 오는 to do는 '~해서'로 해석한다.
(2) would, should 등 조동사 뒤에 오는 to do는 '~라면'으로 해석하고 must be, cannot be가 오면 '~하다니'로 해석한다.
(3) 감탄문의 to do도 '~하다니'로 해석한다.

> 1. He **smiled to** see the monkey.
> 2. I am **glad to** meet you.
> 3. I **should** be very glad **to** go with you.

1. 그는 웃었다 / 원숭이를 보고서.
2. 나는 기쁘다 / 너를 만나게 되어서.
3. 나는 매우 기쁠 것입니다 / 당신과 함께 갈 수 있다면.

1. He **wept to** see the sight.
2. I am **sorry to** give you trouble.
3. **To** tell a lie again, you will be punished.
4. He **must** be foolish **to** say like that.
5. He **cannot** be rich **to** ask you for some money.
6. How foolish I was **to** trust him!

영작

1. 그는 울었다 / 그 광경을 보고서.
2. 죄송합니다 / 폐를 끼쳐서.
3. 만일 다시 거짓말을 하면 너는 벌을 받을 것이다.
4. 그는 바보임에 틀림 없다 / 그렇게 말하다니.
5. 그는 부자일 리가 없다 / 너에게 돈을 부탁하는 것을 보니.
6. 얼마나 어리석었던가 / 그를 믿다니!

11 be to + 시간 / no(not) + be to / if + be to / be never to

(1) be to는 '~해야 한다'나 '~할 수 있다'로 해석한다.
(2) be to + 미래 표시 부사구 = ~할 예정이다
(3) no(not) + be to = ~할 수 없다
(4) if + be to = ~하려면
(4) be never to = ~못할 운명이다

1. You **are to** obey your parents.
2. My house **is to** be seen from the station.
3. The meeting **is to** be held **next Monday**.
4. **If** you **are to** succeed, you must work hard.
5. No one **was to** be seen on the street.
6. He **was never to** see his home again.

1. 너는 순종**해야 한다** / 부모님에게.
2. 내 집은 볼 **수 있다** / 정거장에서.
3. 회의는 열릴 **예정이다** / 다음주 월요일에.
4. 네가 성공**하려면** / 너는 열심히 공부해야 한다.
5. 아무도 볼 **수 없었다** / 그 길에서.
6. 그는 다시 집에 못 돌아올 **운명이다**.

1. Some books **are to** be tasted, others **to** be swallowed, and some few **to** be chewed and digested.
2. President Clinton **is to** go on the air at eight **this evening**.
3. Jonathan took all his courage in hand and walked to the Elder Gull, who, it was said, **was soon to** be moving beyond this world.

영작

1. 어떤 책들은 음미**해야 하며** / 어떤 책은 삼켜**야 하며** / 일부 소수의 책은 / 씹고 소화**해야 한다**
2. 클린턴 대통령이 방송에 나올 **예정이다** / 여덟 시에 오늘 저녁.
3. 조너선은 용기를 다해 걸어갔다 / 장로 갈매기에게, / 들은 바에 의하면 곧 **예정돼 있었던** / 움직일 것으로 / 이 세상 너머로.

12 독립부정사

부정사의 의미상의 주어가 일반인이어서 생략된 경우에는 내용에 따라 '~**하면**' 혹은 '~**하지만**' 으로 해석한다. 회화에서 유용하게 사용할 수 있으므로 잘 익혀두자

1. **To tell the truth**, he is a liar.
2. **To be frank with you**, I am against the plan.
3. **To do him justice**, he is an able man.
4. **To make a long story short**, we agreed to go.
5. **To return to the subject**, what is your point of protest?
6. **To begin with**, I don't like the color.
7. He is, **so to speak**, a grown-up baby.
8. **To make matters worse**, his father failed in his business.
9. **To be sure**, he is dead.
10. **Strange to say**, the light went out of itself.
11. **Needless to say**, because of the accident he had, he'll be off work for a while.
12. He knows French, **not to speak of**(=to say nothing of) English.

영작

1. **사실을 말하면** 그는 거짓말쟁이다.
2. **솔직히 말하면** 나는 그 계획에 반대다.
3. 그를 **공평하게 말하면** 그는 능력 있는 사람이다.
4. **간단히 말하면** 우리는 가기로 결정했다.
5. **본론으로 돌아가면** 당신이 항의하는 요점은 무엇이오?
6. **무엇보다도** 나는 그 색깔을 좋아하지 않는다.
7. 그는 **말하자면** 다 자란 아기다.
8. **설상가상으로** 그의 아버지가 사업에 실패했다.
9. **확실히** 그는 죽었다.
10. **말하기에 이상하지만** 불이 저절로 나갔다.
11. **말할 필요도 없지만** 그가 겪은 사고 때문에 그는 당분간 쉴 것이다.
12. 그는 불어를 잘 안다, 영어는 **말할 필요도 없지만**.

13 -ing + 동사 / 동사 + -ing

-ing가 동사 앞에서 주어 역할을 하거나 동사 뒤에서 보어·목적어 역할을 할 때 '**것**'으로 해석한다.

1. Say**ing** and do**ing** are two things.
2. I remember see**ing** him somewhere.

1. 말하는 것과 행동하는 **것은** 별개의 것이다.
2. 나는 기억한다 / 그를 본 **것을** / 어디에선가.

1. Go**ing** to Harvard or Duke won't automatically produce a better job and higher pay.
2. Understand**ing** is an ongoing process, never ceasing, never absolute.
3. Try**ing** to become like somebody else, or like your ideal, is one of the main causes of contradiction, confusion and conflict.
4. Be**ing** an active citizen requires hav**ing** a flexible intelligence and a mind free, as Matthew Arnold said, of stock notions and habits.
5. Learn**ing** is find**ing** out what you already know. Do**ing** is demonstrat**ing** that you know it. Teach**ing** is remind**ing** others that they know just as well as you.

영작

1. 가는 **것은** 하버드大나 듀크大에 / 자동적으로 만들지는 않는다 / 더 나은 직업과 더 높은 급여를.
2. 이해하는 **것은** 하나의 진행하는 과정이다. / 결코 멈추지 않는 / 결코 절대적이지 않은.
3. 되려고 노력하는 **것은** / 다른 누구처럼 혹은 당신의 이상처럼, / 주요 원인들의 하나다 / 모순, 혼란 그리고 갈등의.
4. 적극적인 시민이 되는 **것은** 요구한다 / 가지는 **것을** / 유연한 지성과 마음을 매튜 아놀드가 말했듯이, / 구태의연한 생각들과 습관들에서 자유로운.
5. 배우는 **것은** 발견하는 **것**이다 / 당신이 이미 알고 있는 **것을**. / 행하는 **것은** 보여주는 **것**이다 / 당신이 그것을 알고 있다는 **것을**. / 가르치는 **것은** 상기시키는 **것**이다 다른 사람들에게 / 그들이 알고 있다는 **것을** / 바로 당신만큼 잘.

14 전치사 + -ing / 명사 + of -ing

(1) 전치사 뒤에 오는 -ing는 전치사의 목적어로서 명사 역할을 한다.
(2) 명사 뒤에 오는 of -ing는 '~(하)는'으로 해석한다.

> 1. He went away **without** say**ing** a word.
> 2. He has a bad habit **of** gett**ing** up late in the morning.

1. 그는 나갔다 / 한 마디 말도 없이.
2. 그는 나쁜 습관을 가지고 있다 / 늦게 일어나**는** / 아침에.

1. I'm not in favor **of** switch**ing** people around.
2. Thank you **for** your answer**ing** so promptly.
3. One of the most familiar methods **of** attract**ing** attention is the use of adornment.
4. He or she may stand before us, but we see only the figure **of** our own mak**ing**.
5. In the process **of** learn**ing**, we, like Twain, continually remake our education, ourselves, and our ways **of** cop**ing** with and understand**ing** the world.
6. That vision **of** learn**ing**, difficult to implement as it is, should be central to schooling.

영작

1. 나는 좋아하지 않는다 / 바꾸는 **것을** 사람을 이리저리.
2. 고맙습니다 / 그렇게 빨리 회답해 줘서.
3. 가장 친숙한 방법들의 하나는 / 관심을 끄**는** / 장식의 사용이다.
4. 그 혹은 그녀가 서있을지도 모르겠다 / 우리 앞에 / 그러나 우리는 본다 / 오직 모습을 / 우리 자신이 만**든**.
5. 배우**는** 과정에서 / 우리는 트웨인처럼 끊임없이 개조한다 / 우리의 교육을, 우리 자신들을, / 그리고 우리의 방법들을 / 세계에 대처하는 그리고 세계를 이해하는.
6. 그런 학습관이 / 시행하기에 어려운/ 그것이 있는 그대로, / 중심이 돼야 한다 / 학교 교육에서.

15 소유격, 목적격 + ing

동명사의 의미상의 주어는 소유격으로 표시하지만 현대 영어에서는 의미상의 주어로 목적격을 더 많이 쓰는 경향이 있다.
해석은 '~**가** …**하는 것을**' 로 한다.

> 1. I don't like go**ing** to such a place.
> 2. I don't like **your** go**ing** to such a place.
> 3. I don't like my **sister** go**ing** to such a place.
> 4. He doesn't like **me** go**ing** to such a place.

1. 나는 좋아하지 않는다 / 그런 곳에 가는 **것을**.
2. 나는 좋아하지 않는다 / 네가 그런 곳에 가는 **것을**.
3. 나는 좋아하지 않는다 / 나의 여동생이 그런 곳에 가는 **것을**.
4. 그는 좋아하지 않는다 / 내가 그런 곳에 가는 **것을**.

1. I don't like **you**(or your) talk**ing** unkindly about my poor friend.
   = I don't like **that** you should talk unkindly about my poor friend.
2. My parents don't like the idea **of me** marry**ing** a foreigner.
3. There is no evidence **of** prehistoric **man**'s hav**ing** made war, for all his flint implements seem to have been designed for hunting, for digging, or for scraping hides.

영작

1. 나는 좋아하지 않는다 / 네**가** 불친절하게 이야기하는 **것을** / 나의 가난한 친구에 대해.
2. 나의 부모님은 좋아하지 않는다 / 생각을 / 내**가** 외국인과 결혼하겠**다는**.
3. 증거는 없다 / 유사 이전의 인간**이** 전쟁을 했**다는** / 왜냐하면 거의 모든 석기는 / 고안된 것처럼 보이기 때문이다 / 사냥을 위해, 땅을 파기 위해 / 혹은 짐승 가죽을 벗기기 위해.

16 동사 + 동명사 / 동사 + 부정사

(1) **동명사**만 목적어로 가지는 동사에는 dislike, mind, avoid, evade, escape, resist, give up, quit, discontinue, deny, postpone, put off, finish, stop 등 **회피·포기** 동사, 그리고 consider, admit, allow, appreciate, enjoy 등이 있다.

(2) **부정사**만 목적어로 가지는 동사에는 wish, want, hope, desire, learn 등 **기대** 동사, decide, promise, agree, refuse 등 **동의·거절** 동사 등이 있다.

(3) **동명사**와 **부정사**를 모두 목적어로 가지는 동사에는 like, hate, prefer, begin, continue, cease, try, propose, intend 등이 있다.

---

1. She **denied** steal**ing** money.
2. What do you **want to** have?
3. He **began to** talk. He **began** talk**ing**.

---

1. 그녀는 **부인했다** / 돈을 훔친 것을.
2. 당신은 무엇을 가지**기를 원합니까**?
3. 그는 말하기 **시작했다**.

(1) 동명사만 목적어로 가지는 동사

1. Believe it or not, each of us... is one day going to **stop** breathing, turn cold, and die.
2. The Smiths are **considering** moving to New York.
3. She **missed** seeing that film when it was at the local cinema.
4. He **enjoys** reading a novel.
5. I don't **mind** taking the bus.
6. Would you **mind** opening the window?
7. He **admitted** having done wrong.
8. I **finished** read**ing** the novel last night.
9. The child barely **escaped** be**ing** run over.
10. He **gave up** drink**ing** by the doctor's advice.
11. She **resisted** be**ing** kissed.

> 영작

1. 믿건 안 믿건 / 우리 각자는... / 어느 날 **멈추고** / 숨쉬는 **것을**, / 몸이 차갑게 되고 죽을 것이다.
2. 스미스 댁은 **고려하고 있다** / 이사가는 **것을** / 뉴욕으로.
3. 그녀는 **놓쳤다** / 보는 **것을** / 그 영화를 / 그것이 지방 극장에서 상영될 때.
4. 그는 **즐긴다** / 소설 읽**기를**.
5. 나는 **싫어하지 않는다** / 버스 타는 **것을**.
6. 문 좀 열어주시겠습니까?
7. 그는 **시인했다** / 잘못했다는 **것을**.
8. 나는 **끝마쳤다** / 소설 읽**기를** / 어젯밤.
9. 그 아이는 가까스로 **피했다** / 차에 치이는 **것을**.
10. 그는 **포기했다** / 음주를 / 의사의 충고에 따라.
11. 그녀는 **저항했다** / 입맞춤 당하는 **것을**.

(2) 부정사만 목적어로 가지는 동사

1. If you **wish to** learn I can teach you how to fly.
2. She **managed to** get on the bus.
3. "I **want to learn to** fly like that," Jonathan said.
4. I **hope to** see you within the next few days.
5. He **refused** to discuss the question.

> 영작

1. 자네가 **원한다면** 배우**기를** / 자네에게 나는 법을 가르쳐 줄 수 있지.
2. 그녀는 **간신히** 그 버스를 **탔다**.
3. 나는 **원합니다** / 나는 **것을 배우기를** / 그렇게 / 조녀선은 말했다.
4. 나는 **희망한다** / 너를 보는 **것을** / 앞으로 수일 내에.
5. 그는 **거절했다** / 그 문제를 토의하는 **것을**.

17 -ing, -ed + 명사

-ing가 명사 앞에 오면 '~하는', -ed가 명사 앞에 오면 '~하게된, 하여진'
으로 해석한다.

> 1. a sleep**ing** baby
> 2. an excit**ing** scene.
> 3. fall**en** leaves
> 4. a brok**en** window
> 5. a blue-ey**ed** girl
> 6. a newly-w**ed** couple
> 7. A roll**ing** stone gathers no moss.

1. 잠자**는** 아기
2. 흥분시키**는** 장면
3. 떨어**진** 잎들
4. 부서**진** 창문
5. 파란 눈을 가**진** 소녀
6. 신혼부부
7. 구르는 돌에는 이끼가 끼지 않는다.

1. I hear the approach**ing** thunder which will destroy us, too.
2. Distill**ed** books are, like common distilled waters, flashy things.
3. I'm young, and I have many buri**ed** qualities.
4. If I speak in the tongues of men and of angels, but have not love, I am only a resound**ing** gong or a clang**ing** cymbal.
5. You have seen hate-fill**ed** policemen curse, kick, brutalize and even kill your black brothers and sisters.

영작

1. 나는 듣는다 / 다가오**는** 천둥소리를 / 우리를 멸망시킬, 역시.
2. 증류**된** 책들은 / 일반 증류수들 같아서 / 섬광적인(일시적으로 화려한) 것들이다.
3. 나는 어리다 / 그리고 나는 가지고 있다 많은 문혀**진** 자질들을.
4. 만약 내가 말해도 / 인간의 언어들로 / 그리고 천사의 (언어들로), / 그러나 가지고 있지 않다면 사랑을. / 나는 단지 울려 퍼지**는** 징 / 혹은 뗑그렁 하고 울리**는** 심벌이다.
5. 당신은 보아왔다 / 증오에 **찬** 경찰관들이 / 저주하고 차고 짐승처럼 대하고 심지어 죽이는 것**을** / 당신의 흑인 형제 자매들을.

PART 2

18 명사 + -ing, -ed + 수식어구

-ing, -ed는 뒤에 수식어구가 오면 명사 뒤에 놓인다. 이 경우 명사와 -ing, -ed 사이에는 'that be'나 'Who be'를 넣을 수 있다. 형용사도 뒤에 수식어구가 올 때는 명사 뒤에 온다.

1. Who is that girl (who is) carry**ing** a racket.
2. I know a Hawaiian girl (who is) call**ed** Bessie.
3. The boy reads the Bible (that is) writt**en** in English.
   Cf. The man (who is) desirous of success must work hard.

1. 누구지 저 소녀는 / 정구채를 들고 있**는**?
2. 나는 알고 있다 / 한 하와이 소녀를 / 베시라고 불리**는**.
3. 그 소년은 읽는다 / 성경을 / 영어로 **된**.
   Cf. 성공을 바라는 사람은 열심히 일해야 한다.

1. Four score and seven years ago our fathers brought forth on this continent, a new nation, (that was) conceiv**ed** in liberty, and dedicat**ed** to the proposition that all men are created equal.
2. The biggest problem (that is) fac**ing** American business today is that most managers have too much information.
3. I simply can't build my hopes on a foundation consist**ing** of confusion, misery, and death.
4. Understanding is an ongoing process, never ceas**ing**, never absolute.

영작

1. 지금으로부터 87년 전 / 우리의 선조는 탄생시켰습니다 / 이 대륙에 / 한 새로운 나라를, / 자유 속에 잉태**된** / 그리고 바쳐**진** / 명제에 / 모든 사람들은 창조됐다는 평등하게.
2. 가장 큰 문제는 / 미국 기업이 직면하고 있**는** 오늘날/ 대다수 경영자들이 가지고 있다는 것이다 / 너무 많은 정보를.
3. 나는 단순히(절대로) 쌓아올릴 수 없다 / 나의 희망들을 / 토대 위에 / 이루어지**는** / 혼란, 비참함, 그리고 죽음으로.
4. 이해하는 것은 진행하는 과정이다. / 결코 멈추지 않**는** / 결코 절대적이지 않**은**.

19 -ing ~, 주어

'-ing ~, 주어'는 '~하는 + 주어'로 해석한다. 흔히 시간, 이유, 조건, 양보 등으로 문맥상 구분해서 해석하지만 의미가 불확실한 경우도 많으므로 '~하는'으로 이해하는 것이 좋다. 만약 글쓴이가 시간, 이유, 조건 등을 분명히 표시할 의도가 있었다면 분사구문을 쓰지 않고 'when/as/if + 주어 + 동사'로 표현했을 것이다.

1. Walk**ing** along the street, I met a friend.
2. (**Being**) warm and full, he soon fell asleep.

1. 거리를 걷고있**던**(걷고 있을 때) 나는 친구를 만났다.
2. 몸이 따뜻하고 배부**른**(배부르니) 그는 곧 잠들었다.

1. Turn**ing** to the left, you will find the post office.
2. Walk**ing** on tiptoe, I approached the window.
3. Liv**ing** near the sea, I cannot swim.
4. Smil**ing** brightly, she came up to me.
5. Startl**ed** to hear a man's voice, Julliet shouted back, "Who's there?"
6. (Being) uncontroll**ed**, the forces of nature may be dangerous and destructive, but once mastered, they can be bent to man's will and desire.
7. Hav**ing** finished his homework, he went to bed.

영작

1. 왼쪽으로 도**는**(돌면) 당신은 우체국을 발견할 것이다.
2. 발끝으로 걸**은**(걸어) 나는 창가에 다가갔다.
3. 바닷가에 사**는**(살지만) 나는 수영을 할 수 없다.
4. 밝게 웃**는**(웃으면서) 그녀는 나에게 다가왔다.
5. 남자의 목소리를 듣고 놀**란** / 줄리엣은 소리쳐 대꾸했다. / "누구세요 거기?"
6. 제어되지 않**은**(않으면) 자연의 힘들은 위험할 지 모른다 / 그리고 파괴적일지도 모른다 / 그러나 일단 정복**된**(정복되면) / 자연의 힘들은 따를 수 있게 된다 / 인간의 의지와 소망대로.
7. 숙제를 끝마**친** (후) 그는 잠자리에 들었다.

20 코머(,)-ing / 명사 + -ing ~, 주어 / with + 명사 + 분사

(1) 코머(,) -ing = 그리고 ~하다
(2) 명사 + -ing ~, 주어 = ~가 …다, ~가 …다
(3) with + 명사 + 분사(전명구) = ~가(을) …하는 채

1. We took a walk together, **enjoying** the fine view around.
2. **School being** over, the boys went home.
3. She looked at me **with** tears runn**ing** down her cheeks.

1. 우리는 함께 걸었다 / **그리고 즐겼다** / 주변의 아름다운 경치를.
2. 학교가 끝났**다**(끝나서), 소년들이 집으로 갔다.
3. 그녀는 나를 바라보았다 / 눈물**이** 빰에 흘러내리는 **채**.

1. "Romeo," he replied, **stepping** out from the shade into the moonlight.
2. Twain learns how to navigate the river at a young age, **learning** every shoal, snag, and sandbar.
3. I wander from one room to another, downstairs and upstairs, **feeling** like a songbird whose wings have been cut and who, in the dark, is throwing herself against her cage.
4. Our dinner be**ing** over, we went out for a walk.
5. Don't leave the room **with** the window open.

영작

1. "로미오입니다" 그가 대답했다 / **그리고 걸어나왔다** / 그늘에서 달빛 속으로.
2. 트웨인은 배운다 / 어떻게 그 강을 항해하는 지를 / 젊은 나이에, / **그리고 배운다** / 모든 얕은 곳, 쓰러진 나무, 모래톱을.
3. 나는 방황한다(왔다갔다한다) / 한 방에서 다른 방으로, / 아래층과 위층을, / **그리고 느낀다** 노래하는 새처럼 / 날개가 짤린 / 그리고 어둠 속에서 던지고(부딪치고) 있**는** / 자신을 새장에다.
4. 식사**가** 끝났**다**, 우리는 산책을 나갔다.
5. 방을 떠나지 말아라 / 창문**을** 열어둔 **채**.

21 독립분사구문

의미상의 주어인 일반인이 생략된 분사구문은 내용에 따라 '**~하면**' 혹은 '**~하더라도**'로 해석한다.

1. **Generally speaking**, the Koreans are a diligent people.
2. **Frankly speaking**, he is not a reliable man.
3. **Strictly speaking**, Great Britain consists of Scotland, Wales and England, and the United Kingdom consists of Great Britain and Northern Ireland.
4. **Judging from** his appearance, he seems to be rich.
5. **Talking of movies**, I don't like sad movies.
6. **Roughly speaking**, this is not correct.
7. **Taking** his age **into consideration**, he looks young.
8. **Granting that** this is true, you are still in the wrong.

영작

1. **일반적으로 말하면** 한국인들은 근면한 국민이다.
2. **솔직히 말하면** 그는 믿을만한 사람이 아니다.
3. **엄격히 말해**, 대브리튼 섬은 스코틀랜드, 웨일즈, 잉글랜드로 이뤄지고 대영제국은 대브리튼 섬과 북아일랜드로 이뤄진다.
4. 그의 외모로 **판단하면** 그는 부자처럼 보인다.
5. 영화**에 관해 말하자면** 나는 슬픈 영화를 좋아하지 않는다.
6. **대강 말하더라도** 이것은 옳지 않다.
7. 그의 나이를 **고려하더라도** 그는 어려 보인다.
8. 이것이 사실**이라 하더라도** 네가 잘못이다.

22 동사 + that + 주어 + 동사

동사 뒤에서 that은 '**것, 다고**' 로 해석한다. 매우 자주 나오는 기본 문형이다.

> 1. We all "know" **that** going to college is essential for economic success.
> 2. I still believe **that** people are really good at heart.

1. 우리 모두 알고 있다 / 대학에 가는 것이 / 필수적이라는 **것을** / 경제적 성공을 위해.
2. 나는 아직 믿는다 / 사람들은 정말 착하**다고** / 마음속은.

1. The conclusion is **that** the Ivy League – a metaphor for all elite schools – has little comparative advantage.
2. "You must begin by knowing **that** you have already arrived..."
3. I've found **that** there is always beauty – in nature, in freedom, in yourself.
4. If I look up into the heavens, I think **that** it will all come out right, **that** this cruelty will end, **that** peace will return again.
5. You see **that** principles, beliefs and ideals must inevitably lead to hypocrisy and a dishonest life.

영작

1. 결론은 이렇다 / 아이비 리그가 – 모든 명문교들의 상징인 – / 거의 상대적인 이점을 가지고 있지 않다는 **것**이다
2. "자네는 시작해야 해 / 앎으로써 / 자네가 이미 도착했다는 **것을**......"
3. 나는 알았다 / 늘 아름다움이 있다는 **것을** / 자연 속에, 자유 속에, 너 자신 속에
4. 내가 쳐다보면 / 하늘을 / 나는 생각한다 / 그 모든 것이 잘 되어 갈 것이**라고** / 이런 잔인성은 끝날 것이**라고**, / 평화가 올 것이**라고** 다시.
5. 당신은 안다 / 원칙들, 신념들 그리고 이상들이 불가피하게 이끈다는 **것을** / 위선과 부정직한 삶으로.

23 It ~ that … / 동사 + it + 보어 + that

(1) 주어로 쓰인 that절이 길 경우 그 자리에 it를 놓고 that절은 문장 뒤로 보낸다.
(2) 목적어로 쓰인 that절이 길 경우에도 그 자리에 it를 놓고 that절을 문장 뒤로 보낸다.

> 1. **That** he is honest is true. = **It** is true **that** he is honest.
> 2. I think **that** our team will win the game.
>   I think **it** certain **that** our team will win the game.

1. (그것은) 사실이다 / 그가 정직하다는 **것은**.
2. 나는 생각한다 / 우리팀이 그 게임에서 이길 것이**라고**.
   나는 생각한다 / (그것은) 확실하다고 / 우리팀이 그 게임에서 이기는 **것은**.

1. **It**'s really a wonder **that** I haven't dropped all my ideals, because they seem so absurd and impossible to carry out.
2. **It** is altogether fitting and proper **that** we should do this.
3. **It** is not what one accomplishes, but what one tries to accomplish, **that** makes a man strong.
4. **It** may also be said that rational, industrious, useful human beings are divided into two classes.
5. **It** may be said that "unceasing effort is the price of success."
6. I take **it** for granted **that** he is honest.

― 영작 ―

1. (그것은) 정말 놀라운 일이다 / 내가 놓지(버리지) 않았다는 **것은** / 모든 나의 이상들을 / 그것들은 보이기 때문에 / 너무 터무니없고 불가능하게 / 실천하기에는.
2. (그것은) 너무 합당하고 적절합니다 / 우리가 그렇게 하는 **것은**.
3. (그것은) 아니다 / 인간이 성취하는 것이 아니라 / 인간이 성취하기 위해 노력하는 것이다 / 사람을 강하게 만드는 **것은**.
4. **역시 말해질 수 있다** / 이성적인, 근면한, 유용한 사람들은 / 나눠진**다고** / 두 가지 부류로.
5. **말해질 수도 있다** / "끊임없는 노력은 성공의 대가다" **라고**.
6. 나는 받아들인다 / (그것을) 당연하게 / 그가 정직하다는 **것을**.

PART 2

24 동사 + (that) + 명사 + 동사

동사와 '명사 + 동사' 사이에는 명사절 접속사인 that가 생략돼 있다.

> He says (**that**) the deepest urge in human nature is "the desire to be important."

그는 말한다 / 가장 깊은 충동은 / 인간 본성에서 / '중요해지려는 욕구' **라고**.

※ 다음 문장들에서 that가 생략된 곳에 체크해 보시오.
1. Most people believe they can prove the intensity of their love when they love nobody except the "loved" person.
2. You know you have to "read between the lines" to get the most out of anything.
3. They believe they're destined for great things, like you.
4. I think this heightened sense of observation of nature is one of the chief delights that have come to me through trying to paint.
5. When there is space between you and the object you are observing you will know there is no love.
6. Remember, Jonathan, heaven isn't a place or a time, because place and time are so very meaningless.

영작

1. 대다수 사람은 믿는다 / 그들이 증명할 수 있**다고** / 그들 사랑의 강렬함을 / 그들이 아무도 사랑하지 않을 때 / '사랑하는' 사람 외에는.
2. 여러분은 안다 / 여러분이 읽어야 한다는 **것을** / 행간을 / 최대의 것을 얻기 위해 / 어느 책에서나.
3. 그들은 믿는다 / 그들이 운명지어졌**다고** / 위대한 일들을 위해, 여러분처럼.
4. 나는 생각한다 / 이런 높아진 자연 관찰의 감각이 / 주요한 기쁨들의 하나**라고** / 나에게 온 / 그림을 그리려는 노력을 통해.
5. 공간이 있을 때 / 당신과 당신이 바라보는 대상 사이에 / 당신은 알 것이다 / 사랑이 없다는 **것을**.
6. 명심하게 조너선, / 하늘나라는 어떤 장소나 어떤 시간이 아니라는 **것을**, / 왜냐하면 장소와 시간은 너무 무의미하니까.

25   5w1h + 주어 + 동사

명사절을 이끄는 who, when, where, why, what, how는 '~지'로 해석한다. 5w1h 앞에는 ask, know, tell, understand, imagine, determine 등 의문과 관련된 동사가 온다.

1. I don't know **who** was nominated.
2. Do you know **when** he will come?
3. Do you know **where** they are?
4. I wanted to know exactly **what** made a winning team.
5. A cloud does not know **why** it moves in just such a direction and at such a speed.
6. I can't imagine **how** the thief got in.

1. 나는 모른다 / **누가** 지명 받았는**지**.
2. 너는 아니 / **언제** 그가 올**지**?
3. 너는 아니 / 그들이 **어디에** 있는**지**?
4. 나는 원했다 정확하게 알기를 / **무엇이** 승리 팀으로 만드는 **지**.
5. 구름은 모른다 / **왜** 그것이 움직이는 **지를** / 바로 그런 방향으로 또 그런 속도로.
6. 나는 상상도 할 수 없다 / **어떻게** 도둑이 들어왔는**지**.

1. What determines **who** finishes?
2. You have a concept of **what** you should be and how you should act, and all the time you are in fact acting quite differently.
3. **What** you choose to do with them is up to you.
4. If then, that friend demand **why** Brutus rose against Caesar, this is my answer: Not that I loved Caesar less, but that I loved Rome more.
5. When you are forever fighting a degenerating sense of "nobodyness" then you will understand **why** we find it difficult to wait.

6. You will know, too soon, **how** truly Tom Moore sang, when he said that there was nothing half so sweet in life.
7. One could show **how** many times peace has been broken, and how many promises rendered worthless, by the faithlessness of princes.
8. One is quite astonished to find **how** many things there are in the landscape, and in every object in it, which one never noticed before.

영작

1. 무엇이 결정하는가 / **누가** (학업을) 마치는**지를**?
2. 당신은 가지고 있다 하나의 생각을 / 당신이 **무엇이** 돼야 하는**지**에 대한 / 그리고 당신이 **어떻게** 행동해야 하는 **지**에 대한 / 그리고 항상 / 당신은 실제로는 행동하고 있다 / 매우 다르게.
3. **무엇을** 당신이 결정할 **지**는 / 그들과 함께 하기로 / 당신에게 달렸다.
4. 그러면 그 친구는 물을 것이오 / **왜** 브루터스가 일어섰는**지를** / 시저에 반대해 / 내 대답은 이렇소: / 내가 시저를 덜 사랑했기 때문이 아니라 / 로마를 더 사랑했기 때문이라고.
5. 당신이 영원히 싸우고 있을 때 / 타락감과 / "보잘 것 없는 놈"이라는 - / 그때 당신은 이해할 것이다 / **왜** 우리들이 생각하는 **지를** / 기다리는 것이 어렵다고.
6. 그대는 알게 될 것이다 곧 / **얼마나** 진실하게 톰 무어가 노래했는**지를**, / 그가 말했을 때 / 절반도 되는 게 없다고 / 사랑의 달콤함의 / 인생에 있어서.
7. 사람들은 보여줄 수 있다 / **얼마나** 여러 번 / 평화가 깨졌는**지를**, / 그리고 **얼마나** 많은 약속들이 / 무가치하게 됐는**지를**, / 군주들의 신의 없음에 의해.
8. 사람들은 크게 놀란다 / 알고서는 / **얼마나** 많은 것들이 있는 **지를** / 풍경 속에, / 그리고 풍경 안에 있는 모든 사물 속에 / 사람들이 전에는 결코 알아채지 못한.

26   whether + 주어 + 동사 / 동사 + if + 주어 + 동사

whether절과 동사 뒤에 오는 if절은 '~인지 아닌지'로 해석한다.
ask, see, know, learn, doubt, wonder 등 의문과 관련된 동사가 whether절과 if절을 이끈다.

1. I don't know **whether** he will succeed (or not).
2. He asked **if** I knew Chinese.

1. 나는 모르겠다 / 그가 성공**할지 어떨지**.
2. 그는 물었다 / 내가 중국어를 **아는지 모르는지**.

1. **Whether** it's true or not is hard to tell.
2. **Whether** you are citizens of America or of the world, ask of us the same high standards of strength and sacrifice that we shall ask of you.
3. Now we are engaged in a great civil war, testing **whether** that nation or any nation so conceived and so dedicated, can long endure.
4. I dont know **if** he would come.
5. He glanced at his mother to see **if** she was watching him.
6. I wonder **if** it isn't time now to think about it.

영작

1. 그것이 진실**인지 아닌지**는 말하기 어렵다.
2. 마지막으로 여러분이 미국 시민**이든** 세계의 시민**이든** / 우리에게 부탁하십시오 / 똑같이 높은 수준의 힘과 희생을 / 우리가 여러분에게 부탁하는.
3. 이제 우리는 참가하고 있습니다 / 거대한 내전에, / 그리고 시험받고 있습니다 / 그런 나라가, 혹은 모든 나라가 / 그렇게 잉태된 그리고 그렇게 바쳐진, / 오랫동안 지탱할 수 있을**지 없을 지를**.
4. 나는 모르겠다 / 그가 **올지 안 올지**.
5. 그는 어머니를 힐끗 바라보았다 / 확인하려고 / 그녀가 자기를 보고 있는지 **아닌지**.
6. 나는 궁금하다 / 지금 생각할 때**인지 아닌지** / 그것에 대해.

27 It is + 강조되는 어구 + that(who)

it-that 강조구문에서 It is와 that를 생략해도 문장은 성립된다. 해석은 있는 그대로 it는 '그것' 으로, that은 '~것은' 으로 한다.

> 1. He broke the window on purpose.
> 2. **It** was he **that**(who) broke the window on purpose.
> 3. **It** was the window **that**(which) he broke on purpose.
> 4. **It** was on purpose **that** he broke the window.

1. 그는 깨뜨렸다 / 그 창을 / 일부러.
2. (그것은) 그였다 / 창을 깬 **사람은** / 일부러.
3. (그것은) 창이었다 / 그가 일부러 깬 **것은**.
4. (그것은) 고의에서였다 / 그가 창을 깬 **것은**.

1. **It** is the simple things **that** really matter.
2. **It** was no mere human creature like ourselves **that** we adored. **It** was a queen **that** we paid homage to, a goddess **that** we worshipped.
3. **It** is this desire **that** makes you want to wear the latest styles.
4. **It** is only with the heart **that** one can see rightly.
5. **It** is not until one gets ill **that** one knows how valuable health is.

영작

1. 단순한 것들이다 / 진짜 중요한 **것은**.
2. (그것은) 하잘 것 없는 인간은 아니었다 / 우리와 같은 / 우리가 경모한 **것은**. // (그것은) 여왕이었다 / 우리가 경의를 표한 **것은** / (그것은) 여신이었다 / 우리가 숭배한 **것은**.
3. (그것은) 이런 욕구다 / 만드는 **것은** / 당신이 원하도록 / 최신형의 옷을 입기를.
4. (그것은) 오직 마음으로지 / 사람이 볼 수 있는 **것은** 올바로.
5. (그것은) 사람들이 병에 들 때까지는 아니다 / 사람들이 아는 **것은** / 건강이 얼마나 귀중한 지를.

28 명사 + who, whose, whom, which, that

명사 뒤에 오는 wh-나 that는 앞의 명사(선행사)를 수식하며(관계) 대신한다고(대명사) 관계대명사란 이름이 붙여졌다. 명사 뒤에 오는 wh-와 that는 무조건 '~하는'으로 해석하는 것이 포인트다. 선행사가 사람인지 사물인지, 주격인지 목적격인지 하는 것은 당장은 몰라도 해석하는 데는 전혀 지장이 없다. 그런 것들은 그때그때 문장 속에서 쓰임을 익히기만 해도 충분하다.

(1) 사람 + who + 동사
(2) 사람 + whose 명사 + 동사
(3) 사람 + whom + 주어 + 동사
(4) 동물, 사물, 형용사, 구, 절 + which (+주어) + 동사
(5) 사람, 동물, 사물 + that (+주어) + 동사

1. This is the reporter **who** has come here to obtain the news.
2. Children **whose** parents are dead are called orphans.
3. He is one of the remarkable men **whom** this century has produced.
4. She came out onto the balcony **which** looked down onto the garden.
5. I never found the companion **that** was so companionable as solitude.

1. 이 분이 그 기자 분입니다 / 여기에 **온** / 취재하러.
2. 부모가 죽**은** 아이는 고아라고 불린다.
3. 그는 뛰어난 사람들 중의 한 명이다 / 이 나라가 배출**한**.
4. 그녀는 나왔다 / 발코니로 / 정원이 내려다 보이**는**.
5. 나는 결코 찾지 못했다 / 말벗을 / 친근**한** / 고독만큼.

29 사람 + who + 동사

(1) who는 앞의 사람을 받아 주어 역할을 하고 뒤에 동사가 온다.
(2) who 앞에 코머(,)가 오면 '~는' 으로 해석한다.

1. He had a son **who** became a teacher.
2. He had a son, **who** became a teacher.

1. 그는 아들 한 명이 있다 / 선생님이 **된**.
2. 그는 아들 한 명이 있다 / **그는** 선생님이 됐다.

1. "It's strange. The gulls **who** scorn perfection for the sake of travel go nowhere, slowly. Those **who** put aside travel for the sake of perfection go anywhere, instantly.
2. Broadly speaking, human being may be divided into three classes: those **who** are toiled to death, those **who** are worried to death, and those **who** are bored to death.
3. Those **who** have courage and faith will never perish in misery.
4. Everybody likes John, **who** is kind.
5. I met a boy, **who** told me the news.

영작

1. "그것 이상해. / 갈매기들은 / 완벽함을 경멸**하는** / 여행을 위해 / 아무 곳도 가지 못해, 천천히라도. // 갈매기들은 / 여행을 제쳐놓**는** / 완벽함을 위해 / 어디든지 가거든, 즉시.
2. 넓게 말하면 / 인간은 나뉘어질 수 있다 / 세 가지 부류로: / 사람들 / 죽도록 일만 **하는**, 사람들 / 죽도록 걱정만 하**는**, / 그리고 사람들 / 죽도록 권태만 느끼**는**.
3. 사람들은 / 용기와 신념을 가**진** / 결코 망하지 않을 것이다 / 비참하게.
4. 모든 사람이 존을 좋아한다, / **그는** 친절하다.
5. 나는 한 소년을 만났다, / **그는** 나에게 말했다 / 그 뉴스를.

30 사람 + whose 명사 + 동사 / 사람 + whom + 주어

(1) whose는 앞의 사람을 받아 소유격 역할을 하고 뒤에 명사가 온다.
(2) whom은 앞의 사람을 받아 목적격 역할을 하고 뒤에 주어가 온다.

> 1. This is the boy **whose** father is a teacher.
> 2. The girl **whom** you met yesterday is my sister.

1. 이 아이의 아버지가 선생님**인** 그 소년이다.
2. 그 소녀는 / 네가 어제 만**난** / 내 여동생이다.

1. It may also be said that rational, industrious, useful human beings are divided into two classes: first, those **whose** work is work and (those) **whose** pleasure is pleasure; and secondly, those **whose** work and pleasure are one.
2. I wander from one room to another, downstairs and upstairs, feeling like a songbird **whose** wings have been cut and who, in the dark, is throwing herself against her cage.
3. Marcel Proust said that love is subjective and that we do not love real people, but only those **whom** we have created in our mind.

영작

1. 역시 말해진다 / 이성적인, 근면한, 유용한 사람들은 / 나눠진다고 / 두 가지 부류로: / 첫째는 사람들이다 / 일은 일**인** / 그리고 즐거움은 즐거움**인**; / 둘째로, 사람들이다 / 일과 즐거움이 하나**인**.
2. 나는 방황한다(왔다갔다한다) / 한 방에서 다른 방으로, / 아래층과 위층을, / 그리고 느껴지는 노래하는 새처럼 / 날개가 잘**린** / 그리고 어둠 속에서 던지고(부딪치고) 있는 / 자신을 새장에다.
3. 마르셀 프루스트는 말했다 / 사랑은 주관적이라고 / 또 우리는 사랑하는 것이 아니라 / 실제 사람을 / 사랑한다고 사람들만 / 우리가 형성**한** / 우리의 마음속에.

PART 2

31 동물, 사물 + which (+주어) + 동사

(1) which는 선행사가 동물이나 사물일 때 쓰인다.
(2) which 앞에 코머(,)가 오면 형용사·구·절도 선행사로 받으며 **'그런데 그것은'** 으로 해석한다.

1. She made a doll **which** had blue eyes.
2. He lent me a book, **which** interested me.

  1. 그녀는 인형을 만들었다 / 푸른 눈을 가**진**.
  2. 그는 나에게 책 한 권을 빌려주었다 / **그런데 그것은** 나의 흥미를 끌었다.

1. To restore mental equilibrium we should call into use those parts of the mind **which** direct both eye and hand.
2. He is rich, **which** I unfortunately am not.
3. You say so, **which** is a clear proof of your honesty.
4. He tried to swim across the river, **which** was impossible.
5. He sometimes speaks German, **which** language I cannot understand.

영작

1. 회복하기 위해서는 정신적인 균형을 / 우리는 사용해야 한다 / 정신의 부분들을 / 지휘**하는** / 눈과 손을 모두.
2. 그는 부자다. / **그런데** 나는 불행하게도 부자가 아니다.
3. 너는 그렇게 말한다. / **그런데 그것은** 명백한 증거다 / 네가 정직하다는.
4. 그는 수영하려 했다 / 그 강을 건너. / **그런데 그것은** 불가능했다.
5. 그는 가끔 독일어를 말한다. / **그런데 그 언어를** 나는 이해할 수 없다.

32 사람, 동물, 사물 + that (+주어) + 동사

(1) that는 소유격을 제외한 어떤 경우에도 사용할 수 있는 약방의 감초격인 '감초 관계사'다.
(2) 제한적 용법으로만 사용되고 한정의 뜻이 강하므로 선행사에 최상급의 형용사, 서수사, the only, the, very, all 등이 올 때 흔히 쓰인다.

1. This is the best music **that** I have ever heard.
2. This is the very film **that** I have wanted to see.

   1. 이것은 가장 좋은 음악이다 / 내가 지금까지 들어**본** 음악 중에서.
   2. 이것이 바로 그 필름이다 / 내가 보기를 원했**던**.

1. Solitude is not measured by the miles of space **that** intervene between a man and his fellows.
2. "Gather ye rosebuds while ye may, old time is still a-flying, and this same flower... **that** smiles today, tomorrow will be dying."
3. One evening the gulls **that** were not night-flying stood together on the sand, thinking.
4. "You will begin to touch heaven, Jonathan, in the moment **that** you touch perfect speed.

영작

1. 고독은 측정되지 않는다 / 공간의 마일(거리)로 / 끼어 **있는** / 한 사람과 그의 동료들 사이에.
2. "거둬라 그대여 장미 봉오리들을 / 그대가 할 수 있을 때 / 오랜 시간이 아직 날고 (흐르고) 있고 / 이 똑같은 꽃이 / 오늘 미소 **짓는** / 내일이면 질 것이다."
3. 어느 날 저녁 / 그 갈매기들이 / 야간 비행을 하지 않고 있**었던** / 함께 섰다/ 모래사장에 / 그리고 생각에 잠겼다.
4. "자네는 접하기 시작하는 거야 하늘나라를, 조너선, / 도달**하는** 순간에 / 완벽한 속도에.

PART 2

33 명사 + (that) + 명사 + 동사

명사가 연이어 나오면 명사 사이에는 관계대명사 that가 생략돼 있다.

> The kind of people (**that**) I look for to fill top management spots are the eager beavers.

종류의 사람은 / 내가 찾**는** / 채우기 위해 최고 경영직에 / 열성적인 비버들(일꾼들)이다.

다음 문장들에서 that가 생략된 곳을 체크해 보시오.
1. Our love was a religion we could have died for.
2. The only way you can motivate people is to communicate with them.
3. The joy we experience cannot be interfered with, because its source is within ourselves.
4. If I give all I possess to the poor and surrender my body to the flames, but have not love, I gain nothing.
5. Dr. Sigmund Freud, one of the most distinguished psychologists of the 20th century, says that everything you and I do springs from the two motives: the sex urge and the desire to be great.

영작

1. 우리의 사랑은 종교였다 / 우리가 죽을 수도 있었**던**.
2. 유일한 방법은 / 여러분이 사람들에게 동기를 부여할 수 있**는** / 대화하는 것이다 그들과.
3. 기쁨은 / 우리가 경험하**는** / 방해받을 수는 없다. / 왜냐하면 그것의 근원이 우리 자신 속에 있기 때문에.
4. 만약 내가 준다해도 / 모든 것을 / 내가 소유하고 있**는** / 가난한 사람들에게 / 그리고 내준다해도 / 나의 몸을 화염에 / 그러나 가지고 있지 않으면 사랑을 / 나는 아무 것도 얻는 것이 없다.
5. 시그먼드 프로이드 박사는 / 가장 저명한 심리학자의 한 사람인 / 20세기의 / 말한다 / 여러분과 내가 **하는** 모든 일은 (튀어)나온다고 / 두 가지 동기들: / 즉 성적 충동과 위대해지려는 욕망으로부터.

34 what + 주어 + 동사

(1) 선행사를 포함한 관계대명사 what은 '(~하는) 것' 으로 해석한다.
(2) ask, wonder, know 등 **의문**과 관련된 동사 뒤에 오는 what은
대체로 '**~지**' 로 해석되는 **의문**대명사다.

> 1. He gave me **what** he had found.
> 2. I asked him **what** he had found.

1. 그는 나에게 주었다 / 그가 발견한 **것**을.
2. 나는 그에게 물었다 / 무엇을 그가 발견했는**지**.

1. **What** is essential is invisible to the eye.
2. You become responsible, forever, for **what** you have tamed.
3. It is not **what** one accomplishes, but **what** one tries to accomplish, that makes a man strong.
4. **What** one learns beyond the basic skills is hard to measure.
5. Learning is finding out **what** you already know.
6. **What** the caterpillar calls the end of the world, the master calls a butterfly.
7. Different as brotherly love and motherly love are from each other, **what** they have in common is that they are not restricted to one person.

영작

1. 중요한 **것은** / 보이지 않는다 / 눈에.
2. 당신은 책임지게 되죠, 영원히, / 당신이 길들인 **것**에.
3. (그것은) 인간이 성취하는 **것이** 아니라 인간이 성취하기 위해 노력하는 **것**이다 / 사람을 강하게 만드는 것은.
4. 사람들이 배우는 **것은** / 기본 기술들을 넘어서 / 어렵다 측정하기가.
5. 배우는 것은 발견하는 것이다 / 당신이 이미 알고 있는 **것**을.
6. 고치가 세상의 끝이라고 부르는 **것을** / 그 스승은 부른다 / 나비라고.
7. 다르지만 / 우애와 모성애는 / 서로 / 그들이 공통으로 가지고 있는 **것은**, / 그들이 국한돼 있지 않다는 것이다 / 한 사람에게.

35　명사 + when, where, why, how

(1) '명사 + -wh'에서 -wh는 무조건 '~**하는**'으로 해석한다.
(2) when 앞에는 시간 표시 명사, where 앞에는 장소 표시 명사, why 앞에는 the reason이 오고 how 앞에는 선행사가 오지 않는다.
(3) 선행사가 생략된 where는 '하는 곳', when은 '하는 때', why는 '하는 이유', how는 '하는 방법'으로 해석한다.
(4) 일반적으로 ask, know, tell 등 의문과 관련된 동사 뒤에 오는 when, where, why는 명사절 접속사로서 '**~지**'로 해석할 수도 있다.

---

1. I like to climb the mountain **where** there is some snow.
2. There are frequent occasions **when** joking is not allowable.
3. Do you know **where** the children play?
4. Do you know **when** he is going to start?
5. Come **when** you wish.
6. Tell me **why** you left me.
7. This is **how** he always treats me.

---

1. 나는 좋아한다 산을 오르는 것을 / 눈이 약간 있**는**.
2. 경우들은 흔하다 / 농담이 허용되지 않**는**.
3. 너는 알고 있니 / 아이들이 노**는 곳**을?
    = 너는 알고 있니 **어디서** 아이들이 놀고 있는**지**?
4. 너는 알고 있니 / 그가 출발할 **때**를? = 너는 알고 있니 **언제** 그가 출발할 **지**?
5. 오라 / 네가 오고싶을 **때**.
6. 나에게 말해주시오 / 당신이 나를 떠**난 이유**를. = 당신이 **왜** 나를 떠났는 **지**를.
7. 이것이 **방식**이다 / 그가 늘 나를 대하**는**.

1. What noble deeds were we not ripe for in the days **when** we loved?
2. Ah, those foolish days, those foolish days, **when** we were unselfish, and pure-minded; those foolish days, **when** our simple hearts were full of truth, and faith, and reverence!
3. There will come a time **when** the clouds roll away and the landscape lies clearly before you.
4. The best thing for those who are afraid or lonely is to go outside, **where** they can be quite alone with the heavens and nature.
5. **Where** there are prophecies, they will cease; **where** there are tongues, they will be stilled, where there is knowledge, it will pass away.
6. When you look at a face opposite, you are looking from a centre and the centre creates the space between person and person, and **that is why** our lives are so empty and callous.

영작

1. 어떤 고상한 행동이라도 / 우리는 할 마음의 준비를 하고 있지 않았던가? 그 시절에는 / 우리가 사랑했**던**.
2. 아, 저 어리석었던 나날이여, 저 어리석었던 나날이여. / 우리들이 비이기적이고 순수했**던** / 우리의 소박한 마음이 가득 찼**던** / 진실과 믿음과 존경으로.
3. 올 것이다 시간이 / 구름들이 걷히**는** / 그리고 풍경이 놓이는(펼쳐지는) 분명하게 / 당신 앞에.
4. 가장 좋은 일은 / 사람들에게 / 두려워하는 혹은 외로운 / 밖에 나가는 것이다 / **그곳에서는** 그들이 완전히 혼자일 수 있다 / 하늘과 자연과 함께.
5. 예언이 있는 **곳에** / 예언은 그칠 것이며 / 방언이 있는 **곳에** / 방언은 조용해질 것이며 / 지식이 있는 곳에 / 지식은 떠나갈 것이다.
6. 당신이 바라볼 때 / 상대방 얼굴을, / 당신은 보고 있다 / 어떤 중심에서 / 그리고 그 중심은 만든다 / 공간을 / 사람과 사람 사이의, / 그리고 **그것이 이유다** / 우리의 삶들이 그렇게 공허하고 무감각**한**.

36 whenever, wherever, however

when, where, how에 -ever가 붙으면 선행사를 포함하는 양보 부사절을 이끈다. whenever는 '**언제나**', wherever는 '**어디든지**', however는 '**아무리**' 로 해석한다.

1. **Whenever** I visited him, he was not at home.
   = No matter when I visited him, he was not at home.
2. **Wherever** you may go, I will follow you.
   = No matter where you may go, I will follow you.
3. **However** rich you may be, you can't buy it.
   = No matter how rich you may be, you can't buy it.

1. 내가 그를 방문할 **때는 언제나**, 그는 집에 없었다.
   = 내가 언제 그를 방문**할지라도**, 그는 집에 없었다.
2. 당신이 가는 **곳이 어디든지**, 나는 당신을 따라가겠어요.
   = 당신이 **어디로** 간다**해도**, 나는 당신을 따라가겠어요.
3. 네가 **아무리** 부자일지**라도**, 너는 그것을 살 수 없다.

1. A man thinking or working is always alone, **wherever** he may be.
2. Without love, **however** hard you try to reform the world or bring about a new social order or **however** much you talk about improvements, you will only create agony.

영작

1. 사람은 / 생각하는 혹은 일하는 / 늘 고독하다 / 그가 있는 곳이 **어디든지**.
2. 사랑 없이는, / **아무리** 열심히 당신이 노력**해도** / 개혁하려고 세상을 / 혹은 형성하려고 / 새로운 사회 질서를 / 혹은 **아무리** 많이 당신이 이야기**해도** / 개선들에 대해, / 당신은 단지 만들 것이다 고뇌를.

37 whoever, whichever, whatever

관계대명사 who, which, what 등에 -ever를 붙이면 선행사를 포함하는 부사절을 이끈다. whoever는 '**누구나**', whichever는 '**어느 것이든**', whatever는 '**무엇이든**'으로 해석한다.

1. **Whoever** wishes to succeed must be industrious.
2. Choose **whichever** you like.
3. I will give you **whatever** you need.

  1. 성공하기를 원하는 사람은 **누구나** / 근면해야 한다.
  2. 선택하라 / **어느 것이든** / 네가 좋아하는.
  3. 나는 너에게 주겠다 / 네가 필요한 것은 **무엇이든**.

1. **Whoever** has to deal with young children soon learns that too much sympathy is a mistake.
2. If a man delights in his wife and children, has success in work, and finds pleasure in the change of day and night, spring and autumn, he will be happy **whatever** his philosophy may be.
3. **Whatever** the worries of the hour or the threats of the future, once the picture has begun to flow along, there is no room for them in the metal screen.
4. A mind that is confused, **whatever** it does, at any level, will remain confused.

영작

1. 어린애를 다뤄야 하는 사람은 **누구나** / 곧 알게된다 / 너무 많은 동정은 잘못이라는 것을.
2. 만일 한 남자가 기쁨을 얻으면 / 그의 아내와 아이들에게서, / 성공하면 / 일에서, / 그리고 느끼면 즐거움을 / 변화에서 / 밤과 낮, 봄과 가을의, / 그는 행복할 것이다 / 그의 인생철학이 **무엇이든**.
3. 당장의 걱정들 / 혹은 장차의 위험들이 **무엇이든** / 일단 그림이 흐르기(그려지기) 시작하면 / 여지가 없다 / 그런 것들을 위한 / 마음의 화면에는.
4. 혼란된 마음은 / 그것이 혼동하는 것이 **무엇이든** / 어떤 수준에서도 / 계속 혼란스러울 것이다.

38 동격 명사 + that

명사 뒤에서 완전한 문장을 이끄는 that절은 앞의 명사와 동격 관계를 형성하고 '~**라는**, **다는**'으로 해석된다.
fact, proof, possibility, proposition, feeling, terror 등의 명사가 동격 명사로 흔히 사용된다.

> 1. No one can deny the fact **that** you are guilty.
> 2. There is no proof **that** he stole it.

1. 아무도 부정할 수 없다 / 네가 유죄**라는** 사실을
2. 아무 증거가 없다 / 그가 그것을 훔쳤**다는**.

1. Juliet was mournful over the irony of her fate, **that** she had fallen in love with a Montague.
2. You want a feeling **that** you are important in your little world.
3. You are harried by day and haunted by night by the fact **that** you are a Negro, living constantly at tiptoe stance.
4. Four score and seven years ago our fathers brought forth on this continent, a new nation, conceived in liberty, and dedicated to the proposition **that** all men are created equal.
5. Among many parents, the terror **that** their children won't go to the "right" college has supported an explosion of guidebooks, counselors and tutoring companies.

영작

1. 줄리엣은 슬퍼했다 / 운명의 얄궂음에 / 그녀가 사랑에 빠졌**다는** / 몬태규 가의 한 사람과.
2. 당신은 원한다 느낌을 / 당신이 중요하**다는** / 당신의 작은 세계에서.
3. 당신이 괴롭힘을 당하고 / 낮이면 / 꿈에 마저 시달리고 / 밤이면 / 사실에 의해 / 당신이 검둥이**라는** / 살아가는 항상 / 발돋움을 한 자세로.
4. 지금으로부터 87년 전 / 우리의 선조는 탄생시켰습니다 / 이 대륙에 / 한 새로운 나라를, / 자유 속에 잉태된, / 그리고 바쳐진 / 명제에 / 모든 사람들은 창조됐**다는** 평등하게.
5. 많은 부모들 사이에서, / 두려움은 / 그들의 자식들이 가지 못할 것이**라는** / 좋은 대학에, / 부추겼다 / 폭발을 / 안내서들, 카운슬러들 그리고 사설 학원들의.

39 as ~ as ⋯ / such ~ as + 명사

(1) as는 '**만큼, 처럼**'으로 해석한다. 'as ~ as ⋯'에서 앞의 as는 형식적인 요소로 무시한다.
(2) 'such ~ as 명사'는 '명사 **같은** ~'로 해석한다.

> 1. My love is **as** deep and boundless **as** the sea.
> 2. We can't trust **such** a man **as** he.

1. 나의 사랑은 깊고 끝이 없답니다 / 바다**만큼**.
2. 우리는 신용할 수 없다 / 그**와 같은** 인간을.

1. Sexual attraction creates the illusion of union. Yet without love this union leaves the lovers **as** far apart **as** strangers.
2. The dilligent student in one of the crowded hives of Cambridge college is **as** solitary **as** a dervish in the desert.
3. What he told me that evening applies **as** much to the business world **as** it does to sports.
4. Teaching is reminding others that they know just **as well as** you.
5. "Is there no **such** place **as** heaven?"
6. There is no **such** thing **as** a problem without a gift for you in its hands.

영작

1. 성적 매력은 형성한다 / 결합의 환상을. // 그러나 사랑이 없다면 / 이런 결합은 / 그 연인들이 / 멀리 떨어져 있게 한다/ 모르는 사람**처럼**.
2. 부지런한 학생은 / 복잡한 벌집(예를 들어 도서관)의 하나에 있는 / 하버드대학(보스턴시 캠브리지 대학촌 소재)의 / 고독하다 / 회교 탁발승**만큼** / 사막에 있는.
3. 그가 나에게 말한 것은 / 그날 저녁 / 적용된다 / 사업계에도 / 그것이 스포츠계에 적용되는**만큼**.
4. 가르치는 것은 상기시키는 것이다 / 다른 사람들에게 / 그들이 알고 있다는 것을 / 바로 당신**만큼** 잘.
5. **그런** 장소는 없는 가요 / 하늘나라 **같은**?"
6. **그런** 것은 없다 / 선물이 없는 문제 **같은** / 당신을 위한 / 그것의 손에는.

40 so(such) ~ that 주어 ⋯/ so that 주어 may(can) ~

(1) so는 '그래서'를 의미하므로 'so ~ that ⋯'은 '**너무 ~해서 ⋯하다**'로 해석한다.
(2) 'so that 주어 may ~'는 일반적으로 '**~ 하기 위해**'로 해석하지만 빠르고 정확한 독해를 위해 '**⋯ 그래서 ~할 수도 있다**'로 있는 그대로 이해하는 것이 좋다.

※ 다음 영문들을 비교해보면 왜 '있는 그대로' 영문을 이해해야 하는지를 잘 알 수 있을 것이다. 이 세상에는 비슷한 것은 많아도 똑 같은 것은 없기 때문이다. 또 '있는 그대로' 이해해야 진정한 의미에서 직독직해가 가능하고 암기의 부담에서도 벗어날 수 있다.

1. It was **so** lovely a day **that** I went out.
   = It was **such** a lovely day **that** I went out.
2. He is **so** rich **that** he **can** buy the book.
   = He is rich **enough to** buy the book.
   = He is **so** rich **as to** buy the book.
3. This stone is **so** heavy **that** I **can not** lift it.
   = This stone is **too** heavy for me **to** lift.
4. He works hard (**so**) **that** he **may** pass the exam.
   = He works hard (**so as**) **to** pass the exam.
5. He works hard (**so**) **that** he **may not** fail.
   = He works hard (**so as**) **not to** fail.
   = He works hard **lest** he **should** fail.

1. **너무** 아름다운 날**이어서** 나는 외출했다.
2. 그는 매우 부자**여서** 그는 그 책을 살 수 있다. =그는 부자다 / 그 책을 살 **정도로**.
   =그는 **매우** 부자다 / 그 책을 살 **만큼**.
3. 이 돌은 **너무** 무거워서 내가 들 수 없다. = 이 돌은 **너무** 무겁다 / 내가 들**기에는**.
4. 그는 열심히 공부한다 **그래서** / 그는 시험에 합격**할 수도 있다**.
   = 그는 열심히 공부한다 / 시험에 합격**하기 위해**.
5. 그는 열심히 공부한다 **그래서** 그는 실패하지 않**을지도 모른다**
   = 그는 열심히 공부한다 / 실패하지 않**기 위해**. = 그는 열심히 공부한다 / 실패하지 않**도록**.

1. Men are **so** simple and **so** ready to obey present necessities, **that** the one who deceives will always find those who allow themselves to be deceived.
2. Photography has been brought to **such** a degree of perfection **that** there is scarcely an object in nature that is beyond the reach of the camera.
3. Be silent (so) **that** you **may** hear.
4. Women put on beautiful gowns and jewels, **that** they **may** be chosen by men.
5. We have come to dedicate a portion of that field, as a final resting place for those who here gave their lives **that** that nation **might** live.

영작

1. 사람들은 **너무** 단순하고 / **기꺼이** 복종할 준비가 돼 있**어** / 현재의 필요성들에, / 속이**는** 사람은 / 항상 발견할 것이다 / 허용**하는** 사람들을 / 자신들이 속아 넘어 가도록.
2. 사진술은 **매우** 완전한 정도에 도달**해서** / 거의 없다 / 자연계에 카메라가 도달할 수 없는 사물은.
3. 조용히 하시오 / 여러분이 들**을 수 있도록**.
4. 여성들은 착용한다 / 아름다운 가운들과 보석들을 / 그들이 선택되**기 위해** / 남성들에 의해.
5. 우리는 왔습니다 / 바치기 위해 / 그 싸움터의 한 부분을 / 마지막 안식처로 / 사람들을 위해 / 여기서 목숨을 바친 / 그 나라가 살 수 있도록 **하기 위해**.

41 either A or B / ,nor / no sooner A than B / A is no more B than C is

(1) either A or B = A나 B 둘 중의 하나
(2) ,nor = 도 또한 않다
(3) no sooner A than B = A하자마자 B하다
(4) A is no more B than C is = A가 B 아닌 것은 C가 B 아닌 것과 같다

1. **Either** uncle **or** aunt may come.
2. I don't love her, **nor** does she love me.
   = I don't love her, **and** she does **not** love me, **either**.
3. He had **no sooner** seen me **than** he ran away.
   = **No sooner** had he seen me **than** he ran away.
   = **The moment(As soon as)** he saw me, he ran away.
4. A whale is **no more** a fish **than** a horse is.
   = A whale is **not** a fish **any more than** a horse is.

1. 아저씨**나** 아주머니 **두 분 중 한 분**이 오실 지 모른다.
2. 나는 그녀를 사랑하지 않는다 / 그리고 그녀**도 또한** 나를 사랑하지 **않는다**.
3. 그가 나를 보**자마자** / 그는 도망쳤다.
   = 그가 나를 보는 순간 / 그는 도망쳤다.
4. 고래가 물고기가 **아닌 것은** 말이 물고기가 **아닌 것과 같다**.

1. In short, one can **either** read, write, and compute, **or** one cannot.
2. Read not to contradict and confute, **nor** to believe and take for granted, **nor** to find talk and discourse, but to weigh and consider.
3. The world will little note, **nor** long remember, what we say here.
4. **Nor** have legitimate grounds ever failed a prince who wished to show colorable excuse for the non-fulfillment of his promise.
5. **No sooner** has he memorized their locations and peculiarities **than** he has to modify or forget them.

6. **The very moment** we break that law, we shall get into endless trouble.
7. **If** you choose your friends on the ground that you are virtuous and want virtuous company, you are **no nearer** to true friendship **than** if you choose them for commercial reasons.
8. We may sometimes think our country has done us personally an injury, but that gives us **no more** a right not to love our country **than** does an injury received from our father or mother give us a right to hate our father or mother.

> 영작

1. 요컨대, 사람들이 읽고, 쓰고, 계산할 수 있**든지**, / 혹은 할 수 없**든지 둘 중 하나다**.
2. 읽지 말라 / 반대하고 논박하기 위해 / **또한** 믿기 위해서**도** (읽지 **말라**), / 그리고 당연한 것으로 받아들이기 위해서도 (읽지 **말라**) / **또한** 찾기 위해서**도** (읽지 **말라**)/ 이야깃거리와 논박할 자료를 / 그러나 (독서를 하라) 고찰하고 숙고하기 위해.
3. 세상은 별로 주목하지 않을 것입니다, / **또한** 오랫동안 기억하지도 **않을** 것입니다, / 우리가 여기서 말하는 것을.
4. **또한** 합법적인 이유들이 저버린 적도 **없다** / 군주를 / 보여주기를 원했던 / 착색할 수 있는(그럴듯한) 변명을 / 그의 약속의 불이행에 대한.
5. 그가 기억**하자마자** / 그것들의 위치들과 특성들을 / 그는 수정하거나 잊어버려야 한다 그것들을.
6. 그러나 **바로 그 순간** / 우리가 그 법칙을 깨는 / 우리는 끝없는 곤란에 빠질 것이다.
7. 만약 당신이 선택한다면 당신의 친구들을 / 근거 하에 / 당신이 미덕이 있다는 / 그리고 원한다면 미덕이 있는 친구를 / 당신이 거리가 **먼 것은** / 진정한 우정**과는** / 마치 당신이 선택한다면 그들을 / 상업적인 이유들 때문에 / 당신이 진정한 우정과 거리가 **먼 것과 같다**.
8. 우리는 때때로 생각할 수도 있다 / 우리 나라가 우리에게 개인적으로 상처를 준 것을, / 그러나 그것이 우리에게 우리나라를 사랑하지 않을 권리를 **주지 않는 것은** / 우리 부모로부터 상처를 입었다고 해서 / 부모를 미워할 권리를 갖지 못하는 **것과 같다**.

42 되다 · 이동 · 정지 · 감각 · 판명 · 인생 동사 + 보어

(1) go, come, run, make, grow, turn 등 위치나 상태의 변화를 나타내는 동사는 '~**되다**' 로 해석한다.
(2) go, come, stand, sit, run, return, lay 등 이동 동사 다음에 오는 보어는 '**~하면서, ~한채** …하다' 로 해석한다.
(3) stay, remain, keep, hold, rest 등 정지 동사는 '**계속** ~하다' 로 해석한다.
(4) seem, look, feel, sound, smell, taste 등 감각 동사는 '**~하게, ~인 것처럼** …하다' 으로 해석한다.
(5) prove, be found, come out, turn out 등 판명동사는 '**~로 밝혀지다**' 로 해석한다.
(6) marry, live, die, part 등 인생사와 관련된 동사는 '**~로, ~인 상태로** …하다' 로 해석한다.

※ 2형식 동사의 예문들은 한 단어로 생각하고 큰 소리로 읽어 외어둘 필요가 있다.

1. He has **grown** old and weak.
2. He **sat** reading the book.
3. He **remained** a bachelor all his life.
4. He **looked** (to be) ill.
5. The bank-note **proved** (to be) a forgery.
6. He **died** a beggar.

1. 그는 늙고 허약**해졌다**.
2. 그는 **앉아 있었다** / 그 책을 읽으**면서**.
3. 그는 **계속** 독신이었다 / 평생 동안.
4. 그는 보인다 / 아픈 **것처럼**.
5. 그 지폐는 **밝혀졌다** / 위조물인 것으로.
6. 그는 죽었다 / 거지**로**.

43 되다 동사 + 보어

위치나 상태의 변화를 나타내는 동사 + 보어 = ~되다

1. He **got** angry with me.
2. Eggs soon **go** bad in hot weather.
3. His dog **went** mad.
4. He **went** blind in his old age.
5. Your dreams will **come** true some day.
6. She will **make** a good wife.
7. Her blood **ran** cold.
8. He **turned** pale.
9. You **become** responsible, forever, for what you have tamed.
10. Believe it or not, each of us... is one day going to stop breathing, **turn** cold, and die.

영작

1. 그는 나에게 화를 **냈다**.
2. 계란은 곧 상한다 / 더운 날씨엔.
3. 그의 개는 미쳤다.
4. 그는 눈이 멀게 **됐다** / 노년에.
5. 너의 꿈은 실현될 것이다 / 언젠가는.
6. 그녀는 좋은 아내가 **될** 것이다.
7. 그녀는 오싹해**졌다**.
8. 그는 창백**해졌다**.
9. 당신은 책임지게 **되죠**, 영원히, / 당신이 길들인 것에.
10. 믿건 안 믿건 / 우리 각자는/ 어느 날 멈추고 / 숨쉬는 것을, / 몸이 차갑게 **되고** 죽을 것이다.

44 이동 · 정지 동사 + 보어

(1) 이동동사 + 보어 = ~하면서, ~한 채 … 하다

1. He **stood** looking at the picture.
2. She **sat** surrounded by her children.
3. He **went** hopeful and **came** back disappointed.
4. He **went** home satisfied with the result.
5. He **came** home crying bitterly.
6. The dog **ran** barking after him.
7. A soldier **lay** dead on the road.
8. He **returned** home a millionaire.

영작

1. 그는 **서있었다** / 그 그림을 보**면서**.
2. 그녀는 **앉아 있었다** / 자기 아이들에게 둘러싸**인 채**.
3. 그는 **갔다** / 희망에 넘친 채 / 그리고 돌아왔다 실망**한 채**.
4. 그는 집으로 **갔다** / 결과에 만족**한 채**.
5. 그는 집에 **왔다** / 몹시 울**면서**.
6. 그 개는 **달렸다** / 그를 향해 짖으**면서**.
7. 한 군인이 **누워있었다** / 죽은 **채** 길에.
8. 그는 집에 **돌아 왔다** / 백만장자가 된 **채**.

(2) 정지 동사 + 보어 = **계속** … 하다

1. They **kept** silent for several hours.
2. You may **rest** assured.
3. This ticket **holds** good for three days.
4. A mind that is confused, whatever it does, at any level, will **remain** confused.
5. He cannot **remain** indifferent.
6. Poetry, beauty, romance, love, these are what we **stay** alive for.

영작

1. 그들은 **계속** 침묵을 지켰다 / 여러 시간 동안.
2. 너는 **계속** 안심해도 된다.
3. 이 티켓은 **계속** 유효하다 / 3일 동안.
4. 마음은 / 혼란된, / 그것이 혼동하는 것이 무엇이든, / 어떤 수준에서도, / **계속** 혼란스러울 것이다.
5. 그는 **계속** 냉담할 수는 없다.
6. 시, 아름다움, 낭만, 사랑, 이것들은 / 우리가 **계속** 살아가는 목적이다.

45 감각동사 + 보어

감각동사 + 보어 = ~인 것처럼(~하게) …하다

1. Always make the other person **feel** important.
2. She **looks** every inch a lady.
3. It's really a wonder that I haven't dropped all my ideals, because they **seem** so absurd and impossible to carry out.
4. A rose by any other name would **smell** as sweet.
5. The music **sounds** sweet.
6. The soup **tastes** of onion.

영작

1. 항상 만들어라 / 다른 사람이 **느끼도록** / 중요**하다고**.
2. 그녀는 보인다 / 어디까지나 귀부인**인 것처럼**.
3. 정말 놀라운 일이다 / 내가 놓지(버리지) 않았다는 것은 / 모든 나의 이상들을 / 그것들은 **보이기** 때문에 / 너무 터무니없고 불가능**한 것처럼** / 실천하기에는.
4. 장미는 어떤 다른 이름이라도 / **냄새나겠지요** / 향기**롭게**.
5. 음악이 **들린다** / 감미**롭게**.
6. 그 수프는 양파 맛이 난다.

46　판명 · 인생동사 + 보어

(1) 판명동사: ~로 밝혀지다

1. The rumor **turned out** (to be) false.
2. The report was **found** (to be) true.
3. The scandal will **come out** (to be) true at the trial.
4. This bud of love may **prove** (to be) / a beautiful flower when we next meet.

> 영작

1. 그 풍문은 **밝혀졌다** / 거짓으로.
2. 그 보도는 **밝혀졌다** / 사실인 것으로.
3. 그 풍문은 사실로 **밝혀질** 것이다 / 재판에서.
4. 이 사랑의 꽃봉오리는 **밝혀질지도** 몰라요 / 한 송이 아름다운 꽃으로 / 우리가 다음에 만날 때.

(2) 인생동사: (명사)로서, (형용사)인 상태로 …하다

1. She **married** young.
2. My teacher **lives** a bachelor.
3. We **parted** the best of friends.
4. He **went** an enemy and **came** back a friend.
5. They were **born** poor, **lived** poor and poor they **died**.

> 영작

1. 그녀는 결혼했다 / 젊어**서**.
2. 나의 선생님은 사신다 / 총각**으로**.
3. 우리는 헤어졌다 / 다정한 친구**로**.
4. 그는 갔다 적**으로** / 그리고 돌아왔다 / 친구**로**.
5. 그들은 태어났다 / 가난**한 상태로** / 살았다 / 가난**한 상태로** / 그리고 가난**한 상태로** 그들은 죽었다.

47 be + 과거분사

(1) 4형식 문형의 수동태는 능동태로 해석하는 것이 자연스러운데 사람은 '~에게', 사물은 '~을'로 해석한다.
(2) 과거분사 thought, believed, called, named, said 등은 생략하고 해석해도 문장을 이해하는 데는 지장이 없다.

---

1. He gave me the book.
   = I was **given** the book by him.
   = The book was **given** (to) me by him.
2. Some think him a good Samaritan.
   = He is **thought** to be a good Samaritan.

---

1. 그가 주었다 나에게 그 책을.
   = 나에게 주었다 그 책을 그가.
   = 그 책을 주었다 나에게 그가.
2. 어떤 사람은 생각한다 그가 자선가라고.(= 그는 자선가다.)

1. I bought her the watch.
   = The watch was **bought** for her by me.
2. I believe him (to be) a teacher.
   = He is **believed** to be a teacher.
3. Adam named his wife Eve.
   = His wife was **named** Eve.
4. He **is said** to be a liar.
   = **It is said that** he is a liar.

영작

1. 나는 사주었다 그녀에게 그 시계를.
   = 그 시계를 사주었다 그녀를 위해 내가.
2. 나는 믿는다 / 그가 선생님이라고.(= 그는 선생님이다.)
3. 아담은 불렀다 / 아내를 이브라고.(= 그의 아내는 이브다.)
4. 그는 거짓말쟁이로 **불려진다**.(= 그는 거짓말쟁이다.)

PART 2

48 타동사 + 목적어

resemble, attend, reach, enter, discuss, excel, marry, leave, cover 등은 타동사이므로 뒤에 전치사가 와서는 안 된다.

1. He **resembles**(=takes after) his father.
2. He **married** a rich girl.
3. He **reached**(=arrived at, got to) the station.
4. He **entered**(=walked into) the room.
5. He **left**(=walked out of) the room.
6. He **attended** the meeting.
7. We **discussed**(=talked over) the problem.
8. She **excels**(=is better than) me in cooking.
9. She **survived** her mother.
10. We are **approaching** the island.
11. If your love is true, and you mean to **marry** me, I will put my future in your hands.
12. It's better to **attend** Yale or Stanford than, say, Arizona State.
13. Jonathan loves to fly and spends all his time trying to **reach** the fastest speed.

영작

1. 그는 그의 아버지를 **닮았다**.
2. 그는 부잣집 아가씨와 **결혼했다**.
3. 그는 역에 **도착했다**.
4. 그는 그 방에 **들어갔다**.
5. 그는 그 방에서 **나갔다**.
6. 그는 그 회의에 **참석했다**.
7. 우리는 그 문제를 **토의했다**.
8. 그녀는 나**보다** 요리 솜씨가 **낫다**.
9. 그녀는 자기 어머니보다 **오래 살았다**.
10. 우리는 섬에 **접근하고** 있다.
11. 만약 당신의 사랑이 진실하다면 / 그리고 당신이 의미(의도)한다면 / **결혼하기를** 나와 / 나는 놓을(맡길) 겁니다 / 나의 미래를 당신의 손에.
12. 더 낫다 / 예일大나 스탠퍼드大를 **다니는** 것이 / 예를 들어 애리조나 주립大보다.
13. 조너선은 나는 것을 좋아한다 / 그리고 온종일 보내는 것을 좋아한다 / 최고의 속도에 **도달하려** 애쓰며.

49 주다동사 + 사람 + 사물

동사 뒤에 '사람 + 사물'이 오면 'A에게(를 위해) B를 **~해주다**'로 해석한다. 사람을 사물 뒤로 보낼 때는 to, for, of 등이 사람 앞에 온다.

(1) A**에게** B를 ~해주다: give, bring, show, send, teach, tell, lend, offer, hand + 사물 + to 사람
(2) A를 **위해** B를 ~해주다: buy, get, make, order, leave, play, save, sing + 사물 + for 사람
(3) ask, inquire + 사물 + of 사람

---

1. I **gave** her the book. = I gave the book to her.
2. He **bought** the girl a red rose.
   =He bought a red rose for the girl.

---

1. 나는 **주었다** / 그녀에게 그 책을.
2. 그는 **사주었다** / 그 소녀를 위해 한송이 빨간 장미를.

1. "Can you **teach** me to fly like that?"
2. I will **lend** you the money that you want.
3. And now I will **show** you the most excellent way.
4. She **handed** the driver a street map.
5. Tomorrow, I will **send** a messenger **to** you.
6. Mary **told** her brothers a fairy tale.
7. Won't you please **play** me a Chopin?
8. May I **ask** you a favor? = May I **ask** a favor **of** you?
9. We **played** him a trick. = We **played** a trick **on** him.

영작

1. "**가르쳐 주시겠어요** / 제가 날도록 그렇게?"
2. 내가 **빌려주겠다** / 너에게 네가 원하는 돈을.
3. 그리고 이제 나는 **보여줄** 것이다 그대들에게 / 가장 훌륭한 방법을.
4. 그녀는 **건네주었다** / 운전 기사에게 거리 지도를.
5. 내일, 나는 **보낼** 거예요 / 심부름꾼을 당신에게.
6. 메리는 **들려주었다** / 동생들에게 동화를.   7. 쇼팽 곡을 **연주해주지** 않겠습니까?
8. 부탁이 한 가지 있습니다.   9. 우리는 그를 속였다.

50 동사 + 명사 + 보어

5형식 문형의 명사(목적어)와 보어는 주어와 술어의 관계에 있다.
5형식 동사는 매우 중요하지만 대충 다뤄온 분야이므로 잘 익혀두자.
다음의 해석은 동사와 연결 지어 말을 만들어 보면 자연스럽게 이해할 수 있다. 특히 보어의 형태에 유의하자.

(1) 생각 동사: think, believe, consider, imagine, find, guess, expect, took, regrad, treat
   명사 + 명사, 형용사, 준동사 = '~가 …라고'
(2) 호칭 동사: call, name
   명사 + 명사 = '~를 …라고'
(3) 임명 동사: elect, appoint, select, choose, make
   명사 + 명사 = '~를 …로'
(4) 명령 동사: order, command, advise, tell, warn, compel, force
   명사 + to do = '~에게 …하라고' '~가 …할 것을'
(5) 허락 동사: allow, forbade, permit, enable
   명사 + to do = '~가 …하는 것을'
(6) 부탁 동사: ask, beg
   명사 + to do = '~에게 …해달라고'
(7) 감각 동사: see, watch, smell, hear, feel
   명사 + 원형부정사(진행형, 분사형) = '~가 …하는 것을'
(8) 사역 동사: have(시키다), make(만들다), let(허락하다)
   명사 + 원형부정사 = '~가 …하게'
(9) 기타: set, help, keep, like, hate, expect, find

1. I **believe** the couple satisfied.
2. They **called** him a liar.
3. We **elected** him as our representative.
4. I **ordered** him to leave the room.
5. He never **allows** me to look untidy.
6. He **asked** her to marry him.
7. I **saw** the bird fly.
8. He **made** me drink on that night.
9. He **set** his dog loose.

1. 나는 믿는다 / 그 부부**가** 만족하고 있**다고**.
2. 그들은 불렀다. / 그를 거짓말쟁이**라고**.
3. 우리는 선출했다 / 그를 우리의 대표**로**.
4. 나는 명령했다 / 그**에게** 방에서 나가**라고**.
5. 그는 결코 허락하지 않는다 / 내**가** 옷을 지저분하게 입는 **것을**.
6. 그는 청혼했다 / 그녀**에게** 자기와 결혼**해달라고** .
7. 나는 보았다 / 새**가** 나는 **것을**.
8. 그는 만들었다 / 내**가** 그날 밤 술을 마시게.
9. 그는 개를 풀어주었다.

51 생각 동사

생각 동사＋ 명사 ＋ 명사, 형용사, 준동사 ＝ '**～가 …라고**' 생각하다

1. Some **think** him a good Samaritan.
2. I **believe** him (to be) a teacher.
3. We **consider** the withdrawal a great shame.
4. I **find** it wholesome to be alone the greater part of the time.
5. I always **imagined** him as a tall man.
6. I **regard** our hiding as a dangerous, romantic adventure.
7. In my diary, I **treat** all difficulties as amusing.

영작

1. 어떤 사람은 생각한다 / 그**가** 자선가**라고**.
2. 나는 믿는다 / 그**가** 선생님이**라고**.
3. 우리는 여기고 있다 / 후퇴**가** 큰 치욕이**라고**.
4. 나는 생각한다 / (그것이) 건전하**다고** / 혼자 있는 **것이** / 대부분의 시간을.
5. 나는 언제나 상상하고 있었다 / 그**가** 키 큰 사람이**라고**.
6. 나는 간주한다 / 우리의 은신**이** / 위험하고 낭만적인 모험이**라고**.
7. 나의 일기에서 / 나는 간주한다 / 모든 어려움들**이** 즐거운 것이**라고**.

52 호칭/임명 동사

(1) 호칭 동사 + 명사 + 명사 = '~를 …라고' 부르다

1. Adam **named** his wife Eve.
2. What the catepillar calls the end of the world, the master **calls** a butterfly.

영작

1. 아담은 불렀다 / 아내를 이브**라고**.
2. 고치가 부르는 것을 / 세상의 끝이라고. / 그 스승은 부른다 / 나비**라고**.

(2) 임명 동사 + 명사 + 명사 = '~를 …로' 임명하다

1. They **appointed** him chairman.
2. Though you may **choose** the virtuous to be(=as) your friends, they may not choose you.
3. I have **made** him my friend.

영작

1. 그들은 임명했다 / 그를 회장**으로**.
2. 비록 당신이 선택할지 모른다 해도 / 미덕을 지닌 사람들을 / 당신의 친구들**로** / 그들은 선택하지 않을 지도 모른다 / 당신을.
3. 그러나 나는 만들었지 / 그를 나의 친구**로**.

53 명령 · 허락 · 부탁 동사

(1) 명령 동사 + 명사 + to do = '~에게 …하라고' '~가 …할 것을' 명령하다

1. He **ordered** his men to fire.
2. The general **commanded** the troops to withdraw.
3. He often **tells** me to keep my mouth shut.
4. I **warned** him not to be late.
5. He **advised** me not to go there.
6. Illness **compelled** me to spend the holiday in bed.
7. You can lead a horse to water, but you can't **force** it to drink.

■ 영작 ■

1. 그는 명령했다 / 부하**에게** 발포**하라고**.
2. 장군은 명령했다 / 군대**에게** 후퇴**하라고**.
3. 그는 종종 말한다 / 나**에게** 입을 닫으**라고**.
4. 나는 경고했다 / 그**에게** 늦지 말**라고**.
5. 그는 충고했다 / 나**에게** 그곳에 가지 말**라고**.
6. 병은 강요했다 / **나에게** 휴일을 침대에서 보내**라고**.
7. 당신은 말을 물가로 끌고 갈 수 있다 / 그러나 당신은 **강요할** 수는 없다 / 말에게 물을 마시**라고**.

(2) 허락 동사 + 명사 + to do = '~가 …하는 것을' 허락하다

1. I will **allow** them to do as they like.
2. I **forbade** him to enter my room.
3. He **permitted** him to depart.
4. Good health **enabled** him to carry out the plan.

■ 영작 ■

1. 나는 내버려둘 것이다 / 그들이 멋대로 **하는 것을**.
2. 나는 금했다 / 그**가** 들어**오는 것을**.
3. 우리는 허락했다 / 그**가** 떠나**는 것을**.
4. 건강은 가능하게 했다 / 그**가** 그 계획을 수행**하는 것을**.

(3) 부탁 동사 + 명사 + to do = '~에게 …해달라고'

1. She **asked** me to hand this package to you.
2. I **begged** my husband to accompany me.

■ 영작 ■

1. 그녀가 부탁했다 / 나에게 전달**해달라고** / 이 꾸러미를 당신에게.
2. 나는 간청했다 / 나의 남편에게 동행**해달라고**.

54 감각동사

감각동사 + 명사 + 원형부정사(진행형, 분사형) = '~가 …하는 것을'

1. **I saw** a man beaten by some people.
2. **Watch** the girl play the violin.
3. We **noticed** someone jump over the fence.
4. We **felt** the house shake.
5. I **heard** my name called.
6. If you listen real close, you can **hear** them whisper their legacy to you.
7. I can't **hear** a single bird singing outside.
8. You have **seen** vicious mobs lynch your mother and father at will.
9. I suddenly **feel** my tongue twisted and your speech stammering when I am humiliated.

영작

1. 나는 **보았다** / 한 남자가 몇 명의 사람에게 맞**는 것을**.
2. 주목하라 / 그 소녀**가** 바이올린을 연주하는 **것을**.
3. 우리는 눈치챘다 / 누군가**가** 담을 뛰어넘는 **것을**.
4. 우리는 느꼈다 / 집**이** 흔들리는 **것을**.
5. 나는 들었다 / 내 이름**이** 불리는 **것을**.
6. 여러분이 듣는다면 / 아주 가까이에서 / 여러분은 들을 수 있다 / 그들**이** 속삭이는 **것을** / 그들의 유산을 / 여러분에게.
7. 나는 들을 수 없다 / 한 마리의 새**가** 노래**하는 것도** 밖에서.
8. 당신이 보아왔다 / 악독한 폭도들**이** 린치하는 **것을** / 당신의 부모를 / 마음대로.
9. 나는 갑자기 느낀다 / 나의 혀**가** 뒤틀리고 나의 말**이** 더듬어지는 **것을** / 모욕을 당할 때.

55 사역동사

사역동사 + 명사 + 원형부정사 = '~가 …하게, 하도록' 시키다

1. They will **have** some one sing.
2. I **had** the man repair my car.
   = I got the man to repair my car.
   = I had my car repaired by the man.
   cf. I had(got) my bag stolen.
3. Always **make** the other person feel important.
4. Would you like to know how to **make** a girl fall in love with you?
5. Students create their own success; this **makes** the schools look good.
6. I **let** him have his own way.
7. **Let** it rather be a moving sea between the shores of your souls.

영작

1. 그들은 시킬 것이다 / 어떤 사람**이** 노래**하게**.
2. 나는 시켰다 / 그 사람**이** 내 차를 수리**하게**.
   cf. 가방을 도둑 맞았다.
3. 항상 만들어라 / 다른 사람**이** 느끼**도록** / 중요하다고.
4. 여러분은 알고 싶은가? / 어떻게 만드는 지를 / 한 소녀**가** 사랑에 빠지**도록** 당신에게.
5. 학생들이 창출한다 / 그들 자신의 성공을; / 이것이 **만든다** / 그 학교들이 좋게 보**이도록**.
6. 나는 허락한다 / 그**가** 하고싶은대로 **하도록**.
7. 그것**이** 차라리 움직이는 바다가 되**게 하라** / 그대 영혼들의 물가 사이에서.

56 기타 5형식 동사

1. I **set** him quickly on his way.
2. I'll **help** her (to) translate the story.
3. He **kept** me waiting long.
4. I **hate** a thing done by halves. If it be right, do it boldly.
5. Many people don't **like** a woman to smoke.
6. I **want** you to do your best.
7. I **would like** you **to** step forward... and peruse some of the faces from the past.
8. My father **expected** me to go to a medical school.
9. We **found** everything in good order.
10. I **found** the cage empty.

영작

1. 나는 그를 서둘러 돌아가**게 했다**.
2. 나는 돕겠다 / 그녀**가** 그 이야기를 번역**하는 것을**.
3. 그는 내**가** 오랫동안 기다리**도록 했다**.
4. 나는 싫어한다 / 일이 행해지는 **것을** / 어중간하게. // 만약 그것이 옳다면 / 실행하라 그것을 대담하게.
5. 많은 사람들이 싫어한다 / 여자**가** 담배 피우는 **것을**.
6. 나는 원한다 / 당신**이** 최선을 다**할 것을**.
7. 나는 바란다 / 여러분**이** 앞으로 다가**오기를**... / 그리고 꼼꼼히 읽기를(쳐다보기를) / 과거의 얼굴들을.
8. 나의 아버지는 기대하셨다 / 내**가** 의대에 가**기를**.
9. 우리는 알았다 / 모든 **것**이 잘 정리돼 있음**을**.
10. 나는 발견했다 / 새장**이** 비워있는 것을.

57 가정법

가정법은 의외로 쉽다. 문형은 시제의 일치에만 유의하면 되고 가정의 정도는 현재보다 과거가 더 강하며 과거완료는 실현불가능한 일을 가정하는 것이라고 알아두면 된다.

(1) 가정법 현재: '~**하면** …**할 것이다**'
   If 주어 + 현재동사, 주어 + 현재조동사
(2) 가정법 과거: '~**하면** …**할 것이다**'
   If 주어 + 과거동사, 주어 + 과거조동사
(3) 가정법 과거완료: '~**했다면** …**했을 것이다**'
   If 주어 + 과거완료, 주어 + 과거조동사 + 완료
(4) 가정법 미래: '**만일**(만에 하나) ~**한다면** …**할 것이다**'.
   If 주어 + **were to**(should), 주어 + **과거**(현재)조동사
(5) 혼합 가정문 = '~**했다면** …**할 것이다**'
   가정법 과거완료 + 가정법 과거

---

1. If he **is** honest, I **will** employ him.
2. If he **were**(was) honest, I **would** employ him.
3. If he **had been** honest, I **would have** employ**ed** him.
4. If I **were to** be young again, I **would** be a teacher.
5. What **should** I do if I **should** lose my sight?
6. If he **had not** been killed in the war, he **would** be **now** thirty years old.

---

1. 그가 정직**하다면** 나는 그를 채용**할 것이다**.
2. 그가 정직**하다면** 나는 그를 채용**할 것이다**.
3. 그가 정직**했다면** 나는 그를 채용**했을 것이다**.
4. **만일** 내가 다시 젊어진다면 나는 교사가 **될 것이다**.
5. 나는 어떻게 해야 하지 / **만일** 시력을 잃어버리면?
6. 그가 죽지 않**았다면** / 전쟁에서 / 그는 **지금은** 30살일 **것이다**.

1. **If I had to** sum up in one word the qualities that make a good manager, **I'd** say that it all comes down to decisiveness.
2. **If** every man **were not**, to a great extent, the architect of his own character, he **would** be a fatalist, an irresponsible creature of circumstances.
3. What noble lives **could** we not **have lived** for her sake (if I **had tried to** do so)?
4. Our love was a religion we **could have died** for.
5. **Had** Graduates of Harvard **chosen** colleges with lesser nameplates, they **would** (on average) **have done** just as well.
6. **Unless** you **had** force of character and physical strength, you **could** not succeed in life.
7. **Without** the rain, we **should have had** a pleasant journey.
8. If you **had listened** to me, you **wouldn't** be in danger now.

영작

1. 내가 요약해야 한**다면** / 한 단어로 / 자질들을 / 좋은 관리자를 만드는 / 나는 말할 **것이다** / 그것 모두 귀결된다고 / 결단력으로.
2. 모든 사람이 **아니라면** / 대단할 정도로 / 그 자신의 성격의 창조자가 / 그는 **될 것이다.** / 숙명론자가 / 책임 없는 피조물인 / 주위 환경에 대해.
3. 무슨 고상한 삶이라도 / 우리는 살 수 있지 않**았던가** / 그녀를 위해서라면?
4. 우리의 사랑은 하나의 종교였다 / 우리가 그것을 위해 죽**을 수도 있었던**.
5. 하버드대 졸업생들이 선택**했다면**(선택했더라도) / 대학들을 / 더 낮은 지명도를 가진, / 그들은 (평균적으로) **해냈을 것이다** / 그만큼은.
6. 인격의 힘과 체력을 갖지 **않으면** 너는 성공할 수 없**을 것이다** / 인생에서.
7. 비가 오지 **않았다면** 우리는 재미있는 여행을 **했을 것이다.**
8. 네가 (그때) 내 말을 들**었다면** 너는 **지금** 위험에 처해 있지 **않을텐데.**

P·A·R·T

 세상에서 가장 아름다운 영어 명문 30

I   세상 사랑하기
II   세상 살기
III 세상 가지기
IV 세상 바꾸기
V   세상 버리기

1. On Being in Love / Jerome Klapka Jerome 우리가 사랑할 때는
2. On Three Kinds of love / Erich Fromm 3가지 종류의 사랑
3. On Love / André Maurois 사랑에 대해
4. Love / from Corinthians 13:1-13 Teachings of Paul the Apostle 사랑이란
5. Romeo and Juliet / Shakespeare 로미오와 줄리엣
6. The Prophet – On Marriage / Kahlil Gibran 예언자 – 결혼에 관해

1. On Being in Love

What noble deeds were we not ripe for in the days when we loved? What noble lives could we not have lived for her sake? Our love was a religion we could have died for. It was no mere human creature like ourselves that we adored. It was a queen that we paid homage to, a goddess that we worshipped. And how madly we did worship! And how sweet it was to worship! Ah, lad, cherish love's young dream while it lasts! You will know, too soon, how truly Tom Moore sang, when he said that there was nothing half so sweet in life.

Even when it brings misery, it is a wild, romantic misery, all unlike the dull, worldy pain of after sorrows. When you have lost her – when the light is gone out from your life, and the world stretches before you a long, dark horror, even then a half enchantment mingles with your despair. Ah, those foolish days, those foolish days, when we were unselfish, and pure-minded; those foolish days, when our simple hearts were full of truth, and faith, and reverence.

Jerome Klapka Jerome (1859~1927)
English novelist and playwright whose humour – warm, unsatirical, and unintellectual. Began work as a railway clerk at age 14. Later found work as a schoolmaster, actor and finally as a journalist. First book published 1888 'On Stage and Off', 1889 published 'The Idle Thoughts of an Idle Fellow' and 'Three Men in a Boat' the later of which has never been out of print in the UK.

> When you have lost her – when the light is gone out from your life, and the world stretches before you a long, dark horror, even then a half enchantment mingles with your despair.

An amusing photograph of Jerome and his wife "Ettie" on a tandem bicycle.

Jerome K. Jerome (left) with 'Harris', George and lady friends on the Thames in the 1880's.

Dictionary

ripe: 1. fully grown or matured and ready for harvest or eating, as grain, fruit, or cheese.
2. ready to do, be done, or have something done to. Ex. The company is ripe for takeover.
homage: deep respect and often praise shown for a person or god.
Ex. On this occasion we pay homage (to him) for his achievements.
adore: 1. to worship as a divinity. Ex. She adores the Lord. 2 to love and honor deeply. Ex. He adores his grandmother.
lad: 1. a boy or young man. 2 a familiar or affectionate term or form of address for a man. Ex. The men in my club are all good lads.
enchant: to have a magical effect on. Ex. His music enchants us.

On Being in Love

What noble deeds / were we not ripe for
in the days / **when** we loved?
What noble lives / **could** we not **have lived** / for her sake?
Our love was a religion / **(that)** we **could have died** / for.
It was no mere human creature / like ourselves / **that** we adored.
It was a queen / **that** we paid homage to,
a goddess / **that** we worshipped.
And how madly / we did worship!
And how sweet / it was **to** worship!
Ah, lad, cherish / love's young dream / while it lasts!
You will know, / too soon, / **how** truly Tom Moore sang,
when he said / **that** there was nothing half / so sweet / in life.
Even when it brings misery,
it is a wild, romantic misery,
all unlike / the dull, worldy pain / of after sorrows.
When you have lost her –
when the light is gone out / from your life,
and the world stretches / before you / a long, dark horror,
even then / a half enchantment mingles / with your despair.
Ah, those foolish days, those foolish days,
when we were unselfish, and pure-minded;
those foolish days,
when our simple hearts were full / of truth, and faith, and reverence!

우리가 사랑할 때는

어떤 고상한 행동이라도 / 할 마음의 준비를 우리는 하고 있지 않았던가
그 시절에는 / 우리가 사랑했**던**?
어떤 고상한 삶이라도 / 우리는 살 수 있지 **않았던가** / 그녀를 위해서라면?
우리의 사랑은 일종의 종교였다 / 우리가 죽을 수도 있었**던** / (그것을) 위해 .
하잘 것 없는 인간은 아니었다 / 우리와 같은 / 우리가 경모한 **것은**.
여왕이었다 / 우리가 경의를 표한 **것은**,
여신이었다 / 우리가 숭배한 **것은**.
그리고 얼마나 미친 듯이 / 우리가 숭배했던가!
그리고 얼마나 달콤했던가 / 숭배한다는 **것이**!
아, 젊은이여, 고이 간직하오 / 사랑의 젊은 꿈을 / 그것이 지속되는 동안!
그대는 알게 될 것이다 곧 / **얼마나** 진실하게 톰 무어가 노래했는**지를**,
그가 말했을 때 / 절반도 되는 게 없**다고** / 사랑의 달콤함의 / 인생에 있어서.
사랑의 꿈이 불행을 가져올 때라도,
그것은 격정적이고 낭만적인 불행이며,
전혀 다르다 / 음침한 세속적인 괴로움과는 / 나중에 오는 슬픔의.
당신이 그녀를 잃었을 때 –
빛이 꺼졌을 때 / 당신의 인생에서,
세상이 드리울 때 / 당신 앞에 / 길고 어두운 공포를.
심지어 그때에도 / 절반의 황홀함이 섞여 있는 것이다 / 당신의 실망에는.
아, 저 어리석었던 나날이여, 저 어리석었던 나날이여,
우리들이 비이기적이고 순수했**던**;
저 어리석었던 나날이여,
우리의 소박한 마음이 가득 찼**던** / 진실과 믿음과 존경으로!

2. On Three Kinds of love

Love is not a relationship with a particular person. It is the attitude of a person towards the world as a whole. Most people believe they can prove the intensity of their love when they love nobody except the "loved" person. This is a fallacy. If someone loves only one other person and is indifferent to everyone else, his "love" is not love, but an enlarged egotism. If I truly love one person, I love all persons. If I can say to somebody else, "I love you", I must be able to say, "I love in you everybody, I love through you the world, and I love in you also myself."

Different as brotherly love and motherly love are from each other, what they have in common is that they are not restricted to one person.

Erotic love, in contrast, is the craving for complete fusion or union with one other person. It is by its very nature exclusive and not universal. It is also, perhaps, the most deceptive form of love there is. Because sexual desire is coupled with the idea of love, people are easily misled to conclude that they love each other when they want each other physically. Sexual attraction creates the illusion of union. Yet without love this union leaves the lovers as far apart as strangers. Sometimes it makes them ashamed of each other, or even makes them hate each other.

Fromm, Erich (1900~1980)
German-born U.S. psychoanalyst and social philosopher who explored the interaction between psychology and society. By applying psychoanalytic principles to the remedy of cultural ills, Fromm believed, mankind could develop a psychologically balanced "sane society."

If someone loves only one other person and is indifferent to everyone else, his "love" is not love, but an enlarged egotism.

Venus and Cupid: Metropolitan Museum of Art, New York City

Dictionary

intense: extreme and forceful or (of a feeling) very strong. Ex. intense cold / hatred
fallacy: an idea that a lot of people think is true but which is false. Ex. It is a common fallacy that women are worse drivers than men.
indifferent: lacking in interest or feeling; unconcerned. Ex. Why don't you vote – how can you be so indifferent (to what is going on)!
egotism: Egotism is the tendency to think only about yourself and consider yourself better and more important than other people.
craving: a strong or uncontrollable desire. Ex. Sometimes she has a craving for chocolate.
fusion: to join or become combined. Ex. nuclear fusion.
exclusive: limited to only one person or group of people. Ex. This room is for the exclusive use of guests.
illusion: a fantasy or idea that results in a mistaken perception of reality.

On Three Kinds of Love

Love is not a relationship / with a particular person.
It is the attitude of a person / towards the world as a whole.
Most people believe / (**that**) they can prove / the intensity of their love
when they love nobody / except the "loved" person.
This is a fallacy.
If someone loves / only one other person
and is indifferent / to everyone else,
his "love" is not love, / but an enlarged egotism.
If I truly love one person, / I love all persons.
If I can say to somebody else, / "I love you",
I must be able to say,
"I love / in you everybody,
I love / through you the world,
and I love in you also myself."
Different as brotherly love and motherly love / are from each other,
what they have in common / is **that** they are not restricted to one person.
Erotic love, in contrast, / is the craving
for complete fusion or union / with one other person.
It is by its very nature exclusive / and not universal.
It is also, perhaps, the most deceptive form / of love / there is.
Because sexual desire is coupled / with the idea of love,
people are easily misled / to conclude / **that** they love each other
when they want each other / physically.
Sexual attraction creates / the illusion of union.
Yet without love
this union leaves / the lovers **as** far apart / **as** strangers.
Sometimes it makes / them ashamed of each other,
or even makes / them hate each other.

세가지 종류의 사랑

사랑은 관계가 아니다 / 어느 특정인과의.
그것은 한 사람의 태도다 / 전체 세계를 향한.
대다수 사람은 믿는다 / 그들이 증명할 수 있**다고** / 그들 사랑의 강렬함을
그들이 아무도 사랑하지 않을 때 / 사랑하는 사람 외에는.
그것이 잘못된 생각이다.
만일 어떤 사람이 사랑한다면 / 다른 한 사람만
그리고 무관심하다면 / 다른 모든 사람 사람들에게는,
그의 '사랑' 은 사랑이 아니라 확대된 이기주의이다.
내가 진짜 한 사람을 사랑한다면 / 나는 모든 사람들을 사랑한다.
만일 내가 다른 누군가에게 말할 수 있다면 / '당신을 사랑한다' 고,
나는 이렇게도 말할 수 있어야만 한다, /
"나는 사랑한다 / 당신 속에서 모든 사람을,
나는 사랑한다 당신을 통해서 세상을,
그리고 나는 사랑한다 / 당신 속에서 역시 나 자신을".
다르지만 / 우애와 모성애는 / 서로,
이 두 가지에 공통적인 것은 / 국한돼 있지 않다는 것이다 / 한 사람에게만
남녀간의 사랑은 이와는 대조적으로 / 열망이다
완전한 융합 또는 결합을 위한 / 다른 사람과의.
그것은 본질상 배타적이다 / 그리고 보편적이지는 않다.
그것은 또한 아마도 가장 속기 쉬운 사랑의 형태다 / (세상에) 존재하는.
왜냐하면 성적 매력은 결합돼 있기 때문에 / 사랑의 개념과,
사람들은 쉽게 잘못 이끌린다 / 결론을 내리도록 / 그들이 서로 사랑한**다고**
그들이 서로를 원할 때 / 육체적으로.
성적 매력은 형성한다 / 결합의 환상을.
그러나 사랑이 없다면
이런 결합은 그 연인들이 멀리 떨어져 있게 내버려둔다 / 모르는 사람**처럼**.
때로 그것은 만든다 / 그들이 서로를 부끄러워하게
혹은 만들기도 한다 / 그들이 서로를 미워하게.

3. On Love

Marcel Proust said that love is subjective and that we do not love real people, but only those whom we have created in our mind. So beauty lies in the eye of the beholder. The actual person will never be seen again. He or she may stand before us, but we see only the figure of our own making. The joy we experience cannot be interfered with, because its source is within ourselves.

One of the most familiar methods of attracting attention is the use of adornment. Flowers, by their brilliant color, attract insects. Women put on beautiful gowns and jewels, that they may be chosen by men. Most of them follow the current fashions to catch the attention of men.

There are several rules which should be followed by both sexes in learning the art of not tiring the loved one. The first is to show in the most intimate moments as much politeness as during the first encounter. The second is to maintain a sense of humor under all conditions. The third is to arouse jealousy with reasonable limits, that is, to avoid indifference. Finally, the last rule, and the least known, is to cling to romance: "Why, when I have won her, do I continue to woo her? Because, though she belongs to me, she is not and never will be mine."

Andre Maurois (1885~1967)
Biographer, novelist, essayist, children's writer. Maurois is best known for his vivid, romantic style biographies of such authors as Shelley, Byron, Balzac, Proust and others. The Quest for Proust is considered by many his finest biography.

We do not love real people, but only those whom we have created in our mind. So beauty lies in the eye of the beholder.

Detail of Lovers from Indian Kishangarh Painting of A Love Scene.

Proust, Marcel (1871-1922)
French novelist, author of A la recherche du temps perdu (1913–27; Remembrance of Things Past), a seven-volume novel based on Proust's life told psychologically and allegorically. In Proust's scheme, the individual is isolated, society is false and ruled by snobbery, and artistic endeavor is raised to a religion.

Dictionary

adornment: decorating; something decorative.   Ex. She never wore make-up, having a classically beautiful face that had little need of adornment.
encounter: to experience (esp. something unpleasant), or to meet (someone) unexpectedly.   Ex. The army is reported to be encountering considerable resistance in some remote rural areas.
brilliant: full of light, shining or bright in colour.   Ex. The sky was a brilliant, cloudless blue.
reasonable: sensible and capable of making rational judgments. not excessive or extreme.   Ex1. a reasonable person.   Ex2. reasonable prices.
indifference: lack of interest in something.   Ex. I can bear love or hate, but not indifference.

On Love

Marcel Proust said / **that** love is subjective
and **that** we do not love / real people,
but only those / **whom** we have created / in our mind.
So beauty lies / in the eye of the beholder.
The actual person will never be seen / again.
He or she may stand / before us,
but we see / only the figure / **of** our own mak**ing**.
The joy / (**that**) we experience / cannot be interfered with,
because its source is / within ourselves.
One of the most familiar methods / **of** attract**ing** attention
is the use of adornment.
Flowers, / by their brilliant color, / attract insects.
Women put on / beautiful gowns and jewels,
(so) **that** they **may** be chosen / by men.
Most of them follow / the current fashions / **to** catch / the attention of men.
There are several rules / **which** should be followed / by both sexes
in learning / the art **of** not tir**ing** / the loved one.
The first is **to** show / in the most intimate moments
as much politeness / **as** during the first encounter.
The second is **to** maintain / a sense of humor / under all conditions.
The third is **to** arouse / jealousy / with reasonable limits,
that is, **to** avoid / indifference.
Finally, the last rule, and the least known, / is **to** cling / to romance:
"Why, when I have won her, / do I continue / to woo her?
Because, though she belongs to me,
she is not and never will be mine."

사랑에 관해

마르셀 프루스트는 말했다 / 사랑은 주관적이**라고**
또 우리는 사랑하지 않**고** / 실제 사람을,
사랑한**다고** 사람들만 / 우리가 형성**한** / 우리의 마음 속에.
그래서 아름다움은 존재한다 / 구경꾼의 눈에 (=제 눈에 안경).
실제 사람은 결코 보이지 않을 것이다 / 다시는.
그 혹은 그녀가 서 있을지 모른다 / 우리 앞에,
그러나 우리는 본다 / 오직 모습을 / 우리 자신이 만**든**.
기쁨은 / 우리가 경험**하는** / 방해받을 수는 없다.
왜냐하면 그것의 근원이 / 우리 자신들 속에 있기 때문에.
가장 친숙한 방법들 중의 하나는 / 관심을 끄**는**
장식의 사용이다.
꽃들은, / 그것들의 빛나는(화려한) 색깔로, / 끈다 곤충들을.
여성들은 착용한다 / 아름다운 가운들과 보석들을,
그들이 선택되**기 위해** / 남성들에 의해.
그들의 대다수는 따른다 / 최근 패션들을 / 끌**기 위해** / 남성들의 관심을.
여러 가지 법칙들이 있다 / 따라야 **할** / 양쪽 성들이.
배우는 데 있어 / 지루하지 않게 **하는** 기술을 / 사랑하는 사람을.
첫 번째는 보여주는 **것**이다 / 가장 친밀한 순간들에도
최대한 정중함을 / 첫 만남 동안**처럼**.
두 번째는 유지하는 **것**이다 / 유머 감각을 / 어떤 상황들 하에서도.
세 번째는 불러일으키는 **것**이다 / 질투심을 / 적당한 한계를 가지고,
즉, 피하는 **것**이다 / 무관심을.
끝으로, 마지막 법칙이자 가장 덜 알려진 법칙은 / 매달리는 **것**이다 / 낭만에:
"왜, 내가 그녀를 쟁취했는데, / 내가 계속하는가 / 구애하는 **것을** 그녀에게?
왜냐하면, 비록 그녀가 내게 속하지만,
그녀는 나의 것이 아니고 결코 되지도 않을 것이기 때문이다."

4. Love-1

from Corinthians 13:1–13 Teachings of Paul the Apostle

And now I will show you the most excellent way.
If I speak in the tongues of men and of angels, but have not love, I am only a resounding gong or a clanging cymbal. If I have the gift of prophecy and can fathom all mysteries and all knowledge, and if I have a faith that can move mountains, but have not love, I am nothing. If I give all I possess to the poor and surrender my body to the flames, but have not love, I gain nothing.

Love is patient, love is kind. It does not envy, it does not boast, it is not proud. It is not rude, it is not self-seeking, it is not easily angered, it keeps no record of wrongs. Love does not delight in evil but rejoices with the truth. It always protects, always trusts, always hopes, always perseveres.

Paul, the Apostle, Saint
1st-century Jew who, after first being a bitter enemy of Christianity, later became an important figure in its history. Paul, the Apostle. "A man small of stature, with a bald head and crooked legs, in a good state of body, with eyebrows meeting and nose somewhat hooked, full of friendliness; for now he appeared like a man, and now he had the face of an angel"(Acts of Paul and Thecla 3).

If I give all I possess to the poor and surrender my body to the flames, but have not love, I gain nothing.

Cupid and Psyche by Antonio Canova in Musee du Louvre

Dictionary

tongue: the language or dialect of a particular area. Ex. She spoke in a foreign tongue.
resound: To be filled with sound; reverberate. Ex. The concert hall resounded with cheers and applause.
gong: A rimmed metal disk that produces a loud, sonorous tone when struck with a padded mallet.
clang: A loud, resonant, metallic sound. Ex. The dinner bell clanged for almost twenty minutes.
fathom: To determine the depth of; sound. Ex. I couldn't fathom why he came back.
surrender: to turn over or yield to the power, control, or possession of another, esp. under compulsion. Ex. They surrendered the documents to the authorities.
self-seeking: interested only in gaining an advantage over others.

Love – 1

And now I will show you / the most excellent way.
If I speak / in the tongues of men / and of angels,
but have not love,
I am only a resounding gong / or a clanging cymbal.
If I have / the gift of prophecy
and can fathom / all mysteries and all knowledge,
and if I have a faith / **that** can move mountains,
but have not love, / I am nothing.
If I give / all (**that**) I possess / to the poor
and surrender / my body / to the flames,
but have not love, / I gain nothing.
Love is patient, love is kind.
It does not envy, / it does not boast, / it is not proud.
It is not rude, / it is not self-seeking,
it is not easily angered,
it keeps no record of wrongs.
Love does not delight / in evil / but rejoices / with the truth.
It always protects, / always trusts,
always hopes, / always perseveres.

사랑 - 1

그리고 이제 나는 보여줄 것이다 그대들에게 / 가장 훌륭한 방법을.
만약 내가 말해도 / 인간의 언어들로 / 그리고 천사의 (언어들로),
그러나 가지고 있지 않다면 사랑을,
나는 단지 울려 퍼지는 징 / 혹은 뗑그렁 하고 울리는 심벌이다.
만약 내가 가지고 있다해도 / 예언의 재능을
그리고 통찰할 수 있다해도 / 모든 신비들과 모든 지식을.
그리고 만약 내가 믿음을 가지고 있다해도 / 산들을 옮길 수 **있는**,
그러나 사랑을 가지고 있지 않으면 / 나는 아무 것도 아니다.
만약 내가 준다해도 / 모든 것을 / 내가 소유하고 **있는** / 가난한 사람들에게
그리고 내준다해도 / 나의 몸을 / 화염에,
그러나 가지고 있지 않으면 사랑을 / 나는 아무 것도 얻는 것이 없다.
사랑은 인내하며, 사랑은 친절하다.
사랑은 시기하지 않으며 / 사랑은 자랑하지 않으며 / 사랑은 자만하지 않는다.
사랑은 무례하지 않으며 / 사랑은 이기적이지 않으며
사랑은 쉽게 성내지 않으며,
사랑은 기록을 간직하지 않는다(앙심을 품지 않는다) / 잘못된 일들의.
사랑은 기뻐하지 않는다 / 불의를 / 그러나 기뻐한다 / 진리과 함께.
사랑은 항상 보호하며 / 항상 신뢰하며,
항상 희망하며 / 항상 인내한다.

Love – 2

Love never fails. But where there are prophecies, they will cease; where there are tongues, they will be stilled; where there is knowledge, it will pass away. For we know in part and we prophesy in part, but when perfection comes, the imperfect disappears. When I was a child, I talked like a child, I thought like a child, I reasoned like a child. When I became a man, I put childish ways behind me. Now we see but a poor reflection as in a mirror; then we shall see face to face. Now I know in part; then I shall know fully, even as I am fully known.

And now these three remains: faith, hope and love. But the greatest of these is love.

Love never fails. But where there are prophecies, they will cease; where there are tongues, they will be stilled; where there is knowledge, it will pass away. For we know in part and we prophesy in part, but when perfection comes, the imperfect disappears.

Detail Showing Figures from Cupid and Psyche by Antonio Canova in the Hermitage Museum.

Detail Showing Psyche's Back from Cupid and Psyche by Antonio Canova in the Hermitage Museum.

Dictionary

cease: to stop or come to an end. Ex. Will this snow never cease?
still: to make silent, quiet.
reason: to think in a logical and orderly manner; to try to understand and to make judgments based on practical facts. Ex. Newton reasoned (that) there must be a force such as gravity, when an apple fell on his head.
childish: marked by immaturity, weakness, or foolishness. Ex. childish behavior.
reflection: the throwing back of heat, light, or an image off an object or surface. Ex. In Greek mythology, Narcissus fell in love with his own reflection which he saw in a pool of water.

Love – 2

Love never fails.
But **where** there are prophecies, / they will cease;
where there are tongues, / they will be stilled;
where there is knowledge, / it will pass away.
For we know in part
and we prophesy in part,
but when perfection comes, the imperfect disappears.
When I was a child,
I talked like a child,
I thought like a child,
I reasoned like a child.
When I became a man, / I put childish ways / behind me.
Now we see but a poor reflection / **as** in a mirror;
then we shall see / face to face.
Now I know / in part;
then I shall know / fully,
even as I am fully known.
and now these three remains: faith, hope and love.
But the greatest of these / is love.

사랑 - 2

사랑은 결코 실패하지(없어지지) 않는다.
그러나 예언이 있는 **곳에** / 예언은 그칠 것이며;
방언이 있는 **곳에** / 방언은 조용해질 것이며;
지식이 있는 **곳에** / 지식은 사라질 것이다.
왜냐하면 우리는 알고 있고 / 부분적으로
우리는 예언하기 때문이다 / 부분적으로,
그러나 완전한 것이 오면 / 불완전한 것은 사라진다.
내가 어린아이였을 때,
나는 말했다 어린아이처럼,
나는 생각했다 어린아이처럼,
나는 사고했다 어린아이처럼.
내가 어른이 됐을 때 / 나는 버렸다 어린 아이 같은 방식을 / 내 뒤에.
지금은 우리가 희미한 반영만 보지만 / 거울에 비추어 보는 것**처럼**;
그 때에는 우리가 볼 것이다 / 얼굴을 맞대고.
지금은 나는 알지만 / 부분적으로;
그때에는 나는 알 것이다 / 완전히
바로 내가 (하느님에게) 완전히 알려진 것처럼.
그래서 이제 이 세 가지가 남는다: 믿음, 소망 그리고 사랑이.
그러나 가장 위대한 것은 이들 중에 / 사랑이다.

5. Romeo and Juliet – 1

Juliet was mournful over the irony of her fate, that she had fallen in love with a Montague. She came out onto the balcony which looked down onto the garden. The moon was shining and everything was silent. Here, in the silvery moonlight, stood Juliet, an angel of a girl. "Ah!" she sighed, and began to say to herself: "Oh, Romeo! Why are you Romeo? What is in a name? A rose by any other name would smell as sweet? Oh, my Romeo? Throw away your name, and take me!" Romeo, unable to hold back any longer, shouted out: "Call me Love, not Romeo!" Startled to hear a man's voice, Julliet shouted back, "Who's there?" "Romeo," he replied, stepping out from the shade into the moonlight.

Juliet: How did you come here, tell me, and why? Are you not afraid of my people?

Romeo: No, I am not. I would rather be killed than live without your love.

Juliet: You overheard my confession of love. I love you. I love you from the bottom of my heart.

Shakespeare, William (1564~1616)
English poet, dramatist, and actor, often called the English national poet and considered by many to be the greatest dramatist of all time.

"Oh, Romeo! Why are you Romeo? What is in a name? A rose by any other name would smell as sweet? Oh, my Romeo? Throw away your name, and take me!"

Dictionary

mournful: extremely sad; sorrowful. Ex. a mournful look.
irony: contrast between expectation and outcome, or an event or situation that contains such contrast.
hold back: Ex. Don't hold (anything) back (=keep information secret) – tell us everything that happened.
overhear: to hear (someone speaking) without his or her knowledge.
confess: to admit that you have done something wrong, esp. when what you have done is secret Ex. She confessed to her husband that she had sold her wedding ring.

Lomeo and Juliet –1

Juliet was mournful / over the irony of her fate,
that she had fallen in love with a Montague.
She came out / onto the balcony / **which** looked down onto the garden.
The moon was shining / and everything was silent.
Here, in the silvery moonlight, / stood Juliet, / an angel of a girl.
"Ah!" she sighed,
and began to say to herself:
"Oh, Romeo! Why are you Romeo? What is in a name?
A rose by any other name / would smell (as) sweet?
Oh, my Romeo? / Throw away your name, / and take me!"
Romeo, / (**who** was) unable to hold back / any longer, / shouted out:
"Call me Love, / not Romeo!"
Startl**ed** / **to** hear a man's voice,
Julliet shouted back, / "Who's there?"
"Romeo," he replied,
stepp**ing** out / from the shade into the moonlight.
Juliet: How did you come here, / tell me, / and why?
            Are you not afraid of / my people?
Romeo: No, I am not.
            I **would rather** be killed / **than** live / without your love.
Juliet: You overheard / my confession / of love.
            I love you.
            I love you / from the bottom of my heart.

로미오와 줄리엣 - 1

줄리엣은 슬퍼했다 / 운명의 얄궂음에
그녀가 사랑에 빠지게 **된** / 몬태규 가의 한 사람과.
그녀는 나왔다 / 발코니로 / 정원이 내려다 보이**는**.
달은 빛나고 있었다 / 그리고 모든 것은 조용했다.
여기 은색 달빛 속에, / 서있었다 줄리엣이, / 천사 같은 소녀인.
"아!"그녀는 한숨을 쉬었다,
그리고 말하기 시작했다 / 그녀 자신에게 :
오, 로미오! 왜 당신은 로미오인가요? 무엇이 있나요 이름에?
장미는 어떤 다른 이름이라도 / 냄새가 나겠지요 향기롭게?
오, 나의 로미오! / 버리세요 당신의 이름을, / 그리고 데려가세요 나를!"
로미오는 / 참을 수 없었**던** / 더 이상 / 소리쳤다:
"부르세요 나를 사랑이라고 / 로미오가 아니라!"
놀란 / 남자의 목소리를 듣**고서**,
줄리엣은 소리쳐 대꾸했다. /"누구세요 거기 ?"
"로미오입니다"그가 대답했다,
그리고 걸어나왔다 / 그늘에서 달빛 속으로.
줄리엣: 어떻게 당신이 왔나요 여기에, / 말해주세요 나에게 / 그리고 왜?
　　　　당신은 두렵지 않으세요 / 나의(우리 집) 사람들이?
로미오: 아니오, 나는 두렵지 않소.
　　　　나는 **차라리** 죽음을 당할 **것이오** / 사느니 **보다** / 당신의 사랑 없이.
줄리엣: 당신은 엿들었군요 / 나의 사랑의 고백을.
　　　　나는 사랑합니다 당신을.
　　　　나는 사랑합니다 당신을 / 내 마음의 바닥에서부터(내 마음 속 깊이).

Romeo and Juliet – 2

Romeo: By that silver moon I swear...:
Juliet: Don't swear by the moon. It waxes and wanes.
Romeo: What shall I swear by?
Juliet: Do not swear at all. It is too rash, too sudden to swear anything now. Let's say good night for the present. This bud of love may prove to be a beautiful flower when we next meet. Till then, good night, Romeo!
Romeo: Oh, must you leave me so soon?
Juliet: Yes, I must. What do you want to have?
Romeo: The exchange of a vow of love with you.
Juliet: I gave it to you before you requested it. Yet I wish to give it again. My love is as deep and boundless as the sea. If your love is true, and you mean to marry me, I will put my future in your hands. Tomorrow, I will send a messenger to you to hear your word, and to fix the time and place for our marriage.
Romeo: Send your nurse at nine in the morning
Juliet: I will not fail. It seems like many years till then. Now it is almost morning. Parting is such sweet sorrow. I must say goodnight for the last time. Romeo! Good night!
Romeo: Sleep well. Good night, sweet lady!

Don't swear by the moon. It waxes and wanes. What shall I swear by? Do not swear at all. It is too rash, too sudden to swear anything now. Let's say good night for the present. This bud of love may prove to be a beautiful flower when we next meet.

Dictionary

wax:	to increase gradually in quantity, strength, volume, or the like.
wane:	1 to decrease gradually, as the illuminated portion of the moon. 2 to become less powerful, prosperous, or strong. Ex. His popularity was waning.
rash:	reckless, ill-considered, or hasty.
boundless:	without bounds or limits. Ex. He has boundless good will.
parting:	the act of departing or taking leave.

Romeo and Juliet – 2

Romeo: By that silver moon / I swear...:
Juliet: Don't swear / by the moon.
        It waxes and wanes.
Romeo: What shall I swear by?
Juliet: Do not swear at all.
        It is too rash, too sudden / **to** swear anything now.
        Let's say good night / for the present.
        This bud of love may prove (to be) / a beautiful flower when we next meet.
        Till then, / good night, Romeo!
Romeo: Oh, must you leave / me so soon?
Juliet: Yes, I must. / What do you want to have?
Romeo: The exchange of a vow of love / with you.
Juliet: I gave / it to you / before you requested it.
        Yet I wish to give / it again.
        My love is **as** deep and boundless / **as** the sea.
        If your love is true,
        and you mean / **to** marry me,
        I will put / my future in your hands.
        Tomorrow, I will send / a messenger to you
        to hear / your word,
        and **to** fix / the time and place / for our marriage.
Romeo: Send your nurse / at nine in the morning.
Juliet: I will not fail. / It seems like many years / till then.
        Now it is almost morning. / Parting is such sweet sorrow.
        I must say goodnight / for the last time.
        Romeo! Good night!
Romeo: Sleep well. Good night, sweet lady!

로미오와 줄리엣 - 2

로미오: 저 은빛 달에 걸고 / 나는 맹세하오...:
줄리엣: 맹세하지 마세요 / 달에 걸고.
　　　　그건 차면 기울지요.
로미오: 무엇에 걸고 내가 맹세를 해야 하지요?
줄리엣: 맹세하지 마세요 결코.
　　　　너무 성급하고 너무 갑작스러워요 / 맹세하는 **것은** 무언가를 지금.
　　　　말합시다 굿 나잇이라고 / 지금으로선.
　　　　이 사랑의 꽃봉오리는 한 송이 아름다운 꽃이 될지도 몰라요 /
　　　　우리가 다음에 만날 때.
　　　　그 때까지, / 굿 나잇, 로미오!
로미오: 오, 당신은 떠나보내야 합니까 / 나를 그렇게 빨리?
줄리엣: 예, 나는 떠나보내야 해요. / 당신은 무엇을 가지기를 원하세요 ?
로미오: 사랑의 언약의 교환이죠 / 당신과.
줄리엣: 나는 주었소 / 그것을 당신에게 / 당신이 요구하기 전에 그것을.
　　　　아직 나는 원해요 주기를 / 그것을 다시.
　　　　나의 사랑은 깊고 끝이 없답니다 / 바다**만큼**.
　　　　만약 당신의 사랑이 진실하다면
　　　　그리고 당신이 의도한다면 / 나와 결혼하**기를**,
　　　　나는 놓을(맡길) 겁니다 / 나의 미래를 당신의 손에.
　　　　내일, 나는 보낼 거예요 / 한 심부름꾼을 당신에게
　　　　듣**기 위해** / 당신의 말을,
　　　　그리고 정**하기 위해** / 시간과 장소를 / 우리의 결혼을 위한.
로미오: 보내세요 당신의 유모를 / 아침 9시에.
줄리엣: 나는 실패하지 않을 겁니다. / 여러 해처럼 느껴지는군요 / 그 때까지는.
　　　　이제 거의 아침입니다. / 이별은 너무 달콤한 슬픔이군요.
　　　　나는 말해야겠어요 굿 나잇이라고 / 마지막으로.
　　　　로미오! 굿 나잇!
로미오: 잘 자요. 굿 나잇, 사랑스런 아가씨!

6. The Prophet – On Marriage

Then Almitra spoke again and said, And what of Marriage, master? And he answered saying: You were born together, and together you shall be forevermore. You shall be together when the white wings of death scatter your days. Ay, you shall be together even in the silent memory of God. But let there be spaces in your togetherness, And let the winds of the heavens dance between you. Love one another, but make not a bond of love: Let it rather be a moving sea between the shores of your souls.

Fill each other's cup but drink not from one cup. Give one another of your bread but eat not from the same loaf. Sing and dance together and be joyous, but let each one of you be alone, Even as the strings of a lute are alone though they quiver with the same music. Give your hearts, but not into each other's keeping. For only the hand of life can contain your hearts.

And stand together yet not too near together: For the pillars of the temple stand apart, And the oak tree and the cypress grow not in each other's shadow.

Gibran, Khalil (1883~1931)
Lebanese-American philosophical essayist, novelist, poet, and artist. The prophet and his other books of poetry are loved by inmumerable Americans. His poetry has been translated into more than twenty languages.

And stand together yet not too near together: For the pillars of the temple stand apart, And the oak tree and the cypress grow not in each other's shadow.

an oak tree

Dictionary

forevermore: for all time to come; forever.
string: a cord or slender rope used for binding or lacing. Ex. Do you think it'll be okay to hang this picture on the wall with a piece of string?
lute: an ancient stringed instrument having a bent, fretted neck and a pear-shaped body.
quiver: to shake slightly, often because of strong emotion. Ex. Lennie's bottom lip quivered and tears started in his eyes.
apart: separated by a distance or, less commonly, by time Ex. Stand with your feet wide apart and lower the top half of your body to the floor.
cypress: one of a group of evergreen trees having tiny scale-like leaves, or the branches or wood of such a tree.

6. The Prophet – On Marriage

Then Almitra spoke again and said,
And what of Marriage, master?
And he answered / saying:
You were born together, / and together you shall be forevermore.
You shall be together
when the white wings of death scatter / your days.
Ay, you shall be together / even in the silent memory of God.
But let there be spaces / in your togetherness,
And let the winds of the heavens dance / between you.
Love one another, / but make not a bond of love:
Let it rather be a moving sea / between the shores of your souls.
Fill each other's cup / but drink not / from one cup.
Give one another of your bread / but eat not / from the same loaf.
Sing and dance together / and be joyous,
but let each one of you be alone,
Even as the strings of a lute are alone
though they quiver / with the same music.
Give your hearts, / but not into each other's keeping.
For only the hand of life can contain / your hearts.
And stand together / yet not   too near together:
For the pillars of the temple stand / apart,
And the oak tree and the cypress grow not / in each other's shadow.

6. 예언자 – 결혼에 대해

그러자 알미트라가 다시 말했다,
그러면 결혼이 무엇입니까, 스승이여?
그래서 그는 대답했다 / 다음과 같이:
그대들은 태어났다 함께, / 그리고 그대들은 함께 있으리라 영원히.
그대들은 함께 있으리라
죽음의 하얀 날개들이 흩뿌릴 때까지 / 그대들의 날들을.
아, 그대들은 함께 있으리라 / 심지어 신의 말없는 기억 속에서까지.
그러나 거리를 두라 / 그대들이 함께 있더라도,
그리고 하늘나라의 바람이 춤추게 하라 / 그대들 사이에서.
사랑하라 서로 / 그러나 만들지 말라 사랑의 속박은:
그것은 차라리 움직이는 바다가 되게 하라 / 그대 영혼들의 물가 사이에서.
서로의 컵을 채워라 / 그러나 마시지 말라 / 어느 한 편의 잔 만을.
주라 서로 그대들의 빵을 / 그러나 먹지 말라 / 어느 한 편의 빵만을.
노래하고 춤추라 함께 / 그리고 기뻐하라,
그러나 그대들 각자는 고독에 잠기게 하라,
심지어 류트의 현들도 혼자 있는 것처럼
그것들이 울릴지라도 / 같은 음악을.
주라 그대들의 마음들을, / 그러나 간직하지는 말라.
왜냐하면 인생의 손길만이 간직할 수 있으므로 / 그대들의 마음을.
그리고 함께 서있되 / 너무 가까이 서 있지는 말라:
왜냐하면 사원의 기둥들도 서있으므로 / 떨어져서,
그리고 참나무와 사이프러스는 자라지 않으므로 / 서로의 그늘 속에서는.

7. The Diary of Anne Frank 안네 프랑크의 일기

8. Walden - To Be Alone / Henry David Thoreau 월든 - 혼자 있는 것

9. On Friendship / A. clutton-Brock 우정에 관해

10. How to Win Friends and Influence People / Dale carnegie
    친구를 얻고 남을 움직이는 비결

11. Little Prince / Antoine de Saint Exupéry 어린 왕자

12. The Conguest of Happiness / Bertrand Russell 행복의 정복

7. The Diary of Anne Frank – 1

October 29, 1943

I can't hear a single bird singing outside, and a deadly silence hangs everywhere. I wander from one room to another, downstairs and upstairs, feeling like a songbird whose wings have been cut and who, in the dark, is throwing herself against her cage, "Go outside, laugh, and breathe the fresh air," a voice cries within me; but I don't even answer it any more. I go and lie down and sleep to make the time, the silence, and the terrible fear pass more quickly. For there is no way of killing them.

February 23, 1944

Nearly every morning, I go to the attic to blow the old air out of my body. I sit on the floor and look up at the blue sky and the bare chestnut tree. On its branches drops of rain shine like silver. Sea gulls glide on the wind. As long as this sunshine and the cloudless sky exist, I cannot be unhappy. The best thing for those who are afraid or lonely is to go outside, where they can be quite alone with the heavens and nature. Only then does one feel that all is as it should be and that God wishes to see people happy. Nature brings comfort in all troubles. I've found that there is always beauty – in nature, in freedom, in yourself. Look for these things, and you will find yourself and God again. Those who have courage and faith will never perish in misery.

Anne Frank(1929-1945)
young Jewish girl whose diary of her family's two years in hiding during the Nazi occupation of The Netherlands became a classic of war literature.

As long as this sunshine and the cloudless sky exist, I cannot be unhappy.

At the Anne Frank House(above) in the center of Amsterdam you can find the hiding place where Anne Frank wrote her famous diary during World War Two. The original of the diary is on display as part of the Anne Frank House's permanent exhibition.

While in hiding Anne Frank keeps a diary. In more than two years she fills several notebooks.

Dictionary

deadly: capable of causing death. Ex. the deadly cobra.
glide: to move in a smooth and seemingly effortless manner.
   Ex. The bird glided through the air.
perish: to decay or pass out of existence or use.
   Ex. Youthful beauty eventually perishes.

The Diary of Anne Frank – 1

October 29, 1943

I can't **hear** / a single bird singing outside,

and a deadly silence hangs / everywhere.

I wander / from one room to another, / downstairs and upstairs,

fee**ling** like a songbird / **whose** wings have been cut

and **who**, in the dark, is throwing / herself against her cage,

"Go outside, / laugh, and breathe the fresh air,"

a voice cries within me; / but I don't even answer it / any more.

I go / and lie down / and sleep

to make / the time, the silence, and the terrible fear pass / more quickly.

For there is no way / **of** kill**ing** them.

February 23, 1944

Nearly every morning, / I go to the attic

to blow / the old air out of my body.

I sit / on the floor and look up at the blue sky / and the bare chestnut tree.

On its branches / drops of rain shine / like silver.

Sea gulls glide / on the wind.

As long as this sunshine and the cloudless sky exist,

I cannot be unhappy.

The best thing / for those / **who** are afraid or lonely / is **to** go outside,

where they can be quite alone / with the heavens and nature.

Only then does one feel / **that** all is / as it should be

and that God wishes **to see** / people happy.

Nature brings comfort / in all troubles.

I've found / **that** there is always beauty

– in nature, in freedom, in yourself.

Look for these things, / and you will find yourself and God again.

Those / **who** have courage and faith / will never perish / in misery.

안네 프랑크의 일기 - 1

October 29, 1943
나는 들을 수 없다 / 단 한 마리의 새**가** 노래하는 것도 밖에서,
그리고 죽음 같은 침묵이 걸려 있다(감돌고 있다) / 사방에.
나는 방황한다(왔다갔다한다) / 한 방에서 다른 방으로, / 아래층과 위층을.
그리고 느껴진다 노래하는 새처럼 / 날개가 짤**린**
그리고 어둠 속에서 던지고(부딪치고) 있**는** / 자신을 새장에다,
"밖으로 나가라, / 웃고 마셔라 신선한 공기를",
어떤 목소리가 소리친다 마음 속에서; / 그러나 나는 대답조차 하지 않는다 / 더 이상.
나는 가서 눕는다 그리고 잔다
만들기 위해 / 시간, 침묵, 무시무시한 공포가 지나가도록 / 더 빨리.
방법이 없기 때문이다 / 그런 것들을 없**애는**.

February 23, 1944
거의 매일 아침 / 나는 간다 / 다락방으로
불기 위해(내보내기 위해) / 오래된 공기를 내 몸 밖으로.
나는 앉아 있다 / 마루에 그리고 쳐다본다 푸른 하늘을 / 그리고 벌거벗은 밤나무를.
그것의 가지들 위에는 / 빗방울들이 빛난다 / 은빛처럼.
갈매기들이 미끄러지듯 지나간다 / 바람을 타고.
이 햇빛과 구름 한 점 없는 하늘이 존재**하는 한**,
나는 불행할 수 없다.
가장 좋은 일은 / 사람들에게 / 두려워하**거나** 외로운 / 나가는 **것**이다 / 밖으로,
그곳에서 그들이 완전히 혼자일 수 있다 / 하늘과 자연과 함께.
오직 그때 사람은 느낀다 / 모든 것이 있**다고** / 있어야 하는 그대로
그리고 신은 보기를 원한**다고** / 사람들이 행복해 하는 것을.
자연은 가져다준다 위안을 / 모든 근심 속에서도.
나는 알았다 / 항상 아름다움이 있다는 **것을**
자연 속에, 자유 속에, 자신 속에.
찾아라 이런 것들을 / 그러면 당신은 발견할 것이다 자신과 신을 다시.
사람들은 / 용기와 신념을 가**진** / 결코 망하지 않을 것이다 / 비참하게.

The Diary of Anne Frank – 2

May 3, 1944

I regard our hiding as a dangerous, romantic adventure. In my diary, I treat all difficulties as amusing. I'm young, and I have many buried qualities. Every day, I feel that I'm developing myself and that the liberation is drawing nearer. Why, then, should I be in despair?

July 15, 1944

It's really a wonder that I haven't dropped all my ideals, because they seem so absurd and impossible to carry out. Yet I keep them because, in spite of everything, I still believe that people are really good at heart. I simply can't build my hopes on a foundation consisting of confusion, misery, and death. I see the world slowly being turned into a wilderness. I hear the approaching thunder which will destroy us, too. I can feel the suffering of millions. And yet, if I look up into the heavens, I think that it will all come out right, that this cruelty will end, that peace will return again.

And yet, if I look up into the heavens, I think that it will all come out right, that this cruelty will end, that peace will return again.

During July of 1942, Otto Frank, Edith Frank and their daughters Margot and Anne hid in the building pictured above this text. Hidden living quarters inside the Anne Frank House. The Frank family fled Nazi Germany and remained in hiding until their capture in August 1944.

Dictionary

regard: to consider with a particular attitude or feeling.   Ex. I regard her highly.
develop: to cause to gain strength; cause to grow.   Ex. Studies develop the mind.
absurd: contrary to rational thought; illogical; ridiculous.   Ex. an absurd statement
wilderness: an uncultivated and generally uninhabited region in its natural state.
         Ex. a wilderness park

The Diary of Anne Frank – 2

May 3, 1944

I **regard** / our hiding as a dangerous, romantic adventure.
In my diary, / I **treat** / all difficulties as amusing.
I'm young, / and I have many bur**ied** qualities.
Every day, / I feel / **that** I'm developing myself
and **that** the liberation is drawing nearer.
Why, then, should I be in despair?

July 15, 1944

It's really a wonder
that I haven't dropped / all my ideals,
because they seem / so absurd and impossible / **to** carry out.
Yet I keep them / because, in spite of everything,
I still believe / **that** people are really good / at heart.
I simply can't build / my hopes
on a foundation / consis**ting** of confusion, misery, and death.
I see / the world slowly being turned / into a wilderness.
I hear / the approaching thunder / **which** will destroy us, too.
I can feel / the suffering of millions.
And yet, if I look up / into the heavens,
I think / **that** it will all come out right,
that this cruelty will end, / **that** peace will return again.

안네의 일기 - 2

May 3, 1944
나는 **간주한다** / 우리의 은신을 / 위험하고 낭만적인 모험으로.
나의 일기에서 / 나는 **다룬다** / 모든 어려움들을 즐거운 일로.
나는 어리다 / 그리고 나는 가지고 있다 많은 문혀**진** 자질들을.
매일 / 나는 느낀다 / 내가 계발하고 있**다고** 나 자신을
그리고 해방의 그 날이 점점 가까워지고 있**다고**.
그런데 왜 내가 절망에 빠지겠는가?

July 15, 1944
정말 놀라운 일이다
내가 놓지(버리지) 않았다는 **것은** / 모든 나의 이상들을,
그것들은 보이기 때문에 / 너무 터무니없고 불가능하게 / 실천하**기에는**.
그러나 나는 간직한다 이상들을 / 왜냐하면 온갖 일에도 불구하고,
나는 아직 믿기 때문이다 / 사람들은 정말 착하**다고** / 마음속은.
나는 단순히(절대로) 쌓아올릴 수 없다 / 나의 희망들을
토대 위에 / 이루어지**는**, 혼란 비참함, 그리고 죽음으로.
나는 본다 / 세계가 천천히 변하고 있는 것을 / 황무지로.
나는 듣는다 / 다가오는 천둥소리를 / 우리를 멸망시**킬**, 또한.
나는 느낄 수 있다 / 수백만 명의 고통을.
그러나 만약 내가 쳐다보면 / 하늘을,
나는 생각한다 / 그 모든 것이 잘 되어 갈 것이**라고**,
이 잔인성은 끝날 것이**라고**, / 평화가 돌아올 것이**라고** 다시.

8. Walden – To be alone

I find it wholesome to be alone the greater part of the time. To be in company, even with the best, is soon wearisome and dissipating. I love to be alone. I never found the companion that was so companionable as solitude. We are for the most part more lonely when we go abroad among men than when we stay in our chambers.

A man thinking or working is always alone, let him be where he will. Solitude is not measured by the miles of space that intervene between a man and his fellows. The diligent student in one of the crowded hives of Cambridge college is as solitary as a dervish in the desert.

Thoreau, Henry David (1817~1862)
American essayist, poet, and practical philosopher, renowned for having lived the doctrines of Transcendentalism as recorded in his masterwork, Walden (1854), and for having been a vigorous advocate of civil liberties, as evidenced in the essay "Civil Disobedience" (1849).

We are for the most part more lonely when we go abroad among men than when we stay in our chambers.

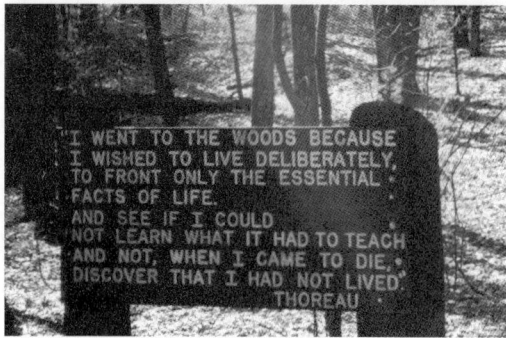

Dictionary

wholesome: promoting or resulting in sound physical or mental health; salutary. Ex. wholesome food; wholesome behavior.
company: an assembled group of people; a guest or guests. Ex. A man is known by the company he keeps.
wearisome: causing fatigue; tiring. Ex. a wearisome day (or book).
dissipating: to disappear by dispersion or dissolution; to waste one's health, money, talent, or the like in the extravagant pursuit of pleasure. Ex. After five years in same job his enthusiasm had finally dissipated.
companion: one who associates with another or others.
Ex. a travel companion; my childhood companion.
dervish: someone who belongs to any of several Muslim religious groups noted for their ascetic practices and for dancing and whirling in religious ecstasy.

Walden – To be alone

I find / **it** wholesome / **to** be alone
the greater part of the time.
To be in company, / even with the best,
is soon wearisome and dissipating
I love / **to** be alone.
I never found / the companion
that was **so** companionable / **as** solitude.
We are for the most part more lonely
when we go abroad / among men
than when we stay / in our chambers.
A man / think**ing** or work**ing** / is always alone,
let him **be where** he will(=**wherever** he may be).
Solitude is not measured / by the miles of space
that intervene / between a man and his fellows.
The diligent student / in one of the crowded hives
of Cambridge college
is **as** solitary / **as** a dervish / in the desert.

월든 - 혼자 있는 것

나는 생각한다 / (그것이) 건전**하다고** / 혼자 있는 **것이**
대부분의 시간을.
사람들과 같이 있는 **것은** / 심지어 최고의 사람들과 같이 있어도,
곧 피로하게 하고 낭비적이다.
나는 좋아한다 / 혼자 있는 **것을**.
나는 결코 찾지 못했다 / 동료를
사귈만한 / 고독**만큼**.
우리는 대개의 경우 더 외롭다
집에서 나와 / 사람들 사이에 있을 때
우리가 머무를 때 보다 / 우리의 방 안에.
사람은 / 생각**하는** 혹은 일**하는** / 항상 고독하다,
그가 **있는 곳이 어디든지**.
고독은 측정되지 않는다 / 공간의 마일(거리)로
끼어 있는 / 한 사람과 그의 동료들 사이에.
부지런한 학생은 / 복잡한 벌집(예를 들어 도서관)의 하나**에 있는**
하버드대학(보스턴시 캠브리지 대학촌 소재)의
고독하다 / 회교 탁발승**만큼** / 사막에 있는.

9. On Friendship

Friendship is above reason, for though you find virtues in a friend, he was your friend before you found them. It is a gift that we offer because we must; to give it as the reward of virtue would be to set a price upon it, and those who do that have no friendship to give.

If you choose your friends on the ground that you are virtuous and want virtuous company, you are no nearer to true friendship than if you choose them for commercial reasons. Besides who are you that you should be setting a price upon your friendship?

It is enough for any man that he has the divine power of making friends, and he must leave it to that power to determine who his friends shall be. For, though you may choose the virtuous to be your friends, they may not choose you; indeed, friendship cannot grow where there is any calculated choice. It comes, like sleep, when you are not thinking about it; and you should be grateful, without any misgiving, when it comes.

By A. clutton-Brock(1868~1924)

Friendship is above reason, for though you find virtues in a friend, he was your friend before you found them.

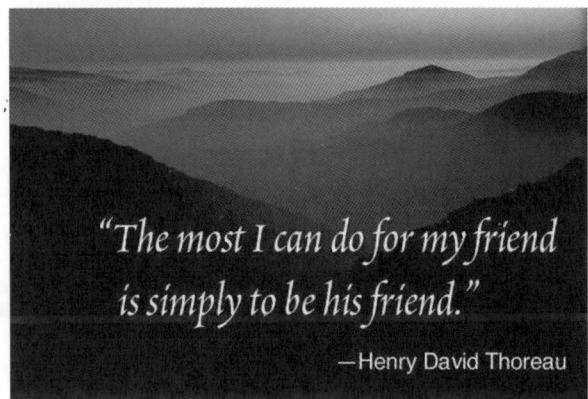

"The most I can do for my friend is simply to be his friend."
—Henry David Thoreau

Dictionary

virtuous: a good moral quality in a person, or the general quality of goodness in a person   Ex. Patience is a virtue.
divine: connected with a god, or like a god.   Ex. The Ayatollah described the Iranian earthquake as a divine test.
calculate: to judge (the number or amount of something) by using the information that you already have, and adding, multiplying, subtracting or dividing numbers   Ex. The cost of the damage caused by the recent storms has been calculated as/at over $5 million.
misgiving: a feeling of regret, doubt, or apprehension.   Ex. I have no misgivings about my decision.

On Friendship

Friendship is above reason,
for though you find virtues / in a friend,
he was your friend / before you found them.
It is a gift / **that** we offer / because we must;
to give it / as the reward of virtue
would be **to** set a price / upon it,
and those / **who** do that
have no friendship / **to** give.
If you choose your friends / on the ground / **that** you are virtuous
and want virtuous company,
you are **no** near**er** / to true friendship
than if you choose them / for commercial reasons.

Besides who are you
that you should be setting a price / upon your friendship?
It is enough / for any man
that he has / the divine power / **of** mak**ing** friends,
and he must leave it / to that power
to determine / **who** his friends shall be.
For, **though** you may **choose** / the virtuous **to** be(=as) your friends,
they may not choose you;
indeed, friendship cannot grow
where there is any calculated choice.
It comes, like sleep,
when you are not thinking / about it;
and you should be grateful,
without any misgiving, / when it comes.

우정에 대해

우정은 이유를 초월한다,
왜냐하면 비록 당신이 발견한다 해도 미덕을 / 한 친구에게서,
그는 이미 당신의 친구였다 / 당신이 발견하기 전에 / 그들을.
우정은 하나의 선물이다 / 우리가 내놓는 / 우리가 그래야 하기 때문에;
그것을 주는 **것은** / 미덕의 보답으로
값을 매기는 **것**이 될 것이다 / 우정에,
그리고 사람들은 / 그런 일을 하**는**
우정을 가지고 있지 않다 / (남에게) **줄**.
만약 당신이 선택한다면 당신의 친구들을 / 근거 하에 / 당신이 미덕이 있**다는**
그리고 원한다면 미덕이 있는 친구를,
당신이 진정한 우정과는 거리가 먼 **것은**
마치 당신이 그들을 선택한다면 / 상업적인 이유들 때문에
당신이 진정한 우정과 거리가 먼 **것과 같다**.
더구나 당신이 뭐가 잘났다고
당신이 값을 매긴단 말인가 / 당신의 우정에 대해?
(그것으로) 충분하다 / 누구에게나
그가 가지고 있다는 **것**으로 / 신성한 힘을 / 친구들을 만드**는**,
그래서 그는 맡겨야 한다 / 그 힘에
결정하는 **것은** / **누가** 그의 친구들이 될 것인**지를**.
비록 당신이 선택한다 하더라도 / 미덕을 지닌 사람들을 / 당신의 친구로,
그들이 당신을 선택하지 않을 지도 모르기 때문이다;
사실 우정은 자랄 수 없다
어떤 것이든 계산적인 선택이 있는 **곳에서는**.
그것은 찾아온다, / 잠자는 것처럼.
당신이 생각하고 있지 않을 때 / 그것에 대해;
따라서 당신은 감사해야 한다,
어떤 의심도 없이, / 우정이 찾아올 때는.

10. How to Win Friends and Influence People

There is one important law of human conduct. If we obey that law, we shall almost never get into trouble. That law, if obeyed, will bring us countless friends and constant happiness. But the very moment we break that law, we shall get into endless trouble. The law is this: Always make the other person feel important.

Dr. Sigmund Freud, one of the most distinguished psychologists of the 20th century, says that everything you and I do springs from the two motives: the sex urge and the desire to be great. Dr. John Dewey, America's most profound philosopher, phrases it a bit differently. He says the deepest urge in human nature is "the desire to be important." Remember that phrase: "the desire to be important." It is significant. You want recognition of your true worth. You want a feeling that you are important in your little world. It is this desire that makes you want to wear the latest styles. All of us have the same desire. So, let's obey the Golden Rule, all the time, everywhere. Would you like to know how to make a girl fall in love with you? Obey the rule and talk to her about herself.

Carnegie, Dale (1888~1955)
American lecturer, author, and pioneer in the field of public speaking and the psychology of the successful personality.

Dr. Sigmund Freud, one of the most distinguished psychologists of the 20th century, says that everything you and I do springs from the two motives: the sex urge and the desire to be great.

Freud, Sigmund(1865~1939)
Austrian neurologist, psychologist and founder of psychoanalysis, is generally recognised as one of the most influential and authoritative thinkers of the twentieth century.

Dewey, John (1859~1952)
American philosopher and educator who was one of the founders of the philosophical school of pragmatism, a pioneer in functional psychology, and a leader of the progressive movement in education in the United States.

Dictionary

distinguished: marked by excellence or renown; eminent.
　　　　　　 Ex. a distinguished family
spring: to originate or develop from someone or something.
urge: an involuntary or natural impulse or desire to do something.
profound: deep; having intellectual insight and depth.　Ex. a profound thought.
phrase: to express or say in a particular way.　Ex. How should I phrase this introduction?
recognition: formal acknowledgment or approval.　Ex. recognition for her achievements.

How to Win Friends and Influence People

There is one important law / of human conduct.
If we obey that law,
we shall almost never get into trouble.
That law, / if obeyed, will bring
us countless friends and constant happiness.
But **the very moment** / **(that)** we break that law,
we shall get into endless trouble.
The law is this:
Always make / the other person feel / important.
Dr. Sigmund Freud,
one of the most distinguished psychologists / of the 20th century, says
that everything **(that)** you and I do / springs / from the two motives:
the sex urge and the desire **to** be great.
Dr. John Dewey, / America's most profound philosopher,
phrases it / a bit differently.
He say / **(that)** the deepest urge / in human nature
is "the desire **to** be important."
Remember that phrase: "the desire to be important."
It is significant.
You want recognition / of your true worth.
You want a feeling / **that** you are important / in your little world.
It is this desire / **that** makes / you want / to wear the latest styles.
All of us have / the same desire.
So, let's obey / the Golden Rule, / all the time, everywhere.
Would you like to know
how to make / a girl fall in love with you?
Obey the rule / and talk to her / about herself.

친구를 얻고 남을 움직이는 방법

한 가지 중요한 법칙이 있다 / 인간 행동의.
만일 우리가 지키면 그 법칙을,
우리는 거의 곤란에 빠지지 않을 것이다.
그 법칙은 / 준수만 된다면 / 가져다 줄 것이다
우리에게 수많은 친구들와 끊임없는 행복을.
그러나 **바로 그 순간** / 우리가 그 법칙을 깨는,
우리는 끝없는 곤란에 빠질 것이다.
그 법칙은 다음과 같다:
항상 만들어라 / 다른 사람이 느끼도록 / 중요하다고.
시그먼드 프로이드 박사는,
가장 저명한 심리학자의 한 사람인 / 20세기의 / 말한다
여러분과 내가 하는 모든 일은 (튀어)나온**다고** / 두 가지 동기들로부터:
즉 성적 충동과 위대해지려**는** 욕망이 그것이다.
존 듀이 박사는 / 미국의 가장 해박한 철학자인,
표현한다 그것을 / 약간 다르게.
그는 말한다 / 가장 깊은 충동은 / 인간 본성에서
'중요해지려**는** 욕구' 라고.
기억하라 그 구절을 / '중요한 인물이 되려는 욕구' 라는.
그것은 의미심장하다.
당신은 원한다 인정을 / 당신의 진짜 가치의.
당신은 원한다 느낌을 / 당신이 중요하**다는** / 당신의 작은 세계에서.
바로 이런 욕구다 / 당신이 원하도록 만드는 **것은** / 최신형의 옷을 입기를.
우리 모두는 가지고 있다 / 똑같은 욕망을.
그러므로 따르자 / 그 황금률을 / 어느 때나 어디에서나.
여러분은 알고 싶은가?
어떻게 만드는 지를 / 한 소녀가 당신에게 사랑에 빠지도록 ?
그 법칙을 지키라 / 그리고 그녀에게 말하라 / 그녀 자신에 대해.

11. The Little Prince – 1

The little prince went away, to look again at the roses. "You are not at all like my rose," he said. "as yet you are nothing. No one has tamed you, and you have tamed no one. You are like my fox when I first knew him. He was only a fox like a hundred thousand other foxes. But I have made him my friend, and now he is unique in all the world." And the roses were very much embarrassed.

"You are beautiful, but you are empty," he went on. "One could not die for you. To be sure, an ordinary passerby would think that my rose looked just like you – the rose that belongs to me. But in herself alone she is more important than all the hundreds of you other roses: because it is she that I have watered; because it is she that I have put under the glass globe; because it is she that I have sheltered behind the screen; because it is for her that I have killed the caterpillars (except the two or three that we saved to become butterflies): because it is she that I have listened to, when she grumbled, or boasted, or even sometimes when she said nothing. Because she is my rose."

Antoine de Saint Exupéry(1900~1944)
French aviator and writer whose works are the unique testimony of a pilot and a warrior who looked at adventure and danger with a poet's.

You are like my fox when I first knew him. He was only a fox like a hundred thousand of other foxes. But I have made him my friend, and now he is unique in all the world."

Dictionary

tame: brought or bred out of the wild state and made tractable; domesticated. Ex. a tame leopard.
embarrass: to shame, disconcert, make ill at ease, or make painfully self-conscious.
globe: a round or spherical object, esp. a ball on which there is a map of the earth. Ex. a celestial(a terrestrial) globe.
shelter: to act as or provide cover, protection, or shelter for.
Ex. I sheltered for some time from the shower under a tree.
caterpillar: a butterfly or moth larva, resembling a worm and often brightly colored.
grumble: to mutter dissatisfaction or complaints. Ex. Don't grumble at the food.

The Little Prince – 1

The little prince went away, **to** look again / at the roses.
"You are not at all like my rose," he said.
"as yet you are nothing.
No one has tamed you, and / you have tamed no one.
You are like my fox / when I first knew him.
He was only a fox / like a hundred thousand of other foxes.
But I have made / him my friend,
and now he is unique / in all the world."
And the roses were very much embarrassed.
"You are beautiful, / but you are empty," / he went on.
"One could not die / for you.
To be sure, an ordinary passerby would think
that my rose looked just / like you
– the rose / **that** belongs to me.
But in herself alone / she is more important
than all the hundreds of you other roses:
because **it** is she / **that** I have watered;
because **it** is she / **that** I have put under the glass globe;
because **it** is she / **that** I have sheltered behind the screen;
because **it** is for her / **that** I have killed the caterpillars
(except the two or three / **that** we saved / to become butterflies):
because **it** is she / **that** I have listened to,
when she grumbled, or boasted,
or even sometimes / when she said nothing.
Because she is my rose."

어린 왕자 - 1

어린 왕자는 다시 보러 갔다 / 그 장미들을.
"너희는 전혀 같지 않아 내 장미꽃과." / 그는 말했다.
"아직 너희는 아무 것도 아니므로.
아무도 길들이지 않았어 너희를 / 그리고 너희도 누구 한 사람 길들이지 않았지.
너희는 내 여우와 같아 / 내가 처음 알았을 때의.
그는 단지 한 마리의 여우였어 / 수백 수천의 다른 여우들처럼.
그러나 나는 만들었지(삼았지) / 그를 나의 친구로,
그리고 이제 그는 하나 밖에 없는 여우가 됐지 / 온 세상에서."
그러자 장미들은 매우 당황하였다.
"너희는 아름답다. / 그러나 마음은 허무할거야" / 그는 말을 계속했다.
"한 사람도 죽지는 않을 거야 / 너희를 위해.
분명히 / 평범한 행인은 생각할 거야
나의 장미꽃도 보였**다고** / 바로 너희처럼
- 그 장미꽃 말이야 / 내 것이 된.
그러나 혼자 있는 내 꽃은 훨씬 더 중요하지
수 많은 너희 장미들 전부보다:
(그것은) 내 장미이기 때문이지 / 내가 물을 준 **것은**;
(그것은) 내 장미이기 때문이지 / 내가 씌워 준 **것은** 유리 덮개를;
(그것은) 내 장미이기 때문이지 / 내가 가려준 **것은** 바람막이 뒤에
(그것은) 내 장미를 위한 것이기 때문이지 / 내가 죽인 **것은** 쐬기 벌레를
(두 세 마리는 제외하고 / 우리가 남겨**둔** / 나비들이 되도록):
(그것은) 내 꽃이기 때문이지 / 내가 귀를 기울인 **것은**,
내 꽃이 불평했거나 자랑했을 때도,
심지어 아무 것도 말하지 않았을 때도 귀를 기울였지.
그 꽃은 내 장미이기 때문에."

The Little Prince – 2

And he went back to meet the fox.

"Goodbye," he said. "Goodbye," said the fox. "And now here is my secret, a very simple secret: It is only with the heart that one can see rightly; what is essential is invisible to the eye."

"What is essential is invisible to the eye," the little prince repeated, so that he would be sure to remember.

"It is the time you have wasted for your rose that makes your rose so important."

"It is the time I have wasted for my rose –" said the little prince, so that he would be sure to remember.

"Men have forgotten this truth," said the fox. "But you must not forget it. You become responsible, forever, for what you have tamed. Your are responsible for your rose..."

"I am responsible for my rose," the little prince repeated, so that he would be sure to remember.

"It is the time you have wasted for your rose that makes your rose so important."

Dictionary

essential: 1. of the highest importance for achieving something. Ex. It is essential that we arrive on time. 2. being the most basic element or feature of something or somebody. Ex. We wanted the biography to tell us the essential nature of the man. 3. something that is necessary or fundamental. Ex. Having your own computer is an essential for this kind of work.
invisible: not able to be seen with the eyes. Ex. invisible to the naked eye.
tame: brought or bred out of the wild state and made tractable; domesticated. Ex. a tame leopard.

The little Prince – 2

And he went back / **to** meet the fox.

"Goodbye," he said.

"Goodbye," said the fox.

"And now here is my secret, a very simple secret:

It is only with the heart **that** one can see rightly;

what is essential is invisible to the eye."

"**What** is essential is invisible to the eye,"

the little prince repeated, **so that** he **would** be sure to remember.

"**It** is the time / **(that)** you have wasted / for your rose

that makes / your rose so important."

"It is the time I have wasted for my rose –" said the little prince,

so that he would be sure to remember.

"Men have forgotten this truth," / said the fox.

"But you must not forget it.

You become responsible, forever, / for **what** you have tamed.

You are responsible / for your rose..."

"I am responsible for my rose," / the little prince repeated,

so that he would be sure to remember.

어린왕자 - 2

그리고 그는 돌아왔다 / 만나**기 위해** 여우를.
"잘 있어" 그가 말했다.
"잘 가" 말했다 여우가.
"이제 내 비밀을 말해주지 / 매우 단순한 비밀이야:
그것은 오직 마음으로 보아야 / 바르게 볼 수 있다는 것이지;
중요한 **것은** / 보이지 않아 눈에."
"중요한 **것은** / 보이지 않는다고 눈에.
어린 왕자는 되풀이했다 / 분명히 기억**하려고**.
(**그것은**) 시간이야 / 바로 네가 바**친** / 너의 장미를 위해
만드는 **것은** / 너의 장미를 그토록 중요하게."
"그것은 시간이라고 / 내가 바친 내 장미를 위해 - " 말했다 어린 왕자는,
분명히 기억하려고.
"인간들은 잊어버렸지 이런 진리를" / 여우가 말했다.
"그러나 너는 잊어서는 안 돼 그것을.
너는 책임지게 되지, 영원히, / 네가 길들인 **것**을.
너는 책임이 있어 / 너의 장미에...."
"나는 책임이 있다고 내 장미에" / 어린 왕자는 되풀이했다,
분명히 기억하기 위해.

12. The Conquest of Happiness

The whole subject of happiness has, in my opinion, been treated too seriously. It has been thought that men cannot be happy without a theory of life or a religion. Perhaps those who have been made unhappy by a bad theory may need a better theory help them recover, just as you may need a tonic when you have been ill. But when things are normal a man should be healthy without a tonic and happy without a theory. It is the simple things that really matter.

If a man delights in his wife and children, has success in work, and finds pleasure in the change of day and night, spring and autumn, he will be happy whatever his philosophy may be. If, on the other hand, he finds his wife hateful, his children's noise unbearable, and the office a nightmare, or if in the daytime he longs for night, and a night he sighs for the light of day then what he needs is not a new philosophy but a different diet, or more exercise, or what not.

Man is an animal, and his happiness depends upon his physiology more than he likes to think. This is a humble conclusion, but I cannot make myself deny it. Unhappy businessmen, I am convinced, would increase their happiness more by walking six miles every day than by any change of philosophy.

Russell, Bertrand(1872~1970)
English logician and philosopher, best known for his work in mathematical logic and for his social and political campaigns, including his advocacy of both pacifism and nuclear disarmament. He received the Nobel Prize for Literature in 1950.

Man is an animal, and his happiness depends upon his physiology more than he likes to think. Unhappy businessmen, I am convinced, would increase their happiness more by walking six miles every day than by any change of philosophy.

Central Park – Couple walking.

Dictionary

tonic: something that refreshes or restores one's strength or vigor; a medicine with this effect.
unbearable: impossible to bear or endure; intolerable.
nightmare: a terrifying or distressing dream; an experience, event, or state of mind suggestive of a terrible dream. Ex. The trip was a nightmare.
diet: the food and drink ordinarily consumed by a person, animal, or group of such. Ex1 a vegetable (a meat) diet. Ex2 She is on a diet.
physiology: the science that deals with the processes and functions of living organisms and their cells, tissues, and parts.

The conquest of Happiness

The whole subject / of happiness
has, in my opinion, been treated / too seriously.
It has been thought / **that** men cannot be happy
without a theory of life or a religion.
Perhaps those / **who** have been made unhappy / by a bad theory
may need / a better theory / **(that)** help / them recover,
just as you may need a tonic / when you have been ill.
But when things are normal a man should be healthy / without a tonic
and happy / without a theory.
It is the simple things / **that** really matter.
If a man delights / in his wife and children,
has success / in work,
and finds pleasure / in the change / of day and night, / spring and autumn,
he will be happy / **whatever** his philosophy may be.
If, on the other hand, he finds his wife hateful,
his children's noise unbearable, and the office a nightmare,
or if in the daytime he longs for / night,
and at night he sighs for / the light of day –
then **what** he needs / is not a new philosophy
but a different diet, / or more exercise, / or what not.
Man is an animal, / and his happiness depends upon / his physiology
more than / he likes to think.
This is a humble conclusion, / but I cannot make myself deny it.
Unhappy businessmen, / I am convinced,
would increase their happiness   more / by walking six miles every day
than by any change of philosophy.

행복의 정복

전체 주제가 / 행복에 관**한**
다뤄져왔다고 생각한다 / 너무 심각하게.
생각돼왔다 / 인간은 행복할 수 없**다고**
어떤 생활 혹은 종교의 이론 없이는.
아마도 사람들은 / 불행하게 만들어**진**(불행해진) / 잘못된 이론에 의해
필요로 할지도 모른다 / 더 좋은 이론을 / 도와주**는** / 그들이 회복하도록,
마치 강장제를 필요로 할지도 모르는 것처럼 / 여러분이 아팠을 때.
그러나 모든 것이 정상일 때 사람은 건강할 것이다 / 강장제 없이도
그리고 행복할 것이다 / 이론 없이도.
단순한 것들이다 / 진짜 중요한 **것은**.
만일 한 남자가 기쁨을 얻으면 / 그의 아내와 아이들에게서,
일에서 성공하면,
그리고 즐거움을 느끼면 / 변화에서 / 밤과 낮, 봄과 가을의,
그는 행복할 것이다 / 그의 인생철학이 **무엇이든**.
한편 그가 생각한다면 / 아내가 밉다고,
아이들의 시끄러운 소리가 참기 어렵다고, / 그리고 직장이 악몽이라고,
혹은 낮에 그가 애타게 바란다면 / 밤을,
그리고 밤에 그가 그리워한다면 / 낮의 빛을 –
그때 그가 필요로 하는 **것은** / 새로운 철학이 아니라
다른 식사, / 혹은 더 많은 운동 등이다.
인간은 동물이다 / 따라서 인간의 행복은 좌우된다 / 인간의 생리에
이상으로 / 그가 생각하고 싶어하는 것.
이것은 보잘 것 없는 결론이다 / 그러나 나는 그것을 부정할 수 없다.
불행한 사업가들은 / 내가 확신컨대
증진시킬 것이다 그들의 행복을 더 많이 / 걸음으로써 6마일씩 매일
철학의 어떤 변화에 의한 것 보다는.

III 세상 가치기

13. Of Studies / Francis Bacon 학문에 대해
14. Dead Poets Society 죽은 시인의 사회
15. The Autobiography of Lee Iacocca / Lee Iacocca 아이아코카 자서전
16. On Achieving Success / Ernest Hemingway 성공하는 것에 대해
17. How to Enjoy Music / George R. Marek 음악을 즐기는 방법
18. Painting As A Pastime / Winston Churchill 취미로서의 그림 그리기

13. Of Studies

Studies serve for delight, for ornament, and for ability. Their chief use for delight is in privateness and retiring; for ornament is in discourse; and for ability is in the judgement and disposition of business; for expert men can execute, and perhaps judge of particulars, one by one: but the general counsels, and the plots and marshalling of affairs come best from those that are learned. To spend too much time in studies is sloth; to use them too much for ornament is affectation; to make judgement wholly by their rules is the humor of a scholar: they perfect nature, and are perfected by experience: for natural abilities are like natural plants, that need pruning by study; and studies themselves do give forth directions too much at large, except they be bounded in by experience.

Bacon, Francis (1618-21)
A lawyer, statesman, philosopher, and master of the English tongue, he is remembered in literary terms for the sharp worldly wisdom of a few dozen essays.

To use them too much for ornament is affectation; to make judgement wholly by their rules is the humor of a scholar: they perfect nature, and are perfected by experience:

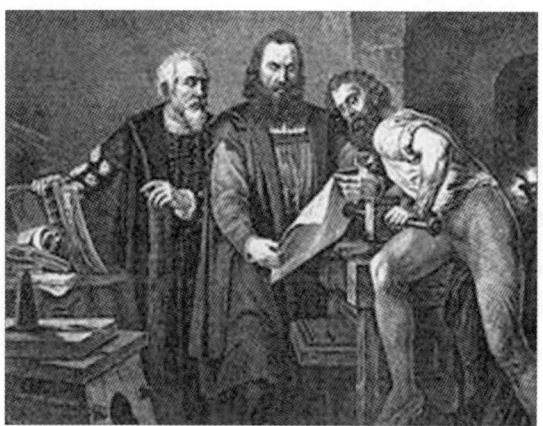
'A Scholar' - 1631; The Hermitage Museum, St. Petersburg

Dictionary

ornament: something that is added to beautify or improve appearance; decoration.
retire: to cease work or active life; to withdraw to seek shelter or seclusion. Ex. I retired to my room.
disposition: a predominant or prevailing mood or temperament, as of a person or the weather; an act of settling a matter.
marshal: to arrange in an orderly fashion or display. Ex. He marshaled his evidence.
sloth: dislike of work or exercise; laziness.
affectation: falseness or superficiality of appearance or behavior; pretense.
prune: to cut or remove dead or unwanted branches, twigs, or the like from; trim.

Of Studies – 1

Studies serve / for delight, for ornament, and for ability.
Their chief use / for delight
is in privateness and retiring(retirement);
(their chief use) for ornament
is in discourse(=conversation);
and (their chief use) for ability
is in the judgement and disposition of business;
for expert men can execute,
and perhaps judge / of particulars, / one by one:
but the general counsels, / and the plots and marshalling of affairs
come best from those that are learned.
To spend too much time / in studies / is sloth;
to use them too much / for ornament / is affectation;
to make judgement wholly / by their rules / is the humor of a scholar:
they perfect nature, / and are perfected / by experience:
for natural abilities are like natural plants,
that need / prun**ing** by study;
and studies themselves do give forth directions / too much at large,
except(=unless, if ~ not) they be bounded in / by experience.

학문에 대해-1

학문은 도움이 된다 / 즐거움을 위해, 장식을 위해, 그리고 능력을 위해.
학문의 주요한 효용은 기쁨을 위한
혼자 은거할 때 있다;
그리고 장식을 위한 주요한 효용은
담화에 있다;
그리고 능력을 위한 효용은
업무의 판단과 배치(처리)에 있다;
왜냐하면 숙련된 사람은 실행할 수 있기 때문이다,
그리고 아마 판단할 수 있기 때문이다 / 특정한 것들에 대해서 / 하나 하나:
그러나 일반적인 조언들과 / 일들의 구상과 정리는
학자들이 가장 낫다.
소비하는 **것은** 너무 많은 시간을 / 학문에 / 게으른 짓이다;
사용하는 **것은** 그것들을 너무 많이 / 장식을 위해 / 허식이다;
판단하는 **것은** 전적으로 / 그것들의 규칙들에 의해 / 학자의 기질이다;
학문들은 완성한다 천성을 / 그리고 학문은 완성된다 / 경험에 의해,
왜냐하면 천성의 능력들은 자연의 식물들과 같기 때문에
필요로 한다 / 가지치**기를** / 학문에 의한;
그리고 학문들 자체는 방향들을 제시한다 / 너무 일반적으로,
학문들이 제한되지 않는 경우 / 경험에 의해.

Of Studies – 2

Crafty men condemn studies, simple men admire them, and wise men use them; for they teach not their own use; but that is a wisdom without them and above them, by observation. Read not to contradict and confute, nor to believe and take for granted, nor to find talk and discourse, but to weigh and consider. Some books are to be tasted, others to be swallowed, and some few to be chewed and digested; that is, some books are to be read only in parts; others to be read but not curiously, and some few to be read wholly, and with diligence and attention. Some books also may be read by deputy, and extracts made of them by others but that would be only in the less important arguments and the meaner sort of books; else distilled books are, like common distilled waters, flashy things.

Reading maketh a full man; conference a ready man; and writing an exact man; and therefore, if a man write little, he had need have a great memory; if he confer little, he had need have a present wit; and if he reads little, he had need have much cunning, to seem to know that he doth not.

Read not to contradict and confute, nor to believe and take for granted, nor to find talk and discourse, but to weigh and consider.

Girl Reading by Renoir.

Dictionary

contradict: to assert the opposite of; deny the truth of.
    Ex. She contradicted my opinion.
confute: to refute or prove incorrect; disprove.
weigh: to ponder carefully before making a decision.
    Ex. I'm weighing the consequences.
deputy: someone authorized to be a substitute or assistant.
extract: to remove or take out by use of force; an excerpt from something written. Ex. make extracts from Shakespeare.

Of Studies – 2

Crafty(=clever) men contemn(=condemn) studies,
simple men admire them;
and wise men use them;
for they teach not / their own use;
but that is a wisdom / without them / and above them, / by observation.
Read not / to contradict and confute,
nor to believe / and take for granted,
nor to find / talk and discourse,
but to weigh / and consider.
Some books **are to** be tasted, others (are) **to** be swallowed,
and some few / (are) **to** be chewed and digested;
that is, / some books **are to** be read / only in parts;
others (are) **to** be read / but not curiously,
and some few (are) **to** be read / wholly,
and with diligence and attention.
Some books / also may be read / by deputy,
and extracts / (**that** is) made of them / by others
but that would be / only in the less important arguments
and the meaner sort of books;
else distilled books / are, like common distilled waters, / flashy things.
Reading maketh / a full man;
conference / a ready man;
and writing / an exact man;
and therefore, if a man write little, / he had need / have a great memory;
if he confer little, / he had need / have a present wit;
and if he reads little, / he had need / have much cunning,
to seem to know / that he doth not.

학문에 대해 - 2

교활한(영리한) 사람은 경멸한다 학문들을,
단순한 사람은 경탄한다 그것들을;
그리고 현명한 사람은 이용한다 그것들을;
왜냐하면 학문들은 가르쳐주지 않기 때문이다 / 그것들 자체 용도를;
그러나 그것은 지혜다 / 학문들 밖의 / 그리고 학문들을 넘어서는, / 관찰에 의한.
읽지 말라 / 반대하고 논박하기 위해,
또한 믿기 위해서도 (읽지 **말라**), / 그리고 당연한 것으로 받아들이기 위해서도,
또한 찾기 위해서도 (읽지 **말라**) / 이야깃거리와 논박할 자료를,
그러나 독서를 하라 무게를 달고(고찰하고) / 숙고하기 위해.
어떤 책들은 음미**해야 하며**, 어떤 책은 삼켜**야 하며**,
그리고 일부 소수의 책은 / 씹고 소화**해야 한다**;
다시 말해 / 어떤 책들은 읽어**야 하며** / 오직 일부만;
어떤 책은 읽어야 하되 / 주의 깊게 읽지 않아도 된다 ,
그리고 일부 소수의 책은 읽**어야 한다** / 전부
성실하고 주의 깊게.
어떤 책들은 / 역시 읽게 할 수도 있다 / 대리로,
그리고 읽어도 된다 / 발췌문들을 / 만들어**진**(뽑은) / 다른 사람들에 의해
그러나 그것은 오직 있을(적용될) 것이다 / 덜 중요한 논의들에
그리고 더 비속한 종류의 책에;
그렇지 않고 증발해 버린 증류한 책들은 / 일반 증류수처럼 / 무미건조한 것이다.
독서는 만든다 / 충실한 사람을;
협의(담론)는 / 준비성 있는 사람을;
그리고 쓰기는 / 정확한 사람을.
따라서, 만약 사람이 글을 적게 쓰면 / 그는 필요가 있다 / 좋은 기억력을 가질;
만약 그가 담론한다면 적게 / 그는 필요성이 있다 / 임기응변의 위트를 가질;
그리고 그가 적게 읽는다면 / 그는 필요가 있다 / 많은 잔꾀를 가질,
보이**기 위해서** 아는 것처럼 / 그가 모르는 것을.

Of Studies – 3

Histories make men wise; poets, witty; the mathematics, subtle; natural philosophy, deep; moral, grave; logic and rhetoric, able to contend, Studies culminate in manners, – nay, there is no impediment in the wit but may be wrought out by fit studies; like as diseases of the body may have appropriate exercise; bowling is good for the stone and reins, shooting for the lungs and breast, gentle walking for the stomach, riding for the head, and the like; so if a man's wit be wandering, let him study the mathematics; for in demonstrations, if his wit be called away never so little, he must begin again; if his wit be not apt to distinguish or find differences, let him study the school-men; for they are cymini sectores.

If he be not apt to beat over matters, and to call up one thing to prove and illustrate another, let him study the lawyers' cases; so every defect of the mind may have a special receipt.

Bowling is good for the stone and reins, shooting for the lungs and breast, gentle walking for the stomach, riding for the head, and the like.

riding

shooting

walking

Dictionary

witty: displaying or characterized by clever, perceptive humor.
Ex. a witty person.
rhetoric: the art, ability, or study of using language effectively in speech or writing, esp. to influence or persuade one's audience.
contend: to strive in argument; dispute; debate. Ex. They angrily contended about which plan was best.
culminate: to arrive at a climax or conclusion. Ex. The celebration will culminate in fireworks.
impediment: an obstacle or hindrance. Ex. He has an impediment in one's walking.
defect: a flaw, error, or other imperfection. Ex. Every man has the defects of his own virtues.

Of Studies - 3

Histories make men wise;
poets, witty;
the mathematics, subtle;
natural philosophy, deep;
moral (philosophy), grave;
logic and rhetoric, able to contend,
Studies culminate / in manners,
- nay, / there is no impediment / in the wit
but may be wrought out(= **that** may not be worked out) / by fit studies;
like / as diseases of the body may have / appropriate exercise;
bowling is good / for the stone and reins(=kidneys),
shooting / for the lungs and breast,
gentle walking / for the stomach,
riding / for the head, and the like;
so if a man's wit be wandering,
let him study / the mathematics;
for in demonstrations,
if his wit be called away / never so little(=**however little it may be**),
he must begin again;
if his wit be not apt / **to** distinguish or find differences,
let him study / the school-men;
for they are cymini sectores(=cutters of cumminin seed, hair-splitters).
If he be not apt / **to** beat over matters,
and **to** call up one thing / **to** prove and illustrate another,
let him study / the lawyers' cases;
so every defect of the mind / may have / a special receipt.

학문에 대하여-3

역사는 / 사람들을 현명하게 만든다 ;
시는, 위트 있게 ;
수학은, 치밀하게 ;
자연 과학은, 깊게 ;
정신과학(윤리학,심리학 등)은, 중후하게 ;
논리학과 수사학은, 논쟁할 수 있게,
학문은 절정에 이르게 한다 / 습관의,
- 아니, / 어떤 장애도 없다 / 정신 속에는
제거될 수 **없는** / 적당한 학문들에 의해 ;
똑같이 / 신체의 질병들이 가지고 있는 것과 / 적당한 운동을 ;
볼링은 좋다 / 결석과 신장에,
사격은 / 폐와 가슴에,
부드러운 걷기는 / 위에,
승마는 머리에, 등 ;
그래서 만약 사람의 정신이 방황하고 있다면(산만하다면),
공부하게 하라 / 수학을 ;
왜냐하면 증명하는 데 있어,
만약 그의 정신이 흩어지면 / **조금이라도**,
그는 시작해야 한다 다시 ;
만약 그의 정신이 적합하지 않다면 / 구분**하기**에 혹은 찾**기**에 차이들을,
공부하게 하라 / 스콜라 학파 사람들을 ;
왜냐하면 그들은 사소한 일도 따지는 사람이기 때문이다.
만약 그가 적합하지 않다면 / 철저히 파헤치**는 데** 문제들을,
그리고 한 가지 사실을 불러내**는 데** / 증명하고 예증하**기 위해** 또 다른 것을,
공부하게 하라 / 판례집을 ;
이처럼 정신의 모든 결함은 / 가지고 있을 지 모른다 / 특별한 처방을.

14. Dead Poets Society – 1

John: Mr. Pitts, will you open your hymnal to page 542. Read the 1st stanza of the poem you find there.

Pitts: "To the virgins to make much of time"?

John: Yes, that's the one. Somewhat appropriate isn't it?

Pitts: "Gather ye rosebuds while ye may, old time is still a-flying, and this same flower... that smiles today, tomorrow will be dying."

John: Thank you, Mr. Pitts. "Gather ye rosebuds while ye may." The latin term for that sentiment is Carpe Diem. Who knows what that means?

Meeks: Carpe Diem. That's seize the day.

John: Very good, Mr....

Meeks: Meeks.

John: Meeks. Another unusual name. "Gather ye rosebuds while ye may." Why does the writer use these lines?

Charlie: He's in a hurry

John: No! Ding! Thanks for playing, anyway. Because we are food for worms, lads. Believe it or not, each of us... is one day going to stop breathing, turn cold, and die.

Directed by Peter Weir. Screenplay by Tom Schulman. Starring: Robin Williams

"Gather ye rosebuds while ye may, old time is still a-flying, and this same flower... that smiles today, tomorrow will be dying."

Herrick, Robert
English cleric and poet, the most original of the "sons of Ben [Jonson]," who revived the spirit of the ancient classic lyric. He is best remembered for the line "Gather ye rosebuds while ye may."

Dictionary

hymnal: a book of church hymns.
stanza: a group of related lines in a poem that are separated typographically from other similar groups and that often have a regular meter and rhyme scheme.
sentiment: emotional feeling. Ex. sentiments of sorrow.
Carpe Diem: seize the day (Latin); the attitude or advice that one should enjoy today, without thought for tomorrow.

Dead Poets Society – 1

John: Mr. Pitts, will you open / your hymnal / to page 542.
          Read the 1st stanza of the poem / (**that**) you find there.

Pitts: "To the virgins to make much of time"?

John: Yes, that's the one.
          Somewhat appropriate isn't it?

Pitts: "Gather ye rosebuds / while ye may,
          old time is still a-flying, and
          this same flower... / **that** smiles today,
          tomorrow will be dying."

John: Thank you, Mr. Pitts.
          "Gather ye rosebuds while ye may."
          The latin term / for that sentiment / is Carpe Diem.
          Who knows **what** that means?

Meeks: Carpe Diem. That's seize the day.

John: Very good, Mr....

Meeks: Meeks.

John: Meeks. Another unusual name.
          "Gather ye rosebuds while ye may."
          Why does the writer use / these lines?

Charlie: He's in a hurry.

John: No! Ding! Thanks for playing, anyway.
          Because we are food for worms, lads.
          Believe it or not,
          each of us... / is one day going to stop / breathing,
          turn cold, and die.

죽은 시인의 사회 - 1

존: 피츠군, 펴보게 / 자네의 찬송가집 / 542쪽을.
　　읽게 그 시의 첫 구절을
피츠: "시간을 버는 천사들에게"말인가요?
존: 맞아, 바로 그거야.
　　적절한 시지, 그렇지 않아?
피츠: "거둬라 그대여 장미 봉우리들을 / 그대가 할 수 있을 때,
　　오랜 시간이 아직 날고(흐르고) 있고
　　이 똑 같은 꽃이 / 오늘 미소 짓는,
　　내일이면 죽을(질) 것이다."
존: 고맙네, 피츠군.
　　"거둬라 그대여 장미 봉우리들을 / 그대가 할 수 있을 때."
　　라틴어 용어(표현)는 / 그 감정에 해당하는 / 카르페 디엠이다.
　　누가 알고 있지 / 그것이 의미하는 **것을**?
믹스: 카르페 디엠. 그것은 '오늘을 잡아라' 입니다.
존: 매우 잘했네, 미스터 누구더라…
믹스: 믹스입니다.
존: 믹스. 또 다른 이상한 이름이군.
　　"모아라 그대여 장미 봉우리들을 / 그대가 할 수 있을 때."
　　왜 글쓴이는 사용하지 / 이런 구절들을?
찰리: 그는 급하거든요.
존: 아니야! 틀렸어! 고맙네 응해준 건, 어쨌든.
　　왜냐하면 우리는 먹이이기 때문이지 / 벌레들을 위한, / 젊은이들이여.
　　믿건 안 믿건,
　　우리 각자는… / 어느 날 멈추고 / 숨쉬는 것을, /
　　몸이 차갑게 되고 죽을 것이다.

Dead Poets Society – 2

John: I would like you to step forward... and peruse some of the faces from the past. You've walked past them, but not really looked at them. They're not that different from you. Same haircut, full of hormones, just like you. Invincible, just like you feel. The world is their oyster. They believe they're destined for great things, like you.

Their eyes are full of hope, just like you. Did they wait until too late... to fulfill one iota of what they were capable? Because, gentlemen, theses boys are now fertilizing daffodils. If you listen real close, you can hear them whisper their legacy to you. Go on, lean in. Listen. You hear it?
Carpe.
Carpe.
Carpe Diem.
Seize the day, boys.
Make your lives extraordinary.

Carpe. Carpe. Carpe Diem. Seize the day, boys. Make your lives extraordinary.

Welton Academy

Dictionary

peruse: to read or examine attentively and in detail.
Invincible: too strong to be defeated, overcome, or surmounted.
  Ex. an invincible enemy.
destined: to ordain in advance, as by fate or divine will.
  Ex. Her efforts were destined to fail.
fertilize: to apply fertilizer to. Ex. He fertilizes his lawn.
extraordinary: far beyond the usual or ordinary.

Dead Poets Society – 2

I would like / you to step forward...
and peruse / some of the faces / from the past.
You've walked / past them, / but not really looked at them.
They're not that different from you.
Same haircut, / full of hormones, / just like you.
Invincible, / just like you feel.
The world is their oyster.
They believe / (**that**) they're destined / for great things, / like you.
Their eyes are full of / hope, / just like you.
Did they wait until too late...
to fulfill / one iota / of **what** they were capable?
Because, gentlemen, / theses boys are now fertilizing / daffodils.
If you listen / real close,
you can hear / them whisper / their legacy / to you.
Go on, lean in. Listen.
You hear it?
Carpe.
Carpe.
Carpe Diem.
Seize the day, boys.
Make your lives extraordinary.

죽은 시인의 사회 - 2

나는 바란다 / 여러분**이** 앞으로 다가오기를...
그리고 꼼꼼히 읽어보기를(살펴보기를) / 그 과거의 얼굴들을.
여러분은 걸어왔다 / 그들 옆을, / 그러나 실제로는 쳐다보지 않았다 그들을.
그들은 그렇게 다르지 않다 / 여러분과.
머리도 같고, / 가득 차 있다 호르몬으로(젊다), / 바로 여러분처럼.
무적이고(패기만만하고), 바로 여러분이 느끼는 것처럼.
세상은 그들의 굴(마음대로 할 수 있는 것)이다.
그들은 믿는다 / 그들이 운명지어졌**다고** / 위대한 일들을 위해, 여러분처럼
그들의 눈은 가득 차 있다 / 희망으로, / 바로 여러분처럼.
그들은 기다렸나 / 너무 늦을 때까지(시기를 놓쳤나)...
채우**기에는** / 아주 조금이라도 / 그들이 할 수 있었던 **것을**?
왜냐하면 신사 여러분, / 이들은 이제 비료가 되고 있기 때문이지 / 수선화들의.
여러분이 듣는다면 / 아주 가까이에서,
여러분은 들을 수 있다 / 그들이 속삭이는 것을 / 그들의 유산을 / 여러분에게.
계속 해서, 기대보라. 들어라.
여러분은 들리는가 이 소리가?
카르페.
카르페.
카르페 디엠.
잡아라 오늘을, 소년들이여.
만들어라 여러분의 인생을 독특하게.

Dead Poets Society – 3

John: We don't read and write poetry because it's cute, but because we are members of the human race. And the human race is filled with passion. Medicine, Law, business, engineering, these are noble pursuits and necessary to sustain life. But poetry, beauty, romance, love, these are what we stay alive for.
To quote from Whitman,
"O me, life
of the questions of these recurring,
of the endless trains of the faithless.
of cities filled with the foolish.
What good amid these o me, o life?"
The answer...that you are here.
That life exists, an identity.
That the powerful play goes on, and
you may contribute a verse.
That the powerful play goes on... and
you may contribute a verse.
What will your verse be?

Whitman, Walt (1819~92)
American poet, journalist, and essayist whose verse collection Leaves of Grass is a landmark in the history of American literature.

Medicine, Law, business, engineering, these are noble pursuits and necessary to sustain life. But poetry, beauty, romance, love, these are what we stay alive for.

Robin Williams

Dictionary

sustain: to provide with the basic necessities of life.
recurring: to occur another time or repeatedly.
train: a long, moving line of persons, animals, or vehicles. Ex. a train of fans.
identity: all of those characteristics by which a person or thing is known to be himself, herself, or itself.
contribute: to give individually or with others to a common fund or collective effort. Ex. We contributed time and money to the campaign.

Dead Poets Society – 3

John: We don't read and write poetry / because it's cute,
but because we are members of the human race.
And the human race is filled / with passion.
Medicine, Law, business, engineering,
these are noble pursuits and / necessary **to** sustain life.
But poetry, beauty, romance, love, these / are what we **stay** alive for.
To quote / from Whitman,
"O me, life
of the questions / of these recurring,
of the endless trains / of the faithless.
of cities / filled with the foolish.
What good / amid these / o me, o life?"
The answer...**that** you are here.
That life exists, an identity.
That the powerful play goes on, and
you may contribute / a verse.
That the powerful play goes on... and
you may contribute a verse.
What will your verse be?

죽은 시인의 사회 - 3

존: 우리가 시를 읽고 쓰지는 않는다 / 그것이 아름답기 때문에,
그러나 우리가 인류의 일원이기 때문에 (시를 읽고 쓴다).
그리고 인류는 넘친다 / 정열로.
의학, 법률, 사업, 기술,
이것들은 숭고한 추구 대상들이고 / 필요하다 삶을 유지하**는 데**.
그러나 시, 아름다움, 낭만, 사랑, 이것들은 / 우리가 계속 살아가는 목적이다.
인용하자면 / 휘트먼의 시에서,
"오 나여, 생명이여
이 의문들 / 순환하는(끝없이 던져지는),
끊임없는 행렬들 / 믿음 없는 자들의.
도시들 / 바보들로 가득 찬.
어떤 좋은 것이 있나 / 이들 속에 / 오 나여, 오 생명이여?"
대답은.. 네가 여기에 존재한다는 **것**.
생명이 존재한다는 **것**, 일종의 정체성.
힘찬 연극은 계속되고,
너는 바쳐질지 모른다는 **것** / 한편의 시로.
힘찬 연극은 계속되고...
너는 바쳐질지 모른다는 **것** / 한편의 시로.
여러분의 시는 어떤 것일까?

15. The Autobiography of Lee Iacocca – 1

Normally, I'm not in favor of switching people around. I'm skeptical of the current fad of rotating people through various departments of a company as though all skills were interchangeable. They're not. It's like taking a cardiologist and saying: He's a great heart surgeon. Next week, let's have him deliver a baby." He'll be the first to tell you that obstetrics is a completely different line of work and that having some expertise in one area doesn't translate into skill or experience in another. The same thing is true in the business world.

If I had to sum up in one word the qualities that make a good manager, I'd say that it all comes down to decisiveness. You can use the fanciest computers in the world and you can gather all the charts and numbers, but in the end you have to bring all your information together, set up a timetable, and act. In addition to being decision-makers, managers also have to be motivators. The only way you can motivate people is to communicate with them.

Iacocca, Lee
American automobile executive who, as president and chairman of the board of the foundering Chrysler Corporation, secured the largest amount of federal financial assistance ever given to a private corporation at that time.

If I had to sum up in one word the qualities that make a good manager, I'd say that it all comes down to decisiveness.

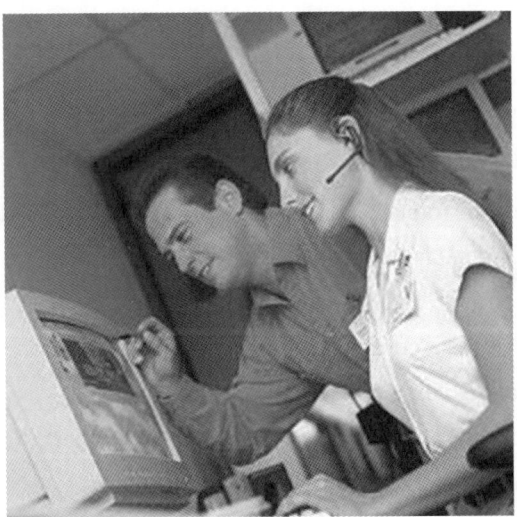

Business people working together at computer.

Dictionary

fad: a fashion or behavior taken up briefly but enthusiastically; craze.
interchangeable: of two things, able to be put or used in place of each other.
cardiology: the medical study of the heart, its normal functioning, and its diseases.
obstetrics: the branch of medicine that deals with pregnancy and childbirth.
expertise: expert knowledge or skill; expertness.
decisiveness: having the power or character to make decisions or end disputes.
  Ex. She is a very decisive person.
motivate: to cause to move or act by giving incentive or inspiration.

15. The Autobiography of Lee Iacocca –1

Normally, / I'm not in favor of / switch**ing** people around.
I'm skeptical of / the current fad
of rotating people / through various departments of a company
as though all skills were interchangeable.
They're not.
It's like taking a cardiologist and saying:
"He's a great heart surgeon.
Next week, / let's have him deliver / a baby."
He'll be the first / to tell you
that obstetrics is a completely different line of work
and **that** having some expertise in one area
doesn't translate / into skill or experience in another.
The same thing is true / in the business world.
If I had to sum up / in one word / the qualities
that make / a good manager,
I'd say **that** it all comes down to decisiveness.
You can use / the fanciest computers / in the world
and you can gather / all the charts and numbers,
but in the end / you have to bring / all your information together,
set up a timetable, / and act.
In addition to being decision-makers,
managers also have to be / motivators.
The only way / (**that**) you can motivate / people
is to communicate with them.

아이아코카 자서전 – 1

일반적으로, / 나는 좋아하지 않는다 / 바꾸는 **것을** 사람을 이리저리.
나는 회의적이다 / 현재의 일시적 유행에 대해
사람을 순환시키는 / 회사의 여러 부서들을 통해서
마치 모든 기능들이 상호교환 가능한 것처럼.
그것들은 그렇지 않다.
그것은 한 심장병 의사를 예로 들어 다음과 같이 말하는 것과 같다:
"그는 위대한 심장 외과 의사다.
다음주에 / 그에게 해산**시키도록 하자** / 아기를."
그는 최초의 사람이 될 것이다 / 여러분에게 말하는
산부인과는 완전히 다른 분야의 일이**라고**
그리고 어떤 전문 기술을 가지는 것은 / 한 분야에서
전이되지 않는**다고** / 다른 분야의 기술 혹은 경험으로.
같은 것이 적용된다 / 사업계에도.
내가 요약해야 한다면 / 한 단어로 / 그 자질들을
좋은 관리자를 만드**는** ,
나는 말할 것이다 / 그 모든 것은 귀결된**다고** / 결단력으로.
여러분은 사용할 수 있다 / 가장 환상적인 컴퓨터들을 / 세상에서
그리고 여러분은 모을 수 있다 / 모든 차트들과 수치들을,
그러나 결국 / 여러분은 취합해서 / 모든 당신의 정보를,
작성해야 한다 시간표를, / 그리고 행동해야 한다.
결단을 내리는 사람이 되는 것 외에,
관리자들은 또한 돼야 한다 / 동기를 부여하는 사람이,
유일한 방법은 / 여러분이 동기를 부여할 수 있**는** / 사람들에게
대화하는 것이다 그들과.

The Autobiography of Lee Iacocca – 2

In corporate life, you have to encourage all your people to make a contribution to the common good and to come up with better ways of doing things. You don't have to accept every single suggestion, but if you don't get back to the guy and say, "Hey, that idea was terrific," and pat him on the back, he'll never give you another one. That kind of communication lets people know they really count.

Always hit him with more while he's up, and never be too tough on him when he's down. When he's upset over his own failure, you run the risk of hurting him badly and taking away his incentive to improve. Or, as Charlie Beacham used to say, "If you want to give a man credit, put it in writing. If you want to give him hell, do it on the phone."

Once, at a private dinner with Vince Lombard, the legendary football coach and a friend of mine, I asked him about his formula for success. I wanted to know exactly what made a winning team. What he told me that evening applies as much to the business world as it does to sports. "The difference between mediocrity and greatness," Lombardi said that night, "is the feeling these guys have for each other. Most people call it team spirit. When the players are imbued with that special feeling, you know you've got yourself a winning team."

"The difference between mediocrity and greatness," Lombardi said that night, "is the feeling these guys have for each other."

Vince Lombardi
Coach in American professional football who became a national symbol of single-minded determination to win. In nine seasons (1959-67) as head coach of the previously moribund Green Bay Packers, he led the team to five championships of the National Football League (NFL). Vince Lombardi After 1968 Super Bowl(above).

Dictionary

credit: approving acknowledgment. Ex. I give him credit for a good job.
formula: an established group of words or symbols used in a procedure; a conventional model for doing something.
mediocre: of average to poor quality; ordinary.
imbue: to inspire or permeate, as with an idea or emotion; deeply influence. Ex. He was imbued with guilt.

The Autobiography of Lee Iacocca – 2

In corporate life, / you have **to** encourage / all your people
to make a contribution / to the common good
and **to** come up with / better ways / **of** do**ing** things.
You don't have to accept / every single suggestion,
but if you don't get back to the guy / and say,
"Hey, that idea was terrific,"
and pat / him on the back,
he'll never give / you another one.
That kind of communication lets people know / (**that**) they really count.
Always hit him / with more / while he's up,
and never be too tough on him / when he's down.
When he's upset / over his own failure,
you run the risk **of** / hurt**ing** him badly
and taking away / his incentive / **to** improve.
Or, as Charlie Beacham used to say,
"If you want **to** give / a man credit, / put it in writing.
If you want **to** give / him hell, / do it on the phone."
Once, at a private dinner / with Vince Lombard,
the legendary football coach and a friend of mine,
I asked him / about his formula / for success.
I wanted **to** know exactly / **what** made a winning team.
What he told me / that evening / applies
as much to the business world / **as** it does to sports.
"The difference between mediocrity and greatness,"
Lombardi said that night, / "is the feeling these guys have for each other.
Most people call / it team spirit.
When the players are imbued / with that special feeling,
you know / (**that**) you've got yourself a winning team."

아이아코카 자서전 - 2

회사 생활에서, / 당신은 격려해야 한다 / 모든 부하 직원들**이**
기여**하도록** / 공동의 선에
그리고 제안**하도록** / 더 좋은 방법들을 / 업무를 처리하는.
당신은 받아들일 필요가 없다 / 모든 단일 제안을,
그러나 만약 당신이 돌아가서 그 사람에게 / 말하지 않는다면
"야, 그 아이디어 멋진데"라고
그리고 두드리지 않는다면 / 그의 등을,
그는 결코 주지 않을 것이다 / 당신에게 다른 아이디어를.
그런 종류의 대화는 / 사람들이 알게 한다 / 그들이 정말 중요하다는 **것을**.
항상 때려라(독려하라) 그를 / 더욱 / 그가 (사기가) 높을 동안,
그리고 결코 너무 심하게 대하지 말라 그에게 / 그가 (사기가) 저하돼 있을 때.
그가 속이 상해 있을 때는 / 그 자신의 실패에 대해,
당신은 위험을 무릅쓰는 것이다 / 상처를 주**는** / 그에게 심하게
그리고 빼앗**는** / 그의 동기를 / 개선하겠**다는**.
혹은, 찰리 비컴이 말하곤 했듯이,
"만약 당신이 주기를 원하면 / 한 사람에게 신뢰(칭찬)를, / 서면으로 하라.
만약 당신이 주기를 원하면 / 그에게 지옥(꾸중)을, / 전화로 하라."
한 번은, 한 사적인 저녁 식사 자리에서 / 빈스 롬발디와의,
전설적인 미식축구 코치이자 나의 친구인,
나는 물었다 그에게 / 그의 방식에 대해 / 성공을 위한.
나는 원했다 **알기를** 정확하게 / 무엇이 승리 팀으로 만드는 **지를**.
그가 나에게 말한 **것은** / 그날 저녁 / 적용된다
사업계에도 / 그것이 스포츠계에 적용되는 **만큼**.
"차이는 / 평범과 위대함 사이의,"
롬바디는 말했다 그날 밤, / "감정이다 / 이들이 있는 서로를 위해.
대다수 사람은 부른다 / 그것을 단체 정신이**라고**.
그 선수들이 물들어 있을 때 / 그런 특별한 감정으로,
당신은 안다 / 승리팀이 된다는 것을."

The Autobiography of Lee Iacocca – 3

I know a man who's been working in the car business all his life. He's highly educated and well organized. He's a brilliant strategist, probably one of the most valuable people in his company. Yet he's never risen to the top ranks, because he just doesn't have the ability to handle people. The best way to develop ideas is through interacting with your fellow managers. This brings us back to the importance of teamwork and interpersonal skills.

The biggest problem facing American business today is that most managers have too much information. It dazzles them, and they don't know what to do with it all. The key to success is not information. It's people. And the kind of people I look for to fill top management spots are the eager beavers. These are the guys who try to do more than they're expected to. They're always reaching. And reaching out to the people they work with, trying to help them do their jobs better. That's the way they're built.

The key to success is not information. It's people. And the kind of people I look for to fill top management spots are the eager beavers.

beaver dam

Dictionary

strategist: an expert in designing strategy, or a maker of strategies.
interpersonal: existing or happening between persons.
dazzle: to dim or confuse the vision of, by blinding light; to confound or greatly impress by brilliance, superior quality or performance, or the like.
Ex1 Outside the cave, the sunlight dazzled us. Ex2. The palace's richness has dazzled many visitors.
beaver: an amphibious rodent with a thick brown pelt, a wide flat tail, and front teeth used as chisels to fell and strip small trees in the building of its damlike habitat.

The Autobiography of Lee Iacocca - 3

I know a man / **who**'s been working / in the car business / all his life.
He's highly educated and well organized.
He's a brilliant strategist,
probably one of the most valuable people / in his company.
Yet he's never risen / to the top ranks,
because he just doesn't have / the ability / **to** handle people.
The best way **to** develop ideas / is through interacting
with your fellow managers.
This brings us back
to the importance / of teamwork and interpersonal skills.
The biggest problem / (that is) fac**ing** American business today
is **that** most managers have / too much information.
It dazzles them,
and they don't know / **what to do** / with it all.
The key to success / is not information. / It's people.
And the kind of people / (**that**) I look for / **to** fill top management spots
are the eager beavers.
These are the guys / **who** try / **to** do more / than they're expected to.
They're always reaching.
And reaching out / to the people / (**whom**) they work with,
trying **to** help / them (to) do their jobs / better.
That's the way / (**that**) they're built.

아이아코카 자서전 - 3

나는 안다 한 남자를 / 일해**온** / 자동차 업계에서 / 모든 그의 인생을(평생을).
그는 높은 교육을 받았고 / 잘 조직되었다(조직적이다).
그는 빛나는(뛰어난) 전략가다,
아마 가장 중요한 사람 중의 한 사람일 것이다 / 그의 회사에서.
그러나 그는 결코 오르지 못했다 / 최고 계급(경영직)에는,
왜냐하면 그는 단지 가지고 있지 않기 때문이다 / 능력을 / 사람을 **다루는**.
가장 좋은 방법은 / 아이디어들을 개발**하는** / 상호작용을 통해서다
당신의 동료 경영자들과.
이것은 일깨워준다 우리에게
팀웍과 대인관계 능력들의 중요성을.
가장 큰 문제는 / 미국 기업이 직면하고 있**는** 오늘날
대다수 경영자들이 가지고 있다는 **것**이다 / 너무 많은 정보를.
그것은 눈부시게(어리둥절) 한다 그들을,
그리고 그들은 모른다 / 해야할 **것을** / 그것 모두를 가지고.
열쇠는 성공으로 가는 / 정보가 아니다. / 그것은 사람이다.
그리고 종류의 사람은 / 내가 찾**는** / **채우기 위해** 최고 경영직에
열성적인 비버들(일꾼들)이다.
이들은 친구들이다 / 노력하**는** / **하기 위해** 더 많이 / 그들이 기대 받는 것보다.
그들은 항상 (손길을) 뻗는다.
그리고 손을 뻗친다 / 사람들에게 / 그들이 함께 일하**는**
그리고 노력한다 도와주**기 위해** / 그들**이 하도록** 그들의 일들을 / 더 잘.
그것이 방식이다 / 그들이 건설되**는**(형성되는).

16. On Achieving Success

We cannot travel every path. Successes must be won along one line. I hate a thing done by halves. If it be right, do it boldly; if it be wrong, leave it undone.

To live with an ideal is a successful life. It is not what one accomplishes, but what one tries to accomplish, that makes a man strong. It may be said that "unceasing effort is the price of success." If we do not work with our might, others will; and they will defeat us in the race and snatch the prize from our grasp. Success grows less and less dependent on luck and chance. Self-distrust is the cause of most of our failures.

The great and indispensable help to success is character. Every character is influenced by heredity, environment and education. But these apart, if every man were not, to a great extent, the architect of his own character, he would be a fatalist, an irresponsible creature of circumstances.

Hemingway, Ernest (1899~1961)
American novelist and short-story writer, awarded the Nobel Prize for Literature in 1954. He was noted both for the intense masculinity of his writing and for his adventurous and widely publicized life. His succinct and lucid prose style exerted a powerful influence on American and British literature.

The great and indispensable help to success is character. ⋯ if every man were not, to a great extent, the architect of his own character, he would be a fatalist, an irresponsible creature of circumstances.

Hemingway's passion for hunting and fishing ran as deeply as his passion for writing. By the mid-1930s, when this picture(left) was taken on a pier in Key West, Florida, he was, in fact, on his way to becoming the best-known fisherman in America.

Dictionary

grasp: to take hold of with or as with a hand.   Ex. grasp the handle of a sword.
defeat: to win a victory over; beat in a game, battle, or the like.   Ex. I defeated her at tennis.
indispensable: absolutely necessary; essential.   Ex. an indispensable responsibility
heredity: the genetic transmission of traits or tendencies from parent to offspring.
fatalist: a belief or doctrine that the events of life are predetermined and cannot be altered by human free will.

On Achieving Success

We cannot travel / every path.
Successes must be won / along one line.
I hate / a thing done / by halves.
If it be right, / do it boldly;
if it be wrong, / leave it undone.
To live with an ideal / is a successful life.
It is not / **what** one accomplishes,
but **what** one tries **to** accomplish,
that makes / a man strong.
It may be said / **that** "unceasing effort is the price of success."
If we do not work / with our might, / others will;
and they will defeat us / in the race
and snatch the prize / from our grasp.
Success grows less and less dependent / on luck and chance.
Self-distrust is the cause / of most of our failures.
The great and indispensable help / to success / is character.
Every character is influenced / by heredity, environment and education.
But these apart, **if** every man **were not**, / to a great extent,
the architect of his own character,
he **would** be a fatalist, / an irresponsible creature / of circumstances.

성공을 이루는 것에 대해

우리는 여행할 수 없다 / 모든 길을.
성공은 이룰 수 있다 / 한 분야를 따를 때.
나는 싫어한다 / 일이 행해지는 것을 / 어중간하게.
만약 그것이 옳다면 / 실행하라 그것을 대담하게;
만약 그것이 옳지 않다면 / 내버려 두라 그것을 하지 않은 채.
산다는 **것은** 이상을 가지고 / 성공적인 삶이다.
인간이 성취하는 **것**이 아니라,
인간이 노력하는 **것**이다 / 성취하**기 위해**,
사람을 강하게 만드는 **것은**.
말해질 수도 있다 / "끊임없는 노력은 성공의 대가다"라고.
우리가 일하지 않는다면 / 전력을 다해 / 다른 사람들이 그렇게 할 것이다;
그래서 그들은 패배시킬 것이다 우리를 / 그 경주에서
그리고 잡아채 갈 것이다 그 상을 / 우리가 움켜잡은 것에서.
성공은 점점 덜 의존하게 된다 / 요행과 우연에.
자기 불신은 원인이다 / 대다수 우리의 실패의.
대단히 크고 필수 불가결한 도움은 / 성공에 / 성격이다.
모든 성격은 영향을 받는다 / 유전, 환경 그리고 교육에 의해.
그러나 이것들과는 별도로 / 모든 사람이 아**니라면** / 대단할 정도로 /
그 자신의 성격의 창조자가,
그는 **될 것이다** 숙명론자가, / 책임 없는 피조물인 / 주위 환경에 대해.

17. How to Enjoy Music – 1

Music may be used in two different ways. The first way is the road taken by the music lover. He need not be able to tell a fugue from a fandango. But to him, the hearing of music is an experience that grips his mind and tears at his heart. He cannot remain indifferent. How does one become a music lover? There is but one way: listen to music! Only direct experience, not study or explanations or any sort of prop, will lead you to music.

I have two suggestions for the beginner. First, listen to the same composition often, until you can respond to it emotionally. Do not expect to encompass a symphony at first hearing. And do not be discouraged or feel guilty if, while listening an unfamiliar symphony, your attention wanders. Initially, absorb from it as much as you can – and coast through the rest. There will come a time when the clouds roll away and the landscape lies clearly before you. In music, the familiar is the enjoyable. Don't dart from one composition to the next. Stay with it!

by George R. Marek

How does one become a music lover? There is but one way: listen to music! Only direct experience, not study or explanations or any sort of prop, will lead you to music.

orchestra

Dictionary

composition: a specific written or musical work.
encompass: to surround or enclose.   Ex. The festival is to encompass everything from music, theatre and ballet to literature, cinema.
coast: to move without continuing to expend effort or energy.
dart;   to move swiftly; spring; dash.   Ex. The lizard darted out of sight.
fugue: a musical form or composition in which one or more themes are stated by one voice and are then restated and modified in counterpoint in strict order by several voices.
fandango: a lively Spanish or Spanish-American dance in triple time for a couple playing castanets, or the music that accompanies this dance.
indifferent: lacking interest or concern; not caring.

How to Enjoy Music – 1

Music may be used / in two different ways.
The first way is the road (that is) **taken** by the music lover.
He need not / be able to tell a fugue from a fandango.
But to him, / the hear**ing** of music / is an experience
that grips his mind / and tears at his heart.
He cannot **remain** indifferent.
How does one become / a music lover?
There is but one way: listen to music!
Only direct experience, / not study or explanations or any sort of prop,
will lead / you to music.
I have / two suggestions / for the beginner.
First, / listen to the same composition / often,
until you can respond to it / emotionally.
Do not expect / **to** encompass a symphony / at first hearing.
And do not be discouraged / or feel guilty
if, while listening / an unfamiliar symphony, / your attention wanders.
Initially, absorb from it / **as** much **as** you can
– and coast through / the rest.
There will come a time / **when** the clouds roll away
and the landscape lies clearly / before you.
In music, the familiar / is the enjoyable.
Don't dart / from one composition to the next.
Stay with it!

음악을 즐기는 방법

음악은 사용될 수 있다 / 두 가지 다른 방법들로.
첫 번째 방법은 길이다 / 음악 애호가가 취**하는** .
그에게는 필요하지 않다 / 구별할 수 있는 능력이 푸가와 판당고를.
그러나 그에게, / 듣는 **것은** 음악을 / 하나의 경험이다.
그의 마음을 잡**는** / 그리고 그의 가슴을 찢**는**.
그는 **계속** 냉담할 수는 없다.
어떻게 사람들은 되는가 / 음악 애호가?
단지 한 가지 길이 있다: 들어라 음악을!
오직 직접적인 경험이, / 연구 혹은 설명들 혹은 어떤 종류의 버팀목(도움)이 아닌,
이끌 것이다 / 여러분을 음악으로.
나는 가지고 있다 / 두 가지 제안들을 / 초보자를 위한.
첫째, / 들어라 같은 곡을 / 자주,
당신이 반응할 수 있을 때까지 그것에 / 감정적으로.
기대하지 말라 / 둘러싸**는**(완전히 이해하는) **것을** 교향곡을 / 처음 들을 때.
그리고 실망하지 말라 / 혹은 죄책감이 드는 것처럼 느끼지도 (말라)
들을 동안 / 익숙지 않은 교향곡을 / 당신의 주의력이 흐트러지**더라도**
처음에는, 흡수하라 그것으로부터 / 당신이 할 수 있는 **만큼**(가능한 한) 많이
– 그리고 연안을 항해하라(적당히 흘려보내라) / 나머지는.
올 것이다 시간이 / 구름들이 걷히**는**
그리고 풍경이 놓이**는**(펼쳐지는) 분명하게 / 당신 앞에.
음악에서는, 친숙한 곡이 / 즐길 수 있는 곡이다.
화살처럼 날아가지 말라(옮기지 말라) / 한 곡에서 다른 곡으로
머물러라 그것과 함께!

How to Enjoy Music – 2

Second, choose – in the beginning, at least, – romantic music.

This is repertoire that begins with Beethoven and ends with Sibelius and that, in its wide orbit, includes the most popular works – those of Schubert, Brahms, Dvorak, Tchaikovsky, verdi, Wagner, Berlioz and a dozen other composers of the 19th century. Such music, with its rich coloring, its exuberance, its sweetness, its exciting oratory, makes an immediate appeal. But it is not safe to predict what you will like. We do know that people tend to respond more easily to Chopin and Puccini than to Handel or Haydn. Yet your experience may differ.

The other way of using music is as background accompaniment – like a tepid bath in which you induce a drowsy reverie. You hardly listen to what you hear, any more than you consciously listen to the surf of the sea. Almost any kind of music can be used for such a purpose, though most people prefer a smooth blend of sound. We meet such music in the most unlikely places – in the dentist's office, in the airport and the bus depot, at the meat market. In factories, such music helps relieve the boredom of routine labor. So it does in the home. Women mix the sound of violins with the sound of the dishwasher.

Such music, with its rich coloring, its exuberance, its sweetness, its exciting oratory, makes an immediate appeal. But it is not safe to predict what you will like.

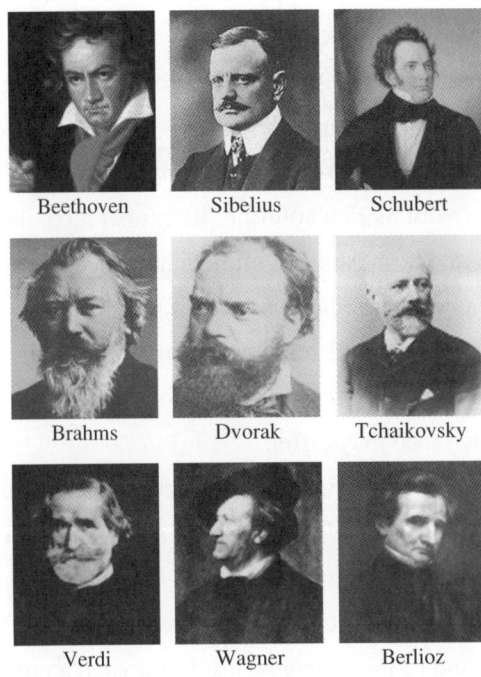

Beethoven   Sibelius   Schubert
Brahms   Dvorak   Tchaikovsky
Verdi   Wagner   Berlioz

Dictionary

exuberant: vigorously enthusiastic or happy; high-spirited; lavish or profuse.
   Ex. exuberant imagination.
oratory: the art of public speaking; eloquence; rhetoric.
accompaniment: part of a musical composition that is intended to support more central parts.
tepid: somewhat warm; lukewarm.
drowsy: nearly asleep.
reverie: a state of daydreaming, reminiscing, or musing.   Ex. be lost in reverie.
depot: a bus or train station.

How to Enjoy Music – 2

Second, choose – in the beginning, at least, – romantic music.
This is repertoire
that begins with Beethoven / and ends with Sibelius
and **that**, in its wide orbit, / includes
the most popular works – those of Schubert, Brahms, Dvorak,
Tchaikovsky, verdi, Wagner, Berlioz
and a dozen other composers / of the 19th century.
Such music, / with its rich coloring, its exuberance, its sweetness,
its exciting oratory, makes / an immediate appeal.
But **it** is not safe / **to** predict / **what** you will like.
We do know / **that** people tend to respond more easily
to Chopin and Puccini / than to Handel or Haydn.
Yet your experience may differ.
The other way **of** us**ing** music / is as background accompaniment –
like a tepid bath / in which you induce / a drowsy reverie.
You hardly listen to / **what** you hear,
any more than / you consciously listen to / the surf of the sea.
Almost any kind of music can be used / for such a purpose,
though most people prefer / a smooth blend of sound.
We meet such music / in the most unlikely places
– in the dentist's office, in the airport
and the bus depot, at the meat market.
In factories, such music helps / relieve the boredom of routine labor.
So it does / in the home.
Women mix / the sound of violins
with the sound of the dishwasher.

음악을 즐기는 법 - 2

두 번째, 선택하라 - 처음에는, 적어도, - 낭만주의 음악을.
이것은 레퍼토리다
시작**하는** 베토벤에서 / 그리고 끝나는 시벨리우스에서
그리고 그것의 넓은 궤도(범위) 내에, 포함하는
가장 인기 있는 작품들을 - 슈베르트, 브람스, 드보르자크,
차이코프스키, 베르디, 바그너, 베를리오즈 등의
그리고 12명의 다른 작곡가들의 / 19세기의.
그런 음악은, 그것의 풍부한 색채, 그것의 풍성함, 그것의 달콤함,
그것의 흥분시키는 웅변(수사) 등과 함께, 만든다 / 직접적인 호소를.
그러나 그것은 위험하다 / 예측하는 **것은** / 무엇을 당신이 좋아하게 될 **지를**.
우리는 안다 / 사람들이 경향이 있다는 **것을** 더 쉽게 반응하는
쇼팽과 푸치니에 / 헨델과 하이든보다.
그러나 당신의 경험은 다를지도 모른다.
다른 방법은 음악을 이용하는 / 배경 반주와 같은 것이다 -
미지근한 목욕물처럼 / 그 속에서 당신은 일으킨다 / 나른한 몽상을.
당신은 거의 주의 깊게 듣지는 않는다 / 당신이 듣는 **것을**,
당신이 주의 깊게 듣는 것 이상으로 / 바다의 파도 소리를.
거의 모든 종류의 음악은 이용될 수 있다 / 그런 목적을 위해,
비록 대다수 사람이 선호하지만 / 소리의 부드러운 혼합을.
우리는 만난다 / 그런 음악을 / 가장 가능성 없는 장소들에서
치과에서, 공항에서
그리고 버스 정류장, 정육점에서.
공장에서도, 그런 음악은 도와준다 / 덜도록 일상적 노동의 지루함을.
마찬가지로 음악은 도와준다 / 집에서도.
여성들은 섞는다(같이 듣는다) / 바이올린의 소리를
식기세척기의 소리와 함께.

18. Painting As A Pastime – 1

Broadly speaking, human being may be divided into three classes: those who are toiled to death, those who are worried to death, and those who are bored to death. It may also be said that rational, industrious, useful human beings are divided into two classes: first, those whose work is work and whose pleasure is leasure; and secondly, those whose work and pleasure are one. Of these the former are the majority. But Fortune's favored children belong to the second class. Their life is a natural harmony. For them the working hours are never long enough.

Yet to both classes, the need of a change of atmosphere is essential. The most common form of diversion is reading. In that vast and varied field, millions find their mental comfort. But reading suffers from one serious defect: books are too nearly akin to the ordinary daily round of the brainworker to give that element of change essential to real relief. To restore mental equilibrium we should call into use those parts of the mind which direct both eye and hand.

Churchill, Sir Winston (1874~1965)
British statesman, orator, and author who as prime minister (1940-45, 1951-55) rallied the British people during World War II and led his country from the brink of defeat to victory.

To restore mental equilibrium we should call into use those parts of the mind which direct both eye and hand.

Sketching Trafalgar Square

Dictionary

toil: long or laborious work or effort. Ex. The students toiled over their workbooks.
industrious: actively productive; hard-working. Ex. He is a very industrious worker.
diversion: something that turns the mind or attention away from serious matters; distraction; amusement. Ex. Sports are good for diversion.
equilibrium: a state in which all acting forces cancel each other to create balance or stability. Ex. the equilibrium of demand and supply.

Painting As a Pastime – 1

Broadly speaking, / human being may be divided / into three classes:
those / **who** are toiled / to death,
those / **who** are worried / to death,
and those / **who** are bored / to death.
It may also **be said**
that rational, industrious, useful human beings
are divided / into two classes:
first, those / **whose** work is work
and (those) / **whose** pleasure is pleasure;
and secondly, those / **whose** work and pleasure are one.
Of these / the former are the majority.
But Fortune's favor**ed** children belong / to the second class.
Their life is a natural harmony.
For them / the work**ing** hours are never long / enough.
Yet to both classes, / the need of a change of atmosphere / is essential.
The most common form of diversion is reading.
In that vast and varied field, / millions find / their mental comfort.
But reading suffers / from one serious defect:
books are **too** nearly akin
to the ordinary daily round of the brainworker
to give that element of change / (**that** is) essential to real relief.
To restore mental equilibrium
we should call into use / those parts of the mind
which direct / both eye and hand.

취미로서의 그림그리기 - 1

넓게 말하면 / 인간은 나누어질 수 있다 / 세 가지 부류로:
사람들 / 죽도록 일만 하는,
사람들 / 죽도록 걱정만 하는,
그리고 사람들 / 죽도록 권태만 느끼는.
역시 **말해질 수 있다**
이성적인, 근면한, 유용한 사람들은
나눠진**다고** / 두 가지 부류로
첫째는 사람들 / 일은 일**인**;
그리고 즐거움은 즐거움**인**
그리고 둘째로, 사람들이다 / 일과 즐거움이 하나**인**.
이들 가운데 / 전자가 대다수다.
그러나 운명이 좋아**하는** 자식들은 속한다 / 두 번째 부류에.
그들의 삶은 자연스러운 조화다.
그들에게는 / 일**하는** 시간이 결코 길지 않다 / 충분히.
그러나 이 두 부류 모두에게, / 분위기 전환의 필요성은 / 필수적이다.
가장 흔한 형태의 기분 전환은 독서다.
광대하고 다양한 분야에서 / 수백만의 사람들이 찾는다 / 그들의 정신적 위안을.
그러나 독서는 피해를 받는다 한 가지 중대한 결점으로(결점을 안고있다):
책은 **너무** 유사하다는 것이다
평범한 매일의 업무 순환(일상 업무)과 / 정신 노동자들의
주기에는 / 변화의 요인을 / 필수적인 / 실제적인 휴식에.
회복하기 **위해서는** 정신적인 균형을
우리는 사용해야 한다 / 정신의 부분들을
지휘하**는** / 눈과 손을 모두.

Painting As a Pastime – 2

To make a plan, thorough reconnaissance of the country is needed. Its fields, its mountains, its rivers, its trees, its flowers, its atmosphere – all require attentive observation from a special point of view. One is quite astonished to find how many things there are in the landscape, and in every object in it, which one never noticed before. I think (that) this heightened sense of observation of nature is one of the chief delights that have come to me through trying to paint. The whole world is open with all its treasures. The simplest objects have their beauty. Every garden presents innumerable fascinating problems. Every piece of land has its own tale to tell. One cannot have several days on one's hands. Good gracious! All there is to admire and how little time there is to see it in!

Painting is complete as a distraction. I know of nothing which more entirely absorbs the mind. Whatever the worries of the hour or the threats of the future, once the picture has begun to flow along, there is no room for them in the metal screen. They pass out into shadow and darkness. All one's mental light, such as it is, becomes concentrated on the task. No one who is fond of painting finds the slightest inconvenience, as long as the interest holds, in standing to paint for three or four hours at a stretch.

One is quite astonished to find how many things there are in the landscape, and in every object in it, which one never noticed before.

An artist paints a miniature landscape on the banks of Talbot Lake in Jasper National Park.

Dictionary

reconnaissance: the act or process of examining an area, esp. to gain militarily useful information.
handicraft: work requiring such skill, such as weaving and woodworking, or the products of such work.
fascinate: to capture and hold the attention and interest of; spellbind.
   Ex. Her beauty fascinated everyone.
distraction: to divert the attention of.   Ex. a distraction after study.
absorb: to take in or soak up; to involve or engage completely.
   Ex. This work really absorbs me.
upright: having an erect posture.   Ex. stand upright.

Painting As a Pastime – 2

To make a plan, / thorough reconnaissance of the country is needed.
Its fields, its mountains, its rivers, its trees, its flowers, its atmosphere
– all require / attentive observation / from a special point of view.
One is quite astonished / **to** find
how many things there are in the landscape,
and in every object in it, / **which** one never noticed / before.
I think (**that**) this heightened sense of observation of nature
is one of the chief delights
that have come to me / through trying to paint.
The whole world is open / with all its treasures.
The simplest objects have / their beauty.
Every garden presents / innumerable fascinating problems.
Every piece of land has / its own tale / **to** tell.
One cannot have several days on one's hands.
Good gracious!
All there is / **to** admire / and how little time there is / **to see** it in!
Painting is complete / as a distraction.
I know of nothing / **which** more entirely absorbs / the mind.
Whatever the worries of the hour / or the threats of the future,
once the picture has begun to flow along,
there is no room / for them / in the metal screen.
They pass out / into shadow and darkness.
All one's mental light,
such as it is, / becomes concentrated / on the task.
No one **who** is fond of painting finds
the slightest inconvenience, / as long as the interest holds,
in standing / **to** paint / for three or four hours at a stretch.

취미로서의 그림그리기 - 2

구상을 **하기 위해서는** / 시골의 철저한 정찰(현지답사)이 필요하다.
들판, 산들, 강들, 나무들, 꽃들, 그 분위기
- 모든 것이 요구한다 / 주의 깊은 관찰을 / 특별한 관점에서.
사람들은 크게 놀란다 / 알고**서는**
얼마나 많은 것들이 있는 **지를** / 풍경 속에,
그리고 모든 사물 속에 그 안의 / 사람들이 결코 알아채지 못**한** / 전에는.
나는 생각한다 / 이런 높아진 감각이 자연 관찰의
주요한 기쁨들의 하나**라고**
나에게 다가**온** / 노력을 통해 그림을 그리려는.
온 세상이 열려 있다 / 모든 보물들을 가진 채.
가장 간단한 사물들도 가지고 있다 / 그 자체의 아름다움을.
모든 정원은 제공한다 / 수많은 매혹적인 문제들을.
어느 땅 조각이든 모두 가지고 있다 / 그것 자체의 이야기를 / 말**할**
사람들은 며칠도 여유가 없다.
아뿔사!
모든 것이 있다 / 찬양**할** / 그런데 얼마나 적은 시간이 있는가 / 들여다 볼!
그림 그리기는 완벽하다 / 기분전환 감으로.
나는 알지 못한다 / 더 완전히 흡수**하는** 것은 / 마음을.
당장의 걱정들 / 혹은 장차의 위험들이 **무엇이든**,
일단 그림이 흐르기(그려지기) 시작하**면**,
여지가 없다 / 그런 것들을 위한 / 마음의 화면에는.
그것들은 사라진다 / 그늘과 어둠 속으로.
모든 사람의 마음의 빛이
그저 그런 대로 / 집중된다 / 그 일에.
좋아하**는** 사람은 그림 그리기를 / 어느 누구도 발견하지(느끼지) 못한다
조금도 불편을 / 흥미가 유지되는 한,
서있는 것에 / 그림을 그리**기 위해** / 서너 시간 동안 단숨에.

19. Why We Cannot Wait / Martin L. King 왜 우리는 기다릴 수 없나

20. Inaugural Address / John F. Kennedy 케네디 대통령 취임사

21. Gettysburg Address / Abraham Lincoln 게티즈버그 연설

22. Julius Caesar / Shakespeare 율리우스 시저

23. The Prince / Machiavelli 군주론

24. Learning and Citizenship / Marvin lazerson, Judith B. McLaughlin, Bruce McPherson 학교 교육은 왜 죽었는가

25. The Worthless Ivy League? / by Robert J. Samuelson 아이비리그는 소용이 없나?

IV 세상 바꾸기

19. Why We Cannot Wait

I guess it is easy for those who have never felt the stinging darts of segregation to say "wait. But when you have seen vicious mobs lynch your mother and father at will and drown your sisters and brothers at whim; when you have seen hate-filled policemen curse, kick, brutalize and even kill your black brothers and sisters; when you suddenly feel your tongue twisted and your speech stammering as you seek to explain to your six-year-old daughter why she can't go to the public amusement park that has just been advertised on television, and see tears welling up in her little eyes when she is told that "Funtown" is closed to colored children, and see the depressing clouds of inferiority begin to form in her little metal sky, and see her begin to distort her little personality by unconsciously developing a bitterness toward white people; when you are humiliated day in and day out by nagging signs reading "white" and colored; when you are harried by day and haunted by night by the fact that you are a Negro, living constantly at tiptoe stance; when you are forever fighting a degenerating sense of "nobodyness" then you will understand why we find it difficult to wait.

I guess it is easy for those who have never felt the stinging darts of segregation to say "wait."

King, Martin Luther, Jr. (1929~68)
eloquent black Baptist minister who led the Civil Rights Movement in the United States from the mid-1950s until his death by assassination in 1968. His leadership was fundamental to that movement's success in ending the legal segregation of blacks in the South.

Dictionary

mob: a large, disorderly, or riotous crowd of people.
whimsy: caprice. a sudden odd or capricious desire. Ex. On a whim, I walked into the nearest store.
brutalize: to treat savagely, mercilessly, or cruelly. Ex. The police brutalized the strikers.
inferior: subordinate in rank, position, or degree. Ex. a sense of inferiority
distort: to twist out of shape; deform the appearance or functioning of. Ex. His face was distorted with (or by) pain.
harry: to attack or annoy repeatedly or constantly; harass.
haunt: to inhabit or frequent as a ghost. Ex. Spirits are supposed to haunt the house.
degenerate: to decline from an original or former condition; change for the worse innature or quality; deteriorate. Ex. Young men of his generation were degenerating.

Why we cannot wait

I guess / **it** is easy / **for** those **who** have never felt
the stinging darts of segregation
to say "wait."
But when you have seen
vicious mobs lynch / your mother and father / at will
and drown your sisters and brothers / at whim;
when you have seen
hate-filled policemen / curse, kick, brutalize and even kill
your black brothers and sisters;
when you suddenly feel
your tongue twisted and your speech stammering
as you seek to explain / to your six-year-old daughter
why she can't go / to the public amusement park
that has just been advertised / on television,
and (when you) **see** / tears welling up / in her little eyes
when she is told / **that** "Funtown" is closed / to colored children,
and (when you) **see**
the depressing clouds of inferiority begin to form
in her little mental sky,
and (when you) **see** / her begin to distort / her little personality
by unconsciously developing a bitterness / toward white people;
when you are humiliated / day in and day out
by nagging signs / read**ing** / "white" and "colored";
when you are harried / by day and / haunted / by night
by the fact / **that** you are a Negro, / liv**ing** constantly at tiptoe stance;
when you are forever fighting / a degenerating sense / of "nobodyness"
then you will understand
why we find / **it** difficult **to** wait.

왜 우리는 기다릴 수 없는가

나는 생각한다 / (그것이) 쉽다고 / 결코 느껴보지 못**한** 사람들이
날카로운 화살들을 인종차별의
"기다려라"라고 말하는 **것은**.
그러나 당신이 보았을 때
악독한 폭도들이 린치하는 것을 / 당신의 부모를 / 마음대로
그리고 물에 빠뜨리는 것을 / 형제자매를 / 기분 내키는 대로;
당신이 보았을 때
증오에 찬 경찰관들이 / 저주하고 차고 짐승처럼 대하고 심지어 죽이는 것을
당신의 흑인 형제 자매들을;
당신이 갑자기 느낄 때
당신의 혀가 뒤틀리는 것을 / 그리고 당신의 말이 더듬어지는 것을
당신이 설명하려고 애쓸 때 / 당신의 여섯 살 난 딸에게
왜 그 아이가 갈 수 없는**지를** / 대공원에
방금 광고**된** / 텔레비전에
그리고 보게될 때 / 눈물이 솟아오르는 것을 / 그 아이의 어린 두 눈에서
그 아이가 들었을 때 / 오락 공원이 닫혔**다고** / 흑인 아이들에게는,
그리고 보게될 때
열등심의 침울한 구름이 형성되기 시작하는 것을
그 아이의 어린 마음의 하늘에,
그리고 보게될 때 / 그 아이가 왜곡시키기 시작하는 것을 / 자신의 어린 성격을
무의식적으로 일으킴으로써 악의를 / 백인에 대해;
당신이 굴욕을 느낄 때 / 해가 뜨나 해가 지나
들볶는 간판들에 의해 / 적혀 **있는** / "백인", "유색인"이라고;
당신이 괴롭힘을 당할 때 / 낮이면 / 꿈에 마저 시달릴 때 / 밤이면
사실에 / 당신이 검둥이**라는** / 살아가는 항상 발돋움을 한 자세로;
당신이 영원히 싸우고 있을 때 / 타락감과 / "보잘 것 없는 놈"이라는 –
그때 당신은 이해할 것이다
왜 우리들이 생각하는 **지를** / 어렵다고 기다리는 것이.

20. Inaugural Address

In the long history of the world, only a few generations have been granted the role of defending freedom in its hour of maximum danger. I do not shrink from this responsibility – I welcome it. I do not believe that any of us would exchange places with any other people or any other generation. The energy, the faith, the devotion which we bring to this endeavor will light our country and all who serve it – and the glow from that fire can truly light the world. And so, my fellow Americans: Ask not what your country can do for you – ask what you can do for your country. My fellow citizens of the world: ask not what America will do for you, but what together we can do for the freedom of man. Finally, whether you are citizens of America or of the world, ask of us the same high standards of strength and sacrifice that we shall ask of you.

Kennedy, John Fitzgerald (1917~63)
35th president of the United States (1961-63), who faced a number of foreign crises, especially in Cuba and Berlin, but managed to secure such achievements as the Nuclear Test-Ban Treaty and the Alliance for Progress. He was assassinated while riding in a motorcade in Dallas.

My fellow Americans: Ask not what your country can do for you – ask what you can do for your country.

John Fitzgerald Kennedy takes the oath of office and becomes the 35th President of the United States of America, January 20, 1961.

Dictionary

grant: to give or agree to give or do (something that another person has asked for). Ex. They granted her an entry visa.
shrink: to (cause to) become smaller. Ex. Your sweater will shrink if you wash it at too high a temperature.
devotion: committed love. deep love and commitment. Ex. Such songs are most apt to stir up devotion.
endeavor: to try (to do something). Ex. Engineers are endeavoring to locate the source of the problem.
sacrifice: giving up of something valued. Ex. I would rather see everything settled with my sacrifice.

Inaugural Address

In the long history / of the world,
only a few generations have been granted
the role of defending freedom / in its hour of maximum danger.
I do not shrink / from this responsibility – I welcome it.
I do not believe
that any of us / would exchange places
with any other people / or any other generation.
The energy, the faith, the devotion / **which** we bring to this endeavor
will light / our country / and all **who** serve it
– and the glow from that fire / can truly light the world.
And so, my fellow Americans:
Ask not / **what** your country can do / for you
– (=but) ask / **what** you can do / for your country.
My fellow citizens of the world:
ask not / **what** America will do for you,
but (ask) / what together we can do / for the freedom of man.
Finally, **whether** you are citizens of America or of the world,
ask of us / the same high standards of strength and sacrifice
that we shall ask of you.

케네디의 취임 연설

오랜 역사에서 / 세계의,
단지 몇 세대만이 부여받아왔습니다,
역할을 / 자유를 수호할 / 매우 위험한 시기에.
나는 회피하지 않습니다 / 이 책임으로부터 / – 나는 환영합니다.
나는 생각하지 않습니다,
우리 가운데 어떤 사람도 / 자리를 바꾸고 싶어한**다고**
어떤 다른 나라 사람과 / 혹은 다른 세대와.
정력, 신념, 헌신은 / 우리가 가져오**는** 이 노력으로 (이 노력을 위해 쏟는)
밝힐 것입니다 / 우리 나라와 / 모든 사람을 우리 나라에 봉사**하는**
그리고 그 불빛은 / 진실로 밝힐 수 있습니다 / 세계를.
그러므로 동포 여러분:
묻지 마십시오 / 무엇을 여러분의 조국이 할 수 있는 **지를** / 여러분을 위해
– 물으십시오 / 무엇을 여러분이 할 수 있는 **지를** / 여러분의 조국을 위해.
세계의 나의 동료 시민들이여:
묻지 마십시오 / 무엇을 미국이 할 수 있는 **지를** / 여러분을 위해,
그러나 물으십시오 / 우리가 함께 무엇을 할 수 있는 **지를** / 인간의 자유를 위해.
마지막으로 여러분이 미국 시민**이든** 세계의 시민**이든**
우리에게 부탁하십시오 / 똑같이 높은 수준의 힘과 희생을
우리가 여러분에게 부탁**하는**.

21. Gettysburg Address – 1

Four score and seven years ago our fathers brought forth on this continent, a new nation, conceived in liberty, and dedicated to the proposition that all men are created equal. Now we are engaged in a great civil war, testing whether that nation or any nation so conceived and so dedicated, can long endure. We are met on a great battlefield of that war. We have come to dedicate a portion of that field, as a final resting place for those who here gave their lives that that nation might live. It is altogether fitting and proper that we should do this. But, in a larger sense, we cannot dedicate – we cannot consecrate – we cannot hallow – this ground. The brave men, living and dead who struggled here, have consecrated it, far above our poor power to add or detract.

Lincoln, Abraham
16th president of the United States (1861-65), who preserved the Union during the Civil War and brought about the emancipation of the slaves.

Our fathers brought forth on this continent, a new nation, conceived in liberty, and dedicated to the proposition that all men are created equal.

Gettysburg Address Memorial(above).

Gettysburg Address on the Wall of Lincoln Memorial(right).

Dictionary

conceive: to give shape to in the mind; to become pregnant with.
    Ex. She conceived a brilliant strategy.
dedicate: to set apart or declare to be for a special use or purpose, as a worthy
    cause, public benefit, or sacred activities.
    Ex. All the profits are dedicated to medical research.
proposition: a plan of action proposed; proposal.; in logic, an affirmative or
    negative statement.
consecrate: to dedicate to the service or worship of a deity; make or declare
    sacred.   Ex. He consecrated his life to church.
hallow: to consecrate or make holy.

Gettysburg Address – 1

Four score and seven years ago
our fathers brought forth / on this continent, / a new nation,
(**that** was) conceiv**ed** / in liberty,
and dedicat**ed** / to the proposition / **that** all men are created equal.
Now we are engaged in / a great civil war,
testing **whether**
that nation or any nation / so conceiv**ed** and so dedicat**ed**,
can long endure.
We are met / on a great battlefield / of that war.
We have come / **to** dedicate / a portion of that field,
as a final resting place
for those / **who** here gave their lives / **that** that nation **might** live.
It is altogether fitting and proper / **that** we should do this.
But, in a larger sense,
we cannot dedicate
– we cannot consecrate
– we cannot hallow – this ground.
The brave men, / living and dead / **who** struggled here,
have consecrated it,
(being) far above / our poor power / **to** add or detract.

게티즈버그 연설 - 1

지금으로부터 87년 전
우리의 선조는 탄생시켰습니다 / 이 대륙에 / 한 새로운 나라를,
잉태**된** / 자유 속에,
그리고 바쳐**진** / 명제에 / 모든 사람들은 평등하게 창조됐다**는**.
이제 우리는 참가하고 있습니다 / 거대한 내전에,
그리고 시험받고 있습니다
그런 나라가, 혹은 모든 나라가 / 그렇게 잉태**된** 그리고 그렇게 바쳐**진**,
오랫동안 지탱할 수 있을**지를**.
우리는 만났습니다 / 큰 싸움터 위에서 / 그 전쟁의.
우리는 왔습니다 / 바치**기 위해** / 그 싸움터의 한 부분을 /
마지막 안식처로
사람들을 위해 / 여기서 목숨을 바친 / 이 나라가 살 수 있도록 **하기 위해**.
너무 합당하고 적절합니다 / 우리가 그렇게 하는 **것은**.
그러나 더 넓은 의미에서,
우리는 바칠 수도 없습니다
- 우리는 신성하게 할 수도 없습니다
- 우리는 거룩하게 할 수도 없습니다 - 이 땅을.
그 용감한 사람들이 (생존한 그리고 사망한) 목숨 바쳐 싸웠**던** 여기서
신성하게 했습니다 이 땅을,
그리고 훨씬 넘어섭니다 / 우리의 미천한 힘을 / 더하거나 혹은 **빼는**.

Gettysburg Address – 2

The world will little note, nor long remember, what we say here, but it can never forget what they did here. It is for us the living, rather, to be dedicated here to the unfinished work which they who fought here have thus far so nobly advanced. It is rather for us to be here dedicated to the great task remaining before us, – that from these honored dead we take increased devotion to that cause for which they gave the last full measure of devotion, – that we here highly resolve that these dead shall not have died in vain – that this nation, under God, shall have a new birth of freedom and – that government of the people, by the people, for the people, shall not perish from the earth.

···government of the people, by the people, for the people, shall not perish from the earth.

Statue of Gettysberg Soldiers.

Dictionary

advance: to move or send forward. Ex. He advanced his troops as far as the riverside.
devotion: great attachment; strong affection; ardent or zealous concern for.
  Ex1 devotion to his cause. Ex2 a scholar's devotion to study.
  Ex3 the devotion of Romeo for Juliet.
measure: the size, quantity, or amount thus calculated. Ex. waist measure.
resolve: to reach a firm or final decision about.
  Ex. He resolved that nothing should hold him back.

Gettysburg Address – 2

The world will little note,
nor long remember,
what we say here,
but it can never forget / **what** they did here.
It is for us the living, rather,
to be dedicated here / to the unfinished work
which they **who** fought here / have thus far so nobly advanced.
It is rather for us
to be here dedicated / to the great task / remain**ing** before us,
– **that** from these honored dead
we take / increased devotion
to that cause / for **which** they gave / the last full measure of devotion,
– **that** we here highly resolve
that these dead shall not have died / in vain
(= We will not allow these dead to have died in vain.)
– **that** this nation, / under God, / shall have / a new birth of freedom
– and **that** government / of the people, by the people, for the people,
shall not perish / from the earth.

게티즈버그 연설 - 2

세상은 별로 주목하지 않을 것입니다,
또한 오랫동안 기억하지도 **않을** 것입니다,
우리가 여기서 말하는 것을,
그러나 세상은 결코 잊지 않을 것입니다 / 그들이 행한 **것을** 여기서.
(그것은) 우리 살아있는 자들의 의무입니다, 오히려,
헌납돼야 하는 **것은** 여기서 / 그 끝나지 않은 일에
여기서 싸운 그들이 / 여기까지 그토록 고결하게 진전시**킨**.
(그것은) 오히려 우리들의 의무입니다
여기서 헌신하는 **것은** / 그 위대한 과업에 / 남아있**는** 우리 앞에,
– 이들 명예로운 전사자들로부터
우리가 떠 안는다는 **것은** / 증대된 헌신을(=더욱 헌신해야 하는 과업을)
대의를 위해 / 그들이 **바친** / 마지막까지 가득 찰 정도의 헌신을(신명을),
– 우리가 여기서 높게(굳게) 결의하는 **것은**
이들 전사자들의 죽음을 헛되이 하**지 않도록**
– 이 나라에 / 신의 가호 아래 / 새로운 자유를 탄생시키겠다고 결심하는 **것은**
– 그리고 정부가 / 국민의, 국민에 의한, 국민을 위한,
사라지지 않도록 굳게 결심하는 **것은** / 지구상으로부터.

22. Julius Caesar

Romans and countrymen!
You now may hear my explanation,
And be silent that you may hear.
If there be any dear friend of Caesar's here, to him I say
That Brutus' s love for caesar was no less than his.
If then, that friend demand why Brutus rose against Caesar
This is my answer:
Not that I loved Caesar less, but that I loved Rome more.
would you rather have caesar living, die as slaves,
Or caesar dead and live as free men?
As caesar loved me, I weep for him:
As he was fortunate, I rejoice at it;
As he was brave, I honour him;
But as he was ambitious, I killed him.
There is tears for his love; Joy for his fortune;
Honour for his bravery; And death for his ambition.
I will finish with these words:
I killed my best friend for the good of Rome,
but I have the same sword for myself
When it shall please my country to need my death.

By Shakespeare

Brutus, Marcus Junius
A leader of the conspirators who assassinated the Roman dictator Julius Caesar in March 44 BC. The son of Marcus Junius Brutus (d. 77), he acquired the alternative name Quintus Caepio through adoption by his uncle, Quintus Servilius Caepio.

> If then, that friend demand why Brutus rose against Caesar
> This is my answer: Not that I loved Caesar less, but that I loved Rome more.

Caesar, Julius
Celebrated Roman general and statesman, the conqueror of Gaul (58-50 BC), victor in the Civil War of 49-46 BC, and dictator (46-44 BC), who was launching a series of political and social reforms when he was assassinated by a group of nobles in the Senate House on the Ides of March.

Dictionary

weep: to show strong emotions, such as joy or grief, by shedding tears; cry.
   Ex. weep at sad news.
rejoice: to be joyful or take pleasure.
   Ex. We rejoiced over the news of their victory.
ambition: a strong desire to become famous, wealthy, or powerful, or to reach a specific goal. Ex. ambition for distinction.
fortune: luck, whether good or ill. Ex. bad(or ill) fortune.

JULIUS CAESAR

Romans and countrymen!
You now may hear / my explanation,
And be silent / (so) **that** you **may** hear.
If there be any dear friend of Caesar's / here, / to him I say
That Brutus's love for caesar was no less / than his.
If then, that friend demand / **why** Brutus rose against Caesar
This is my answer:
Not that I loved Caesar less, / **but that I** loved Rome more.
Would you rather **have** caesar living, / die as slaves,
or caesar dead and / live as free men?
As caesar loved me, / I weep for him;
As he was fortunate, / I rejoice at it;
As he was brave, / I honour him;
But as he was ambitious, / I killed him.
There is tears / for his love; / Joy for his fortune;
Honour / for his bravery; / And death / for his ambition.
I will finish / with these words:
I killed / my best friend / for the good of Rome,
but I have the same sword / for myself
When **it** shall please my country / **to** need my death.

율리우스 시저

로마 시민 여러분, 동포 여러분!
여러분은 이제 들어보시오 / 내 설명을 .
조용히 해주십시오 / 여러분이 들을 **수 있도록.**
만일 시저의 절친한 친구가 있다면 / 여기에 / 그에게 말하리라
시저에 대한 브루터스의 사랑이 못하지 않았**다고** / 그의 사랑보다.
그러면 그 친구는 물을 것이오 / 왜 브루터스가 일어섰는**지를** / 시저에 반대해
내 대답은 이렇소:
내가 시저를 덜 사랑했기 **때문이 아니라** / 로마를 더 사랑했기 **때문이라고.**
여러분은 시저를 살려 / 노예로 죽고싶소,
아니면 시저를 죽이고 / 자유민으로 살고싶소?
시저가 나를 사랑했기에 / 나는 그를 위해 눈물 흘리고;
그가 행복했기에 / 나는 그것을 기뻐하고;
그가 용감했기에 / 나는 그를 존경합니다;
그러나 그가 야심을 가졌기에 / 나는 그를 죽였습니다.
눈물이 있습니다 / 그의 사랑에 대해선; / 기쁨이 / 행운에 대해선;
존경이 / 용맹에 대해선; / 죽음이 있는 것이오 / 야심에 대해선.
나는 끝내겠습니다 / 이런 말들로:
나는 죽였습니다 / 가장 절친한 친구를 / 로마를 위해,
그러나 나는 같은 칼을 받겠습니다 / 내 자신에 대해서도
(그것이) 나의 조국을 기쁘게 할 때는 / 나의 죽음을 요구하는 **것이.**

23. The Prince – 1

There are two methods of fighting, the one by law, the other by force; the first method is that of men, the second of beasts; but as the first method is often insufficient, one must have recourse to the second. It is therefore, necessary for a prince to know well how to use both the beast and the man.

This was covertly taught to rulers by ancient writers, who relate how Achilles and many others of those ancient princes were given Chiron the centaur to be brought up and educated under his discipline. The parable of this semi-animal, semi-human teacher is meant to indicate that a prince must know how to use both natures, and that the one without the other is not durable.

A prince, being thus obliged to know well how to act as a beast, must imitate the fox, and the lion, for the lion cannot protect himself from traps, and the fox cannot defend himself from wolves. Those that wish to be only lions do not understand this.

Machiavelli, Niccolo (1469~1527)
Italian writer and statesman, Florentine patriot, and original political theorist whose principal work, The Prince, brought him a reputation of amoral cynicism.

The parable of this semi – animal, semi – human teacher is meant to indicate that a prince must know how to use both the beast and the man.

Chiron

In Greek mythology, one of the Centaurs, the son of the god Cronus and Philyra, a sea nymph. Chiron lived at the foot of Mount Pelion in Thessaly and was famous for his wisdom and knowledge of medicine. Many Greek heroes, including Heracles, Achilles, Jason, and Asclepius, were instructed by him.

Dictionary

insufficient: inadequate in number, degree, amount, or quality; not sufficient.
　　　Ex. an insufficient sum ; an insufficient idea.
recourse: the act of seeking help, protection, or legal assistance.
discipline: training of the body or mind according to rules or regulations.
parable: a brief story told as a moral or religious lesson, esp. one that uses allegory or symbolism.
durable: not easily worn out; long-lasting; sturdy.

The Prince – 1

There are two methods of fighting,
the one by law, / the other by force;
the first method is that of men, / the second of beasts;
but as the first method is often insufficient,
one must have recourse / to the second.
It is therefore, necessary / **for** a prince **to** know well
how to use / both the beast and the man.
This was covertly taught / to rulers
by ancient writers, / **who** relate
how Achilles and many others of those ancient princes were given
Chiron the centaur
to be brought up and educated / under his discipline.
The parable of this semi-animal, semi-human teacher
is meant to indicate
that a prince must know / **how to** use both natures,
and **that** the one without the other / is not durable.
A prince, / being thus obliged to know well
how to act / as a beast,
must imitate / the fox, and the lion,
for the lion cannot protect himself / from traps,
and the fox cannot defend himself / from wolves.
Those **that** wish / to be only lions / do not understand this.

군주론 - 1

두 가지 방법이 있다 싸움의,
그 하나는 법에 의한 것이요 / 다른 하나는 힘에 의한 것이다;
그 첫째 방법은 인간의 것이요, / 둘째 방법은 짐승들의 것이다;
그러나 그 첫째 방법이 흔히 불충분하므로
사람들은 의지해야 한다 / 두 번째 방법에.
그러므로, 필요하다 / 군주**가** 잘 아는 **것은**
어떻게 사용**할 지를** / 짐승과 인간 모두를.
이것은 은밀하게 가르쳐졌다 / 통치자들에게
고대 문인들에 의해 / 이야기**하는**
어떻게 아킬레스와 많은 다른 고대 통치자들에게 주어졌는지
반인반마의 괴물인 카이런**이**
(그들이) 양육되**기 위해** 그리고 교육받**기 위해** 카이런의 훈련 하에서.
이 반인반마 교사에 대한 우화는
암시하고 있다
군주가 알아야 한다는 **것을** / **어떻게** 두 가지 성질들을 이용하는 **지를**
그리고 하나는 다른 하나가 없이 / 지속적이지 않다는 **것을**.
군주는, / 따라서 잘 알아야 하는
어떻게 행동하는 **지를** / 짐승으로서
모방해야 한다 / 여우와 사자를,
왜냐하면 사자는 방어할 수 없기 때문에 자신을 / 덫으로부터,
그리고 여우는 방어할 수 없기 때문에 자신을 / 늑대들로부터.
원하**는** 사람들은 / 오직 사자이기를 / 이해하지 못한다 이것을.

The Prince – 2

Therefore, a prudent ruler ought not to keep faith when by doing so it would be against his interest, and when the reasons which made him bind himself no longer exist. If men were all good, this precept would not be a good one; but as they are bad, and would not observe their faith with you, so you are not bound to keep faith with them. Nor have legitimate grounds ever failed a prince who wished to show colorable excuse for the non-fulfillment of his promise. Of this one could furnish as infinite number of examples, and show how many times peace has been broken, and how many promises rendered worthless, by the faithlessness of princes, and those that have best been able to imitate the fox have succeeded best. But it is necessary to be able to disguise this character well, and to be a great feigner and dissembler, and men are so simple and so ready to obey present necessities, that the one who deceives will always find those who allow themselves to be deceived.

…those that have best been able to imitate the fox have succeeded best … men are so simple and so ready to obey present necessities, that the one who deceives will always find those who allow themselves to be deceived.

Dictionary

prudent: showing wisdom and caution in practical matters; sensible.
Ex. prudent advice.
colorable: able to be colored; plausible.   Ex. His excuse for lateness was barely colorable.
fulfill: to effect or bring to realization or completion.   Ex. fulfill one's promise
feign: to pretend; to imitate in order to deceive; put on or give a false appearance of.   Ex. She feigned indifference to his compliments.
dissembler: to conceal one's true motives, opinions, or feelings by a pretense.
Ex. dissemble one's sorrow with a smile

The Prince – 2

Therefore, a prudent ruler / ought not to keep faith
when by doing so / it would be against his interest,
and when the reasons / **which** made him bind himself
no longer exist.
If men **were** all good, / this precept **would not** be a good one;
but as they are bad, / and would not observe their faith / with you,
so you are not bound to keep faith with them.
Nor have legitimate grounds ever failed
a prince / **who** wished to show / colorable excuse
for the non-fulfillment of his promise.
Of this / one could furnish / as infinite number of examples,
and show / **how** many times / peace has been broken,
and **how** many promises / rendered worthless,
by the faithlessness of princes,
and those / **that** have best been able to imitate / the fox
have succeeded / best.
But **it** is necessary / **to** be able to disguise / this character well,
and **to** be a great feigner and dissembler,
and men are **so** simple
and **so** ready to obey / present necessities,
that the one **who** deceives / will always find
those / **who** allow / themselves to be deceived.

군주론 - 2

따라서, 현명한 통치자는 / 신의를 지켜서는 안 된다
그렇게 함으로써 / 그것이 배치될 때는 그의 이익에,
그리고 그 이유들이 / 그가 그 자신을 묶도록 만**든**
더 이상 존재하지 않을 때는.
만약 사람들이 모두 선**하다면**, / 이 교훈은 좋은 것이 **못될 것이다**;
그러나 그들이 악할 때 / 그리고 지키지 않으려 할 때 그들의 신의를 / 당신과
당신은 의무가 없다 그들과 신의를 지킬.
또한 합법적인 이유들이 저버린 적도 **없다**
군주를 / 원했**던** 보여주기를 / 착색할 수 있는(그럴듯한) 변명을
그의 약속의 불이행에 대한.
이런 것에 대해 / 사람들은 제공할 수 있다 / 수많은 예들을,
그리고 보여줄 수 있다 / **얼마나** 여러 번 / 평화가 깨졌는지를,
그리고 **얼마나** 많은 약속들이 / 무가치하게 됐는**지를**,
군주들의 신의 없음에 의해,
그리고 사람들이 / 가장 잘 모방할 수 있었**던** / 여우를
성공을 거둬왔다 / 가장 잘.
그러나 (그것은) 필요하다 / 위장할 능력이 있는 **것은** / 이런 성질을 잘,
그리고 가장 잘 하고 시치미를 잘 떼는 사람이 되는 **것은**,
그리고 사람들은 **너무** 단순하고
기꺼이 복종할 준비가 돼 있**어** / 현재의 필요성들에,
속이는 사람은 / 항상 발견할 것이다
허용하는 사람들을 / 자신들이 속아 넘어 가도록.

24. Learning and Citizenship – 1

In his description of how he became a master riverboat pilot in Life on the Mississippi, Mark Twain gave us a vision of learning that incorporates basic skills and the capacity and commitment to go beyond them. Twain's experience in getting to know the river, Joseph Featherstone tells us, is a classic American expression of a metaphor for learning. Twain learns how to navigate the river at a young age, learning every shoal, snag, and sandbar. These are the basic skills. But no sooner has he memorized their locations and peculiarities than he has to modify or forget them, and learn other spots, for the river never stops changing its course. Twain must simultaneously remember the reality of what exists in the river and imagine how different forces and conditions are likely to change it. He can never know the river completely or certainly; knowledge about the river is always provisional. The point can be generalized; as in Twain's education as a river boat pilot, action and understanding depend on mastered skills and memory.

By Marvin lazerson, Judith B. McLaughlin, Bruce McPherson

Twain, Mark (1835~1910)
American humorist, writer, and lecturer who won a worldwide audience for his stories of youthful adventures, especially The Adventures of Tom Sawyer (1876), Life on the Mississippi (1883), and The Adventures of Huckleberry Finn (1884).

Twain learns how to navigate the river at a young age, learning every shoal, snag, and sandbar. These are the basic skills. But no sooner has he memorized their locations and peculiarities than he has to modify or forget them, and learn other spots, for the river never stops changing its course.

The Mark Twain River Boat.

Dictionary

pilot : one who guides a ship into or out of a harbor.
incorporate: to blend parts together or to include parts in a larger whole.
  Ex. I'll incorporate your suggestions into my report.
commitment: an obligation to fulfill a promised act or function.
shoal: a shallow area within a body of water.
snag: a submerged tree, stump, branch, or root that hinders navigation.
snadbar: a ridge of sand deposited in a river or near a seashore ; shoal.
peculiarity: the state or fact of being odd or strange.
  Ex. His peculiarity was quickly noticed.
modify: to alter somewhat; make changes in.
  Ex. To cut costs, they modified the plans for the house.
provisional: adopted on a temporary or tentative basis; conditional.
  Ex. This is only a provisional solution.

Learning and Citizenship – 1

In his description / of **how** he became / a master riverboat pilot
in 'Life on the Mississippi',
Mark Twain gave us
a vision of learning / **that** incorporates
basic skills and the capacity / and commitment / **to** go beyond them.
Twain's experience / in getting to know the river,
Joseph Featherstone tells us,
is a classic American expression / of a metaphor for learning.
Twain learns / **how to** navigate the river / at a young age,
learning every shoal, snag, and sandbar.
These are the basic skills.
But **no sooner** has he memorized their locations and peculiarities
than he has to modify or forget them,
and learn other spots,
for the river never stops / chang**ing** its course.
Twain must simultaneously remember
the reality / of **what** exists in the river
and imagine
how different forces and conditions are likely to change it.
He can never know the river / completely or certainly;
knowledge about the river / is always provisional.
The point can be generalized;
as in Twain's education / as a riverboat pilot,
action and understanding depend on / mastered skills and memory.

학교 교육은 왜 죽었는가 - 1

그의 묘사에서 / **어떻게** 그가 능숙한 도선사가 됐는**지에** 대한
'미시시피강에서의 생활'이란 작품에서,
마크 트웨인은 주었다 / 우리에게
학습의 비전을 / 통합하**는**
기본적 기술들과 능력 / 그리고 헌신을 / 그것들을 넘어서**기 위해**.
트웨인의 경험은 / 그 강에 대해 알게되는,
(조셉 페더스톤이 말하는 바에 따르면 우리에게,)
고전적인 미국적 표현이다 / 배움을 위한 비유의 .
트웨인은 배운다 / **어떻게** 항해하는 **지를** 그 강을 / 젊은 나이에,
그리고 배운다 / 모든 얕은 곳, 쓰러진 나무, 모래톱을.
이런 것들은 기본적 기술들이다.
그러나 그가 기억**하자마자** / 그것들의 위치들과 특성들을.
그는 수정하거나 잊어버려야 한다 그것들을,
그리고 배워야 한다 다른 위치들을,
왜냐하면 강은 결코 멈추지 않기 때문이다 / 바꾸는 **것을** 그것의 코스를.
트웨인은 동시에 기억해야 한다
현실을 / 강에 존재하는 **것의**
그리고 상상해야 한다
어떻게 다른 힘들과 상태들이 / 그것을 변화시킬 가능성이 있는 **지를**.
그는 결코 알 수 없다 그 강을 / 완전히 혹은 확실히;
지식은 강에 대한 / 항상 일시적이다.
그 요점은 일반화될 수 있다;
즉 트웨인의 교육에서처럼 / 강 도선사로서,
행동과 이해는 의존한다 / 숙달된 기술들과 기억에.

Learning and Citizenship – 2

Yet knowledge is fluid, not set in stone; understanding is an ongoing process, never ceasing, never absolute. In the process of learning, we, like Twain, continually remake our education, ourselves, and our ways of coping with and understanding the world.

Twain's metaphor offers us a far more complicated but richer vision of learning that the traditional approach of most classrooms, wherein learning is perceived as the transfer of material from teacher to students, and knowledge is sharply defined, highly structured, even considered permanent. In such classrooms, once one has this knowledge, it does not go away; it is quite specific and easily measured. In short, one can either read, write, and compute, or one cannot. In Twain's vision, learning involves these basic skills and competencies, but it also evolves from them. As Dewey taught us, experience is inextricably involved in any education.

In short, one can either read, write, and compute, or one cannot. In Twain's vision, learning involves these basic skills and competencies, but it also evolves from them.

Inside Classroom 1917

Dictionary

fluid: not stable; changeable. Ex. a fluid approach to problem solving.
ongoing: existing continuously from some time in the past into the future. Ex. an ongoing investigation.
metaphor: a figure of speech in which a word or phrase is used to describe one thing in terms of another in a nonliteral way, such as drowning in "work."
evolve: to develop or change by an evolutionary process.
inextricable: that one cannot free oneself from. Ex. an inextricable maze.

Learning and Citizenship – 2

Yet knowledge is fluid, / not set in stone;
understand**ing** is an ongoing process,
never ceas**ing**, / never absolute.
In the process **of** learn**ing**, / we, like Twain, continually remake our education, ourselves,
and our ways / **of** cop**ing** with and understand**ing** / the world.
Twain's metaphor offers us
a far more complicated but richer vision of learning
than the traditional approach / of most classrooms,
wherein learning is perceived
as the transfer of material / from teacher to students,
and knowledge is sharply defined, / highly structured,
even considered permanent.
In such classrooms, / **once** one has / this knowledge,
it does not go away; / it is quite specific and easily measured.
In short, one can **either** read, write, and compute,
or one cannot.
In Twain's vision, / learning involves
these basic skills and competencies,
but it also evolves / from them.
As Dewey taught us,
experience is inextricably involved / in any education.

학교 교육은 왜 죽었는가 - 2

그러나 지식은 유동적이다 / 고정된 것은 아니다 바위에;
이해하는 **것은** 하나의 진행하는 과정이다,
결코 멈추지 않**는** / 결코 절대적이지 않은.
배우**는** 과정에서 / 우리는 트웨인처럼 끊임없이 개조한다
우리의 교육을, 우리 자신들을,
그리고 우리의 방법들을 / 대처**하는** 그리고 이해**하는** / 세계를.
트웨인의 비유는 제공한다 / 우리에게
훨씬 더 복잡한 그러나 더 풍부한 학습관을
전통적인 시도보다 / 대다수 교실들의,
그곳에서 학습은 인식된다
지식의 이전으로 / 교사에서 학생들로의,
그리고 지식은 예리하게 규정되고, / 고도로 정형화되고,
심지어 간주된다 불변하는 것으로.
그런 교실들에서 / **일단** 사람들이 가지게되**면** / 이런 지식을,
그것은 가버리지 않는다; / 그것은 매우 분명하고 쉽게 측정된다.
요컨대, 사람들이 읽고, 쓰고, 계산할 수 있든**지**,
혹은 학습자가 할 수 없든**지 둘 중 하나다**.
트웨인의 학습관에서 / 학습은 포함한다
이런 기본적 기술들과 능력들을,
그러나 그것은 역시 발전한다 / 그것들로부터.
듀이가 우리에게 가르쳤듯이,
경험은 뗄레야 뗄 수 없이 관련돼 있다 / 어떤 교육에서든.

Learning and Citizenship – 3

What one learns beyond the basic skills is hard to measure; it is constantly shifting and being transformed. No single test can measure all its various dimensions. What one knows must be manifested time and again, adjusted to new situations, criticized, evaluated, expanded upon. That vision of learning, difficult to implement as it is, should be central to schooling.

Learning involves seeing other points of view; understanding, even celebrating, differences; being able to see through stereotypes; being able to transcend custom where it is appropriate, or support it and its meaning when that is appropriate; recognizing the patterns among the fragment we see and experience. It involves using a variety of means for describing and engaging with the world. To do this, we need to learn ideas and to learn how to abandon and transform ideas when they no longer suffice. We need to risk developing our powers of mind to lead us to "deeper and more gripping and subtler ways of knowing the world and ourselves". Being an active citizen requires having a flexible intelligence and a mind free, as Matthew Arnold said, of stock notions and habits. The key to flexible intelligence is imaginative and critical thinking.

Arnold, Matthew 1822-1888
English Victorian poet and literary and social critic, noted especially for his classical attacks on the contemporary tastes and manners of the "Barbarians" (the aristocracy), the "Philistines" (the commercial middle class), and the "Populace."

Being an active citizen requires having a flexible intelligence and a mind free, as Matthew Arnold said, of stock notions and habits. The key to flexible intelligence is imaginative and critical thinking.

Student at Haverford College.

Dictionary

dimension: scope, as of a problem. Ex. The dimensions of the scandal slowly became clear.
manifest: to evidence or prove. Ex. The evidence manifests his remark.
adjust: to bring to a more fitting or more correct state, relationship, position.
implement: to carry out or put into effect. Ex. I want to implement this plan.
schooling: education or training, esp. formal instruction in a school.
grip: a firm grasp, or the pressure of such a grasp.
  Ex. The scene gripped the spectators.
subtle: difficult to detect or define; elusive or ambiguous. Ex. a subtle change.
stock: often used; commonplace. Ex. stock jokes.

Learning and Citizenship – 3

What one learns / beyond the basic skills / is hard **to** measure;
it is constantly shifting and / being transformed.
No single test can measure / all its various dimensions.
What one knows / must be manifested time and again,
adjusted to new situations, / criticized, evaluated, expanded upon.
That vision **of** learn**ing**, / **(that** is) difficult / **to** implement / as it is,
should be central / to schooling.
Learning involves / see**ing** other points of view;
understand**ing**, even celebrat**ing**, / differences;
being able to see through / stereotypes;
being able to transcend custom / **where** it is appropriate,
or (**being** able to) support / it and its meaning / **when** that is appropriate;
recogniz**ing** the patterns / among the fragment / **(that**) we see and experience.
It involves / us**ing** a variety of means
for describing and engaging with the world.
To do this, / we need / **to** learn ideas
and **to** learn / **how to** abandon and transform / ideas
when they no longer suffice.
We need to risk / developing our powers of mind
to lead us / to "deeper and more gripping and subtler ways
of know**ing** / the world and ourselves".
Be**ing** an active citizen requires
hav**ing** a flexible intelligence and a mind
(**that** is) free, / as Matthew Arnold said, / of stock notions and habits.
The key to flexible intelligence / is imaginative and critical thinking.

학교 교육은 왜 죽었는가 - 3

사람들이 배우는 **것은** / 기본 기술들을 넘어서 / 어렵다 측정**하기에**;
그것은 끊임없이 움직이고 / 변형되고 있다.
한 번의 시험으로는 측정할 수 없다 / 그것들의 모든 다양한 측면들을.
사람들이 아는 **것은** / 입증돼야 하고 반복적으로,
조정돼야 하고 새로운 상황들에 / 비판받고 평가받고 확장돼야 한다.
그런 학습관이 / 어려**운** / 시행**하기에** / 그것이 있는 그대로,
중심이 돼야 한다 / 학교 교육에서.
학습은 포함한다 / 보는 **것을** 다른 시각들을;
이해하는 **것을**, 심지어 찬양하는 **것을** / 다른 것들을;
꿰뚫어 볼 수 있는 **것을** / 틀에 박힌 **것을**;
초월할 수 있는 **것을** 관습을 / 그것이 적절한 **곳에서**,
혹은 지지할 수 있는 **것을** / 그것과 그것의 의미를 / 그것이 적절할 때;
인식하는 **것을** 형태들을 / 파편 가운데서 / 우리가 보고 경험**하는**.
그것은 포함한다 / 사용하는 **것을** 다양한 수단들을
묘사하기 위해 세상사를 / 그리고 관계하기 위해 세상사에.
이것을 하**기 위해** , / 우리는 필요로 한다 / 배우는 **것을** 아이디어들을
그리고 배우는 **것을** / **어떻게** 포기하고 변형할 지 / 아이디어들을
그것들이 더 이상 만족시키지 못할 때.
우리는 모험을 할 필요가 있다 / 우리의 정신력을 계발하는
우리를 이끌**기 위해** / "보다 깊고 보다 흥미를 끌고 보다 민감한 방법들로
세계와 우리 자신들을 알게**하는**."
적극적인 시민이 되는 **것은** 요구한다
가지는 **것을** / 유연한 지성과 마음을
매튜 아놀드가 말했듯이, / 구태의연한 생각들과 습관들에서 자유로**운** .
유연한 지성의 열쇠는 / 상상력이 풍부하고 비판적인 사고다.

25. The Worthless Ivy League? – 1

We all "know" that going to college is essential for economic success. The more prestigious the college, the greater the success. It's better to attend Yale or Stanford than, say, Arizona State. People with the same raw abilities do better and earn more by graduating from an elite school. The bonus flows (it's said) from better connections, brighter "peers," tougher courses or superior professors. Among many parents, the terror that their children won't go to the "right" college has supported an explosion of guidebooks, counselors and tutoring companies to help students in the admissions race.

The trouble is that what everyone knows isn't true. Going to Harvard or Duke won't automatically produce a better job and higher pay. Graduates of these schools generally do well. But they do well because they're talented. Had they chosen colleges with lesser nameplates, they would (on average) have done just as well. The conclusion is that the Ivy League – a metaphor for all elite schools – has little comparative advantage. But the schools don't make the students' success. Students create their own success; this makes the schools look good.

By Robert J. Samuelson

The schools don't make the students' success. Students create their own success; this makes the schools look good.

Stanford University

Harvard University

Dictionary

prestigious: having prestige; highly esteemed.
connection: one with whom one is associated, esp. a family member or person of influence.
   Ex. He used his connections to get that job.
peer: a person of the same rank, status, age group, ability as another person.
nameplate: a piece of metal or wood on which a name is inscribed.
Ivy League: an association of eight prestigious colleges and universities in the northeastern United States, including Brown, Columbia, Cornell, Dartmouth, Harvard, Princeton, Pennsylvania, and Yale.
stimulate: to incite or rouse to activity, action, or increased action; animate.
   Ex. Praise stimulates students to work hard.

The Worthless Ivy League? – 1

We all "know"
that go**ing** to college / is essential / for economic success.
The more prestigious the college, the greater the success.
It's better / **to** attend Yale or Stanford / than, **say**, Arizona State.
People with the same raw abilities / do better and earn more
by graduating from an elite school.
The bonus flows (it's said)
from better connections, / brighter "peers," / tougher courses
or superior professors.
Among many parents,
the terror / **that** their children won't go / to the "right" college
has supported / an explosion
of guidebooks, counselors and tutoring companies
to help students / in the admissions race.
The trouble is / **that what** everyone knows / isn't true.
Go**ing** to Harvard or Duke / won't automatically produce
a better job and higher pay.
Graduates of these schools / generally do well.
But they do well / because they're talented.
Had they **chosen** / colleges **with** lesser nameplates,
they **would** (on average) **have done** / just as well.
The conclusion is **that**
the Ivy League – a metaphor for all elite schools –
has little comparative advantage.
But the schools don't make / the students' success.
Students create / their own success;
this makes / the schools look good.

아이비 리그는 무의미한가? - 1

우리 모두 알고 있다
대학에 가는 **것이** / 필수적이라는 **것을** / 경제적 성공을 위해.
명성이 **높을수록** 대학이 / 그만큼 **더 크다** 성공은.
더 낫다 / 다니는 **것이** 예일大나 스탠퍼드大를 / **예를 들어** 애리조나 주립大보다.
사람들은 원래 같은 능력을 가진 / 더 잘 하고 더 많이 돈을 번다
졸업함으로써 명문대를.
보너스가 흘러 들어온**다고 한다**
더 나은 연줄, / 더 영리한 급우들, / 더 어려운 교과과정
혹은 우수한 교수진으로부터.
많은 부모들 사이에서,
두려움은 / 그들의 자식들이 가지 못할 것이**라는** / 좋은 대학에
부추겼다 / 폭발을 /
안내서들, 카운슬러들 그리고 사설 학원들의
학생들을 돕는 / 입시 경쟁에서.
문제는 / 모든 사람들이 알고 있는 **것이** / 사실이 아니라는 **것**이다.
가는 **것이** 하버드大나 듀크大에 / 자동적으로 만들지는 않는다
더 나은 직업과 더 높은 급여를.
졸업생들은 이들 학교들의 / 일반적으로 일을 잘 해낸다.
그러나 그들은 잘 한다 / 왜냐하면 그들이 재능이 있기 때문에.
그들이 선택**했다면**(선택했더라도) / 대학들을 더 낮은 지명도를 **가진**,
그들은 (평균적으로) **해냈을 것이다** / 그만큼은.
결론은 이렇다
아이비 리그가 - 모든 명문교들의 상징인 -
거의 가지고 있지 않다는 **것**이다 상대적인 이점을.
그러나 그 학교들은 만들지 않는다 / 학생들의 성공을.
학생들이 창출한다 / 그들 자신의 성공을;
이것이 만든다 / 그 학교들이 좋게 보이도록.

The Worthless Ivy League? – 2

If you can't (or won't) take advantage of what Princeton offers, Princeton does no good. What students bring to college matters more than what colleges bring to students. The lesson has relevance beyond elite schools. As a society, we've peddled college as a cure for many ills. Society needs more skilled workers. So, send more students to college. College graduates earn much more than high-school graduates. So – to raise incomes – send more students to college. In that, we've succeeded. Perhaps three quarters of high-school graduates go to college, including community colleges.

But half or more don't finish. A new study from the Department of Education reports that these students achieve only modest gains in skills and income. What determines who finishes? In another report, a senior researcher at the Department of Education finds that the most powerful factor is the difficulty of high-school courses. Not having enough money explains few dropouts. Tough courses do more than transmit genuine skills. They provide the experience – and instill the confidence – of completing something difficult. How to motivate students to do their best? This is a hard question for parents and society as a whole. If the answers were self-evident, we'd have already seized them. But going to college – even Harvard – is no shortcut. (from Newsweek).

What determines who finishes? ···the most powerful factor is the difficulty of high-school courses. Tough courses do more than transmit genuine skills. They provide the experience - and instill the confidence - of completing something difficult.

Yale University

Dictionary

relevance: related to or connected with the present matter; pertinent.
peddle: to offer (goods) for sale on the street or from door to door; to offer, dispense, or disseminate.   Ex. They peddle their intolerance to anyone who will listen.
modest: moderate in quantity, size, value, or the like; not extreme.
Ex. a modest income.
instill: to implant gradually in someone's mind or feelings.   Ex. They instilled a sense of honor in their children.
shortcut: a quicker or more direct route.

The Worthless Ivy League? – 2

If you can't (or won't) take advantage of / what Princeton offers,
Princeton does no good.
What students bring / to college
matters more / than **what** colleges bring / to students.
The lesson has relevance / beyond elite schools.
As a society, / we've peddled college / as a cure / for many ills.
Society needs / more skilled workers.
So, send / more students / to college.
College graduates earn / much more / than high-school graduates.
So – **to** raise incomes – / send more students / to college.
In that, / we've succeeded.
Perhaps three quarters / of high-school graduates
go to college, / including community colleges.
But half or more / don't finish.
A new study / from the Department of Education reports
that these students achieve / only modest gains / in skills and income.
What determines / **who** finishes?
In another report, a senior researcher at the Department of Education finds
that the most powerful factor / is the difficulty of high-school courses.
Not having enough money / explains few dropouts.
Tough courses do more / than transmit genuine skills.
They provide the experience – / and instill the confidence
– of completing / something difficult.
How to motivate students / to do their best?
This is a hard question / for parents and society as a whole.
If the answers **were** self-evident,
we**'d have** already **seized** them.
But go**ing** to college / – even Harvard – / is no shortcut.

아이비리그는 무의미한가? - 2

당신이 이용할 수 없다면 / 프린스턴大가 제공하는 것을,
프린스턴大도 아무 소용이 없다.
학생들이 가져오는 **것이** / 대학으로
중요하다 더 / 대학들이 가져오는 **것**보다 / 학생들에게.
그 교훈은 가지고 있다 관련성을 / 명문교들 밖에서도.
하나의 사회로서, / 우리는 홍보해왔다 대학을 / 치유 수단으로 / 많은 병폐의.
사회는 필요로 한다 / 더 많은 숙련된 인력을.
그래서 보낸다 / 더 많은 학생들을 / 대학으로.
대학 졸업자들이 번다 / 더 많이 / 고등학교 졸업생들보다.
그래서 올려주**기 위해** 수입을 / 보낸다 더 많은 학생들을 / 대학으로.
그런 점에서 / 우리는 성공했다.
아마 4분의 3은 / 고등학교 졸업생들의
간다 대학에 / 전문대학들을 포함한.
그러나 절반 혹은 그 이상은 / 끝마치지 못한다.
한 최신 연구는 / 美 교육부의 / 보고한다
이 학생들은 얻는**다고** / 오직 약간의 이익을 / 기술들과 수입에서.
무엇이 결정하는가 / **누가** (학업을) 마치는**지를**?
또다른 보고서에서, 교육부의 한 수석 연구원은 밝혀냈다
가장 힘있는(중요한) 요인은 / 고교 교과과정의 난이도라는 **것을**.
충분한 돈이 없다는 것이 / 중퇴의 원인이 되는 경우는 별로 없다.
어려운 교과과정은 (제공)한다 더한 것을 / 전하는 것보다 / 진짜 기술들을.
그것들은 제공한다 경험을 / - 그리고 불어넣는다 자심감을
- 완수하는 것에 대한 / 무엇인가를 어려운.
동기를 부여**하는** 방법은 (무엇인가) / 학생들이 최선을 다하도록?
이것은 어려운 질문들이다 / 부모들과 사회 전체에는.
그 대답들이 자명**하다면**,
우리는 이미 잡았을(해결했을) **것이다** 그것들을.
그러나 가는 **것이** 대학에 / - 하버드대조차도 - / 지름길은 결코 아니다.

26. Freedom From The Known / J. Krishnamurti 아는 것으로부터의 자유
27. Jonathan Livingston Seagull / Richard Bach 조너선 리빙스턴 시걸
28. Illusions / Richard Bach 환영
29. The Ascent of F6 / W.H. Auden (and Christopher Isherwood) F6의 상승
30. Divinity Dolth Hedge a King / Walter Pater 신성이 왕을 둘러싸다

26 Freedom From The Known – 1

Beauty lies in the total abandonment of the observer and the observed. Say you are walking by yourself or with somebody and you have stopped talking. You are surrounded by nature and there is no dog barking, no noise of a car passing or even the flutter of a bird. You are completely silent and nature around you is also wholly silent. In that state of silence both in the observer and the observed – when the observer is not translating what he observes into thought – in that silence there is a different quality of beauty. There is neither nature nor the observer. When you love, is there an observer? There is an observer only when love is desire and pleasure.

When you look at a face opposite, you are looking from a centre and the centre creates the space between person and person, and that is why our lives are so empty and callous.

When there is space between you and the object you are observing you will know there is no love, and without love, however hard you try to reform the world or bring about a new social order or however much you talk about improvements, you will only create agony.

When you love, is there an observer? There is an observer only when love is desire and pleasure.

J. Krishnamurti
Indian spiritual teacher who rejected organizations, religions and beliefs. In 1909, He was adopted by Mrs. Annie Besant, President of the Theosophical Society. She was convinced that he was to become a great spiritual teacher. Three years later she took him to England to be educated in preparation for his future role. An organization was set up to promote this role. In 1929, after many years of questioning himself and the destiny imposed upon him, Krishnamurti disbanded this organisation, turning away all followers saying:

"Truth is a pathless land, and you cannot approach it by any path whatsoever, by any religion, by any sect. Truth, being limitless, unconditioned, unapproachable by any path whatsoever, cannot be organized; nor should any organization be formed to lead or to coerce people along any particular path."

Dictionary

abandon: to leave (a place, thing or person) forever, or to stop doing (something) before you have finished it.   Ex. She abandoned her husband and children and went off with another man.
flutter: to move swiftly back and forth or up and down in a jerky or irregular manner; flap. Ex. The banners fluttered in the wind.
callous: insensitive; unfeeling; hardhearted.
Ex. a callous disregard for others' suffering.

Freedom From The Known – 1

Beauty lies / in the total abandonment
of the observer and the observed.
Say you are walking / by yourself
or with somebody / and you have stopped / talk**ing**.
You are surrounded / by nature / and there is no dog barking,
no noise of a car passing / or even the flutter of a bird.
You are completely silent / and nature around you is also wholly silent.
In that state of silence / both in the observer and the observed
_ when the observer is not translating / **what** he observes / into thought
– in that silence / there is a different quality of beauty.
There is **neither** nature **nor** the observer.
When you love, / is there an observer?
There is an observer / only when love is desire and pleasure.
When you look / at a face opposite,
you are looking / from a centre / and the centre creates
the space / between person and person,
and **that is why** our lives are so empty and callous.
When there is space / between you and the object / you are observing
you will know / (**that**) there is no love,
and without love, / **however** hard you try / to reform the world
or bring about / a new social order
or **however** much you talk / about improvements,
you will only create agony.

아는 것으로부터의 자유 - 1

아름다움은 달려있다 / 완전한 포기에
관찰자와 관찰되는 것의.
예를 들어 당신이 걷고 있다고 하자 / 혼자
혹은 누군가와 함께 / 그리고 당신은 멈췄다 / 말하는 **것을**.
당신은 둘러싸여 있다 / 자연에 의해 / 그리고 개 짖는 소리도 없다.
지나가는 차의 소음도 없다 / 혹은 새의 퍼덕거리는 소리조차도.
당신은 완전히 말이 없다 / 그리고 당신 주변의 자연도 완전히 말이 없다.
그런 침묵의 상태에서 / 관찰자와 관찰 대상 모두에게
- 관찰자가 번역하지 않을 때 / 그가 관찰하는 **것을** / 생각으로
- 그런 침묵에는 / 다른 질의 아름다움이 있다.
자연도 관찰자도 없다.
당신이 사랑할 때 / 관찰자가 있는가?
관찰자가 있다 / 다만 사랑이 욕망이고 쾌락일 때.
당신이 바라볼 때 / 상대방 얼굴을,
당신은 보고 있다 / 어떤 중심에서 / 그리고 그 중심은 만든다
공간을 / 사람과 사람 사이의,
그리고 **그것이 이유다** / 우리의 삶들이 그토록 공허하고 무감각한.
공간이 있을 때 / 당신과 대상 - 당신이 바라보**는** - 사이에
당신은 알 것이다 / 사랑이 없다는 **것을**.
그리고 사랑 없이는, / **아무리** 열심히 당신이 노력**해도** / 개혁하려고 세상을
혹은 형성하려고 / 새로운 사회 질서를
혹은 **아무리** 많이 당신이 이야기**해도** / 개선들에 대해,
당신은 단지 만들 것이다 고뇌를.

Freedom From The Known – 2

The observer is always adding to and subtracting from what he is. He is a living thing all the time weighing, comparing, judging, modifying and changing as a result of pressures from outside and within.

The observer has always said, "I must do something about these images, I must suppress them or give them a different shape; He is always active in regard to the observed, acting and reacting passionately or casually, and this action of like and dislike on the part of the observer is called positive action – 'I like, therefore I must hold. I dislike therefore I must get rid of.' But when the observer realizes that the thing about which he is acting is himself, there is no conflict between himself and the image. He is that. He is not separate from that.

If something is you, What can you do? You cannot rebel against it or run away from it or even accept it. It is there. So all action that is the outcome of reaction to like and dislike has come to an end. Then you will find that there is an awareness that has become tremendously alive. It is not bound to any central issue or to any image – and from that intensity of awareness there is a different quality of attention and therefore the mind – because the mind is this awareness – has become extraordinarily sensitive and highly intelligent.

> When the observer realizes that the thing about which he is acting is himself, there is no conflict between himself and the image. He is that. He is not separate from that.

J. Krishnamurti

Dictionary

weigh: to ponder carefully before making a decision.   Ex. I'm weighing the consequences.
suppress: to keep back, as an emotion or urge.   Ex. He couldn't suppress his grin.
passionate: capable of or showing strong emotions.   Ex. a passionate love
aware: knowing or mindful; conscious.   Ex. He became aware of my intention.
tremendous: extraordinarily large in degree or size.   Ex. a tremendous crowd.
sensitive: very responsive to and affected by sense impressions.
　　　　　Ex. a sensitive child

Freedom From The Known – 2

The observer is always adding to and subtracting / from what he is.
He is a living thing
all the time weighing, comparing, judging, modifying and chang**ing**
as a result of pressures / from outside and within.
The observer has always said,
"I must do something / about these images,
I must suppress them / or give them / a different shape;
He is always active / in regard to the observed,
act**ing** and react**ing** / passionately or casually,
and this action of like and dislike / on the part of the observer
is called / positive action
– 'I like, therefore I must hold.
I dislike therefore I must get rid of.'
But when the observer realizes
that the thing about / **which** he is acting / is himself,
there is no conflict / between himself and the image.
He is that. He is not separate / from that.
If something is you, / What can you do?
You cannot rebel / against it / or run away from it
or even accept it. / It is there.
So all action / **that** is the outcome of reaction / to like and dislike
has come to an end.
Then you will find
that there is an awareness / **that** has become tremendously alive.
It is not bound / to any central issue or to any image
– and from that intensity of awareness
there is a different quality of attention
and therefore the mind – because the mind is this awareness –
has become extraordinarily sensitive / and highly intelligent.

아는 것으로부터의 자유 - 2

관찰자는 늘 더하고 빼고 있다 / 자신의 있는 그대로에서.
그는 살아있는 존재다
항상 저울질하고 비교하고 판단하고 한정하고 변경**하는**
압력의 결과로 / 바깥과 안으로부터의.
관찰자는 늘 말해왔다,
내가 해야 한다 뭔가를 / 이들 이미지들에 대해,
나는 억압해야 한다 그것들을 / 혹은 줘야 한다 그것들에게 / 다른 형태를;
그는 늘 능동적이**고** / 관찰되는 것에 관해,
그리고 행동하고 반응한다 / 정열적으로 혹은 무심코,
그리고 호불호(好不好)의 이런 행동은 / 관찰자 쪽의
불린다 / 적극적인 행동이라고
- '나는 좋아한다, 따라서 나는 붙잡아야 한다.
나는 싫어한다, 따라서 버려야 한다.'
그러나 관찰자가 깨달을 때
그가 행동하고 있는 대상이 / 자신이라는 **것을**,
아무런 갈등이 없다 / 그 자신과 그 이미지 사이에는.
그가 그것이다. 그는 분리돼 있지 않다 / 그것으로부터.
무엇인가가 당신이라면, / 무엇을 당신은 할 수 있는가?
당신은 반역할 수 없다 / 그것에 대항해 / 혹은 도망갈 수도 없다 그것으로부터
혹은 받아들일 수도 없다 그것을,/ 그것은 있다 그곳에.
따라서 모든 행동은 / 반응의 결과**인** / 좋아하는 것과 싫어하는 것에 대한
끝나게 된다.
그때 당신은 알게 될 것이다
하나의 인식이 있다는 **것을** / 엄청나게 살아있**는**.
그것은 묶여있지 않다 / 어떤 중심 문제 혹은 어떤 이미지에도
- 그리고 그 인식의 강렬함으로부터
다른 질의 주의력이 있다(나온다).
그리고 따라서 마음은 - 마음은 이런 인식이기 때문에 -
엄청나게 민감해진다 / 그리고 고도로 총명해진다.

Freedom From The Known – 3

Do you use the opposite as a means of avoiding the actual which you don't know how to deal with? Or is it because you have been told by thousands of years of propaganda that you must have an ideal – the opposite of 'what is' – in order to cope with the present? When you have an ideal you think it helps you to get rid of "what is', but it never does. You may preach non-violence for the rest of your life and all the time be sowing the seeds of violence.

You have a concept of what you should be and how you should act, and all the time you are in fact acting quite differently; so you see that principles, beliefs and ideals must inevitably lead to hypocrisy and a dishonest life. It is the ideal that creates the opposite to what is, so if you know how to be with 'what is', then the opposite is not necessary. Trying to become like somebody else, or like your ideal, is one of the main causes of contradiction, confusion and conflict. A mind that is confused, whatever it does, at any level, will remain confused. I see this very clearly; I see it as clearly as I see an immediate physical danger. So what happens? I cease to act in terms of confusion any more. Therefore inaction is complete action.

You have a concept of what you should be and how you should act, and all the time you are in fact acting quite differently.

Meditationh Pond: Portland.Or.

Dictionary

propaganda: information, allegations, or opinions that are deliberately and methodically disseminated to promote or attack a particular doctrine, movement, nation.
contradict: to assert the opposite of; deny the truth of. Ex. The facts contradict your theory; She contradicted my opinion.
confuse: to combine in a disordered, unclear way; fail to distinguish between or among. Ex. He confused gratitude with love.
conflict: to be in strong opposition or disagreement; differ. Ex. His testimony conflicts with yours.
inaction: lack of action; passiveness or idleness.

Freedom From The Known - 3

Do you use / the opposite as a means of avoiding
the actual / **which** you don't know / **how** to deal with?
Or is it because you have been told by thousands of years of propaganda
that you must have an ideal – the opposite of 'what is' –
in order to cope with the present?
When you have an ideal
you think / (**that**) it helps / you to get rid of / 'what is',
but it never does.
You may preach non-violence / for the rest of your life
and all the time be sowing / the seeds of violence.
You have a concept
of **what** you should be / and **how** you should act,
and all the time / you are in fact acting / quite differently;
so you see / **that** principles, beliefs and ideals must inevitably lead
to hypocrisy and a dishonest life.
It is the ideal / **that** creates / the opposite / to what is,
so if you know / **how to** be / with 'what is',
then the opposite is not necessary.
Try**ing** to become / like somebody else, / or like your ideal,
is one of the main causes / of contradiction, confusion and conflict.
A mind / **that** is confused, / **whatever** it does, / at any level,
will **remain** confused.
I see this / very clearly;
I see it / **as** clearly **as I** see / an immediate physical danger.
So what happens?
I cease **to** act / in terms of confusion / any more.
Therefore inaction is complete action.

아는 것으로부터의 자유 - 3

당신은 사용하는가 / 반대되는 것을 피하는 수단으로
실제적인 것을 / 당신이 모르**는 / 어떻게** 다뤄야 할 지를?
혹은 그것은 당신이 들어왔기 때문인가 / 수천년의 선전에 의해
당신이 가져야 한**다는** / 이상을 - 있는 것의 반대인 -
대처**하기 위해** 현실에?
당신이 가질 때 이상을
당신은 생각한다 / 그것이 도와준**다고** / 당신이 제거하도록 / 있는 것을,
그러나 그것은 결코 그런 적이 없다.
당신은 설파할지도 모른다 비폭력을 / 당신 인생의 나머지 기간 동안
그리고 언제나 뿌리고 있는지도 모른다 / 폭력의 씨앗들을.
당신은 가지고 있다 하나의 생각을
당신이 **무엇이** 돼야 **지**에 대한 / 그리고 **어떻게** 행동해야 하는 **지**에 대한,
그리고 항상 / 당신은 실제로는 행동하고 있다 / 매우 다르게;
따라서 당신은 안다 / 원칙, 신념 그리고 이상이 불가피하게 이끈다는 **것을**
위선과 부정직한 삶으로.
(그것은) 이상이다 / 만드는 **것은** / 반대되는 것을 / 있는 것에,
따라서 당신이 안다면 / **어떻게** 존재하는 **지**를 / 있는 것과 함께,
그때 반대되는 것은 필요하지 않다.
노력하는 **것** 되려고 / 다른 누구처럼 / 혹은 당신의 이상처럼,
주요 원인들의 하나다 / 모순, 혼란 그리고 갈등의.
마음은 / 혼란**된**, / 그것이 **무엇을** 혼동**하더라도**, / 어떤 수준에서도,
계속 혼란스러울 것이다;
나는 안다 이것을 / 아주 분명히;
나는 안다 그것을 / 분명히 내가 아는 것**만큼** / 즉각적인 신체적 위험을.
그러면 어떤 일이 일어나는가?
나는 멈춘다 행동하는 **것을** / 혼란의 견지에서 / 더 이상.
따라서 무위는 완전한 행동이다.

27 Jonathan Livingston Seagull – 1

One evening the gulls that were not night-flying stood together on the sand, thinking. Jonathan took all his courage in hand and walked to the Elder Gull, who, it was said, was soon to be moving beyond this world.

"Chiang..." he said, a little nervously.

The old seagull looked at him kindly. "Yes, my son?"

Instead of being enfeebled by age, the Elder had been empowered by it; he could outfly any gull in the flock, and he had learned skills that the others were only gradually coming to know.

"Chiang, this world isn't heaven at all, is it?"

The Elder smiled in the moonlight. "You are learning again, Jonathan Seagull," he said.

"Well, what happens from here? Where are we going? Is there no such place as heaven?"

"No, Jonathan, there is no such place. Heaven is not a place, it is not a time. Heaven is being perfect." He was silent for a moment.

"You are a very fast flier, aren't you?"

"I...I enjoy speed Jonathan said, taken aback but proud that the Elder had noticed.

Richard Bach
In spite of being criticized for sharing simple philosophies on life, love, and reincarnation in Jonathan Livingston Seagull and The Bridge Across Forever, new age American author, Richard Bach, inspires and encourages readers to appreciate life, never give up, and discover one's true potential.

Is there no such place as heaven?" "No, Jonathan, there is no such place. Heaven is not a place, it is not a time. Heaven is being perfect."

Many of us find similarities to Jonathan in that we don't always "fit in" with what everyone else does. Few of us, though, have the courage he has to defy the accepted ways and strive for what we feel is right for us.

Dictionary

enfeeble: to take away the strength of; make feeble, as from age or disease.
empower: to grant legal power or authority to; authorize. Ex. The president is empowered to veto a bill which has passed through the Congress.
outfly: To fly faster than another; to advance before in flight or progress.
flock: a group of sheep, goats or birds, or a group of people
Ex. Flocks of geese often fly in a V-shaped formation.

Jonathan Livingston Seagull – 1

One evening / the gulls / **that** were not night-flying
stood together / on the sand, / thinking.
Jonathan took / all his courage / in hand
and walked / to the Elder Gull,
who, it was said, / **was soon to** / be moving / beyond this world.
"Chiang..." he said, / a little nervously.
The old seagull looked at him / kindly.
"Yes, my son?"
Instead of being enfeebled / by age,
the Elder had been empowered / by it;
He could outfly / any gull / in the flock,
and he had learned skills
that the others were only gradually coming to know.
"Chiang, this world isn't heaven at all, is it?"
The Elder smiled / in the moonlight.
"You are learning again, Jonathan Seagull," he said.
"Well, what happens / from here?
Where are we going?
Is there no **such** place / **as** heaven?"
"No, Jonathan, there is no such place.
Heaven is not a place, / it is not a time.
Heaven is being perfect."
He was silent / for a moment.
"You are a very fast flier, aren't you?"
"I...I enjoy speed" Jonathan said,
taken aback but proud / **that** the Elder had noticed.

조너선 리빙스턴 시걸-1

어느 날 저녁 / 갈매기들이 / 야간 비행을 하지 않고 있었**던**
섰다 함께 / 모래사장에 / 그리고 생각에 잠겼다.
조너선은 취했다 / 모든 그의 용기를 / 손에 (용기에 차서 손을 불끈 쥐었다)
그리고 걸어갔다 / 그 원로 갈매기에게,
들은 바에 의하면 곧 **예정돼 있었던** / 옮겨갈 것으로 / 이 세상 너머로.
"치앙..." 그는 말했다, / 약간 초조하게.
원로 갈매기는 그를 바라보았다 / 상냥하게.
"그래, 젊은이?"
허약해진 **대신에** / 나이 때문에
그 원로는 강인해져 있었다 / 나이로 인해;
그는 더 잘 날 수 있었다 / 어느 갈매기보다 / 그 갈매기 떼의,
그리고 그는 배웠었다 기술들을
다른 갈매기들은 오직 단계적으로 알게되었**던**,
"치앙, 이 세상은 결코 하늘나라가 아니죠, 그렇죠?"
그 원로는 미소지었다 / 달빛 속에서.
"너는 배우고 있다 다시 , 조너선 시걸," 그는 말했다.
"그럼, 무슨 일이 일어나죠 / 여기에서?
우리는 어디로 가고 있죠?
그런 장소는 없는 가요 / 하늘나라 **같은**?"
"없지, 조너선, 그런 장소는 없어.
하늘나라는 장소가 아니야, / 그것은 어떤 시간이 아니야.
하늘나라는 완벽한 것이지."
그는 말이 없었다 / 잠시 동안.
"자네는 매우 **빠른** 새야, 안 그런가?"
"저는......저는 즐깁니다 스피드를" 조너선은 말했다,
깜짝 놀랐으나 자랑스러웠다 / 장로 갈매기가 알아보았다는 **것이**.

Jonathan Livingston Seagull – 2

"You will begin to touch heaven, Jonathan, in the moment that you touch perfect speed. And that isn't flying a thousand miles an hour, or a million, or flying at the speed of light. Because any number is a limit, and perfection doesn't have limits. Perfect speed, my son, is being there."

Without warning, Chiang vanished and appeared at the water's edge fifty feet away, all in the flicker of an instant. Then he vanished again and stood, in the same millisecond, at Jonathan's shoulder. "It's kind of fun," he said.

Jonathan was dazzled. He forgot to ask about heaven.

"How do you do that? What does it feel like? How far can you go?"

"You can go to any place and to any time that you wish to go," the Elder said. "I've gone everywhere and everywhen I can think of." He looked across the sea.

"It's strange. The gulls who scorn perfection for the sake of travel go nowhere, slowly. Those who put aside travel for the sake of perfection go anywhere, instantly.

You will begin to touch heaven, Jonathan, in the moment that you touch perfect speed. And that isn't flying a thousand miles an hour, or a million. Because any number is a limit.

Dictionary

vanish: to disappear quickly from sight. Ex. The ghost appeared and then vanished.
flicker: to burn, shine, or move like a flame in quickly changing forms of light and dark. Ex. Candles flickered on all the tables in the restaurant.
millisecond: a unit of time which is equal to 0.001 seconds.
travel: to make a journey, usually over a long distance Ex. As a young man he had travelled the world.

Jonathan Livingston Seagull – 2

"You will begin to touch heaven, Jonathan,
in the moment / **that** you touch / perfect speed.
And that isn't flying / a thousand miles an hour, or a million,
or flying / at the speed of light.
Because any number is a limit,
and perfection doesn't have / limits.
Perfect speed, my son, is **being** there."
Without warning, / Chiang vanished
and appeared / at the water's edge / fifty feet away,
all in the flicker of an instant.
Then he vanished again / and stood,
in the same millisecond, / at Jonathan's shoulder.
"It's kind of fun," he said.
Jonathan was dazzled.
He forgot / to ask about heaven.
"How do you do that?
What does it feel like?
How far can you go?"
"You can go / to any place
and to any time / **that** you wish / **to** go," the Elder said.
"I've gone / everywhere and everywhen / (**that**) I can think of."
He looked / across the sea.
"It's strange.
The gulls / **who** scorn perfection / for the sake of travel
go nowhere, slowly.
Those / **who** put aside travel / for the sake of perfection
go anywhere, instantly.

조너선 리빙스턴 시걸 - 2

"자네는 접하기 시작하는 거야 하늘나라를, 조너선.
순간에 / 자네가 도달**하는** / 완벽한 속도에.
그리고 그것은 나는 것은 아니지 / 시속 1,000마일이나 혹은 백만 마일로,
혹은 나는 것도 (아니지) / 빛의 속도로.
왜냐하면 어떤 숫자도 한계이기 때문이지,
그리고 완벽함은 가지고 있지 않기 때문이지 / 한계를.
완벽한 속도란, 여보게 젊은이, 그 곳에 **존재하는 것**이네."
예고도 없이 / 치앙은 사라졌다
그리고 나타났다 / 물가에 / 50피트 떨어진,
그런데 모든 것이 눈 깜빡할 사이에 일어났다.
그런 다음 그는 다시 사라졌다 / 그리고 섰다,
같은 1,000분의 1초 내에 / 조나단의 어깨에.
"그것은 일종의 장난일세" 그는 말했다.
조나단은 눈이 부셨다(압도됐다).
그는 잊어버렸다 / 물어보는 것을 하늘나라에 관해.
"어떻게 당신은 그렇게 하시죠?
어떤 느낌이 드는가요?
얼마나 멀리 당신은 갈 수 있죠?"
"자네는 갈 수 있어 / 어떤 장소에도
그리고 어느 시간으로도 / 자네가 원**하는** / 가**기를**," 원로 갈매기는 말했다.
"나는 가보았지 / 모든 장소와 모든 시간에 / 내가 생각해낼 수 있**는**."
그는 바라보았다 / 바다를 가로질러.
"그것 참 이상해.
갈매기들은 / 완벽함을 경멸**하는** / 여행을 위해
아무 곳도 가지 못해, 천천히라도.
갈매기들은 / 여행을 제쳐놓**는** / 완벽함을 위해
어디든지 가거든, 즉시."

Jonathan Livingston Seagull – 3

"Rember, Jonathan, heaven isn't a place or a time, because place and time are so very meaningless. Heaven is..."

"Can you teach me to fly like that?" Jonathan Seagull trembled to conquer another unknown.

"Of course, if you wish to learn."

"I wish. When can we start?"

"We could start now, if you'd like."

"I want to learn to fly like that," Jonathan said, and a strange light glowed in his eyes. "Tell me what to do."

Chiang spoke slowly and watched the younger gull ever so carefully. "To fly as fast as thought, to anywhere that is," he said, "You must begin by knowing that you have already arrived..."

The trick, according to Chiang, was for Jonathan to stop seeing himself as trapped inside a limited body that had a forty-two-inch wingspan and performance that could be plotted on a chart. The trick was to know that his true nature lived, as perfect as an unwritten number, everywhere at once across space and time.

"To fly as fast as thought, to anywhere that is," he said, "You must begin by knowing that you have already arrived..."

Dictionary

tremble: to shake slightly, usually because you are cold, frightened, or very emotional   Ex. He's trembling with cold.
trick: an effective or quick way of doing something. Ex. He is familiar with the tricks of the trade.
trap: a device or hole for catching animals or people and preventing their escape.   Ex. The farmer sets traps to catch rats in his barns.
wingspan: the distance between the ends of the wings of a bird, insect or aircraft.
plot: to mark or draw on a piece of paper or a map. Ex. Radar operators plotted the course of the incoming missile.

Jonathan Livingston Seagull – 3

"Remember, Jonathan, / (**that**) heaven isn't a place or a time,
because place and time are so very meaningless. / Heaven is..."
"Can you **teach** / me **to** fly like that?"
Jonathan Seagull trembled / to conquer another unknown.
"Of course, if you wish **to** learn."
"I wish. When can we start?"
"We could start now, / if you'd like."
"I want / **to** learn / **to** fly like that," / Jonathan said,
and a strange light glowed / in his eyes.
"Tell me / **what** to do."
Chiang spoke slowly
and watched the younger gull / ever so carefully.
"**To** fly / **as** fast **as** thought, / to anywhere / **that** is," / he said,
"You must begin / by knowing / **that** you have already arrived..."
The trick, according to Chiang, / was **for** Jonathan **to** stop
see**ing** / himself as trapped
inside a limited body
that had / a forty-two-inch wingspan and performance
that could be / plotted / on a chart.
The trick was **to** know
that his true nature lived, / **as** perfect / **as** an unwritten number,
everywhere at once / across space and time.

조너선 리빙스턴 시걸 - 3

"명심하게 조너선, / 하늘나라는 장소나 시간이 아니라는 **것을**,
왜냐하면 장소와 시간은 너무 무의미하니까. / 하늘나라는……"
"가르쳐 주시겠어요 / 제가 날도록 그렇게?"
조너선 시걸은 몸을 부르르 떨었다 / 정복하려고 또 다른 미지의 세계를.
"물론 자네가 원한다면 배우**기를**."
"저는 원합니다. 언제 우리는 시작할 수 있습니까?"
"우리는 시작할 수 있다 지금, / 자네가 좋다면."
"저는 원합니다 / 배우**기를** / 그렇게 나는 **것을**," / 조나단은 말했다,
그리고 어떤 이상한 빛이 번득였다 / 그의 눈에.
"말해주세요 나에게 / **무엇을** 해야하는**지를**."
치앙은 말했다 천천히
그리고 지켜보았다 그 젊은 갈매기를 / 그 어느 때보다 매우 주의 깊게.
"**날기 위해서는** / 매우 빨리 생각**만큼**, / 어느 곳으로든지 / 존재**하는**" /
그는 말했다,
"자네는 시작해야 해 / 앎으로써 / 자네가 이미 도착했다는 **것을**……"
그 비결은, 치앙에 따르면, / 조나단**이** 멈추는 **것**이었다
보는 **것을** / 그 자신**이** 갇혀 있**다고** / 제한된 몸 속에
가**진** / 42인치의 날개 길이와 동작을
표시될 수 있**는** / 차트 위에.
그 비결은 아는 **것**이었다
그의 진짜 본질이 살아 있었다는 **것을** / 매우 완벽하게 / 써지지 않은 숫자**만큼**,
어느 곳에서든 당장 / 시간과 공간을 가로질러.

28 Illusions – 1

Learning is finding out what you already know.
Doing is demonstrating that you know it.
Teaching is reminding others that they know
just as well as you.
You are all learners, doers, teachers.

Your only obligation in any lifetime
is to be true to yourself.
Being true to anyone else or anything else
is not only impossible, but the mark of a false messiah.

The bond that links your true family
is not one of blood, but of respect and joy in each other's life.
Rarely do members of one family grow up
under the same roof.

There is no such thing as a problem without a gift
for you in its hands.
You seek problems because you need their gifts.

by Richard Bach

Learning is finding out what you already know.
Doing is demonstrating that you know it. Teaching is reminding others that they know just as well as you.

Christ Teaching

Dictionary

demonstrate: to show it and explain how it works.   Ex. The teacher demonstrated how to use the equipment.
obligation: the act of binding oneself legally or morally to do or to refrain from doing something; contract.
messiah: In the Christian religion, the Messiah is Jesus Christ. In the Jewish religion, the Messiah is the king of the Jews who is still to come.
bond: a close connection joining two or more people.   Ex. the bond(s) of friendship/love.

Illusions – 1

Learning is find**ing** out / **what** you already know.
Doing is demonstrat**ing** / **that** you know it.
Teach**ing** is remind**ing** others / **that** they know
just **as well as** you.
You are all learners, doers, teachers.

Your only obligation / in any lifetime
is **to** be true / to yourself.
Being true / to anyone else or anything else
is not only impossible, / but the mark of a false messiah.

The bond / that links your true family
is not one of blood, / but of respect and joy
in each other's life.
Rarely do members of one family grow up
under the same roof.

There is no **such** thing / **as** a problem without a gift
for you / in its hands.
You seek problems / because you need / their gifts.

환영 - 1

배우는 **것은** 발견하는 **것**이다 / 당신이 이미 알고 있는 **것을**.
행하는 **것은** 보여주는 **것**이다 / 당신이 그것을 알고 있다는 **것을**.
가르치는 **것은** 상기시키는 **것**이다 다른 사람들에게 / 그들이 알고 있다는 **것을**
바로 당신**만큼** 잘.
당신들은 모두 배우는 자들이오, 행하는 자들이오, 가르치는 자들이다.

당신의 유일한 의무는 / 일생에서
진실해지는 **것**이다 / 당신 자신에게.
진실해지는 **것은** / 다른 어떤 사람이나 다른 어떤 일에
불가능할 뿐 아니라 / 거짓 메시아의 징표이다.

인연은 / 당신의 진짜 가족을 연결하는
혈연이 아니라 / 존경과 기쁨의 결속이다
각자의 인생에 있는.
한 가족의 구성원들은 거의 자라지 않는다
같은 지붕 밑에서.

그런 것은 없다 / 선물이 없는 문제 **같은**
당신을 위한 / 그것의 손에는.
당신은 찾는다 문제들을 / 당신이 필요하기 때문에 / 그것들의 선물들이.

Illusions – 2

The mark of your ignorance is the depth of your belief
in injustice and tragedy.
What the caterpillar calls the end of the world,
the master calls a butterfly.

You are never given a wish
without also being given the power to make it true.
You may have to work for it, however.

Every person, all the events of your life,
are there because you have drawn them there.
What you choose to do with them is up to you.

A cloud does not know why it moves
in just such a direction and at such a speed,
it feels an impulsion....
this is the place to go now.
But the sky knows the reason and the patterns behind all clouds,
and you will know, too
when you lift yourself high
enough to see beyond horizons.

> What the caterpillar calls the end of the world,
> the master calls a butterfly.

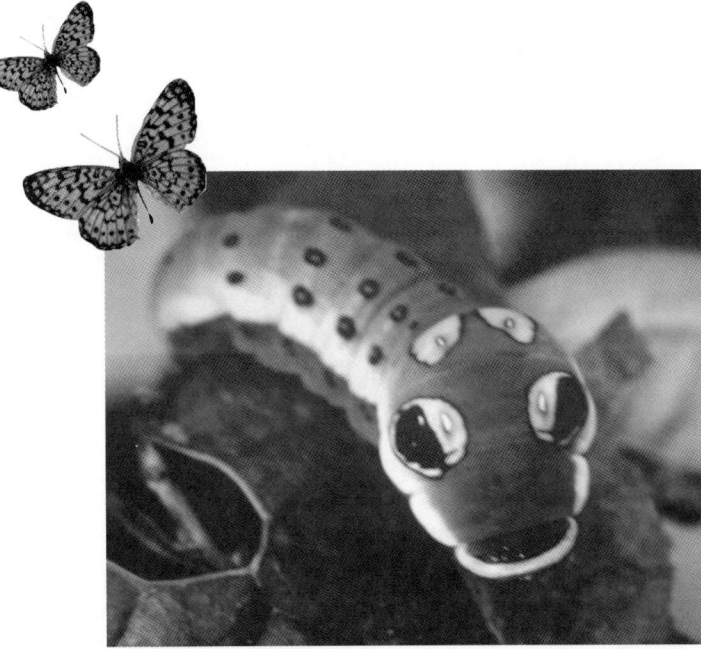

A Carterpillar and butterflies.

Dictionary

direction: the position towards which someone or something moves or faces.
   Ex. They drove away in opposite directions.
impulsion: Influence on the mind; impulse.
injustice: unfairness and lack of justice. Ex. They were aware of the injustices of the system.
caterpillar: a small long animal with many legs which feeds on the leaves of plants and develops into a butterfly or moth.

Illusions – 2

The mark of your ignorance / is the depth of your belief
in injustice and tragedy.
What the caterpillar calls / the end of the world,
the master **calls** / a butterfly.

You are never given / a wish
without also being given / the power to make it true.
You may have to work / for it, / however.

Every person, / all the events of your life,
are there / because you have drawn them there.
What you choose / to do with them / is up to you.

A cloud does not know / **why** it moves
in just such a direction / and at such a speed,
it feels an impulsion....
this is the place / **to** go now.
But the sky knows the reason and the patterns / behind all clouds,
and you will know, too
when you lift yourself / high / **enough to** see beyond horizons.

환영 - 2

당신의 무식의 징표는 / 당신의 믿음의 깊이다
부정과 비극에 대한.
고치가 부르는 **것을** / 세상의 끝이라고 ,
그 스승은 **부른다** / 나비라고.

당신에게 결코 주진 않았다 / 소망을
힘을 주지 않으면서 / 그것을 실현할.
당신은 일해야 할 지 모른다 / 그것을 위해, / 그러나.

모든 사람, / 당신 인생의 모든 사건들은,
그곳에 있다 / 당신이 끌어들였기 때문에 그것들을 그 곳에.
당신이 무엇을 하기로 결정할 **지는** / 그것들과 함께 / 당신에게 달렸다.

구름은 모른다 / **왜** 그것이 움직이는 **지를**
바로 그런 방향으로 / 그리고 그런 속도로,
그것은 하나의 충동을 느낀다...
이곳은 장소다 / 지금 진행되고 있**는**.
그러나 하늘은 안다 / 그 이유와 그 형태들을 / 모든 구름들 뒤에 있는,
그리고 당신은 알 것이다, 역시
당신이 들어올릴 때 당신 자신을 / 높게 / 수평선 너머 **볼 정도로**.